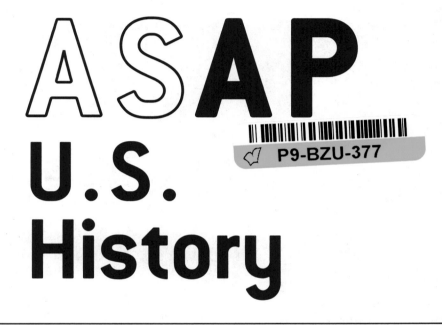

ASAP
U.S.
History

By the Staff of The Princeton Review

princetonreview.com

The Princeton Review
110 East 42nd Street, 7th Floor
New York, NY 10017
Email: editorialsupport@review.com

Published in the United States by Penguin
Random House LLC, New York, and in Canada
by Random House of Canada, a division of
Penguin Random House Ltd., Toronto.

Terms of Service: The Princeton Review Online
Companion Tools ("Student Tools") for retail
books are available for only the two most recent
editions of that book. Student Tools may be
activated only twice per eligible book purchased
for two consecutive 12-month periods, for a
total of 24 months of access. Activation of
Student Tools more than twice per book is in
direct violation of these Terms of Service and
may result in discontinuation of access to
Student Tools Services.

ISBN: 978-1-5247-5767-0
eBook ISBN: 978-1-5247-5772-4
ISSN: 2574-4763

AP and Advanced Placement are registered
trademarks of the College Board, which is not
affiliated with The Princeton Review.

The Princeton Review is not affiliated with
Princeton University.

Editor: Meave Shelton
Production Editors: Melissa Duclos and
                    Kathy G. Carter
Production Artists: Deborah A. Silvestrini and
                    Craig Patches

Printed in the United States of America.

10 9 8 7 6 5 4 3 2 1

Editorial

Rob Franek, Editor-in-Chief
Casey Cornelius, VP Content Development
Mary Beth Garrick, Director of Production
Selena Coppock, Managing Editor
Meave Shelton, Senior Editor
Colleen Day, Editor
Sarah Litt, Editor
Aaron Riccio, Editor
Orion McBean, Associate Editor

Penguin Random House Publishing Team

Tom Russell, VP, Publisher
Alison Stoltzfus, Publishing Director
Jake Eldred, Associate Managing Editor
Ellen Reed, Production Manager
Suzanne Lee, Designer

Acknowledgments

The Princeton Review would like to extend special thanks to the content development team for their hard work, brilliant ideas, enthusiasm, and above-and-beyond dedication to this project: Gina Donegan, Kevin Kelly, Erik Kolb, and Christine Lindwall.

A big round of applause is due to our stellar production artists, Debbie Silvestrini and Craig Patches, for their layout and design wizardry, and to production editors Melissa Duclos and Kathy G. Carter for their careful attention to every page.

Contents

Get More (Free) Content

1 Go to **PrincetonReview.com/cracking.**

2 Enter the following ISBN for your book: 9781524757670.

3 Answer a few simple questions to set up an exclusive Princeton Review account. (If you already have one, you can just log in.)

4 Click the "Student Tools" button, also found under "My Account" from the top toolbar. You're all set to access your bonus content!

Need to report a potential **content** issue?

Contact **EditorialSupport@review.com**.
Include:
- full title of the book
- ISBN number
- page number

Need to report a **technical** issue?

Contact **TPRStudentTech@review.com** and provide:
- your full name
- email address used to register the book
- full book title and ISBN
- computer OS (Mac/PC) and browser (Firefox, Safari, etc.)

Once you've registered, you can...

- Get valuable advice about the college application process, including tips for writing a great essay and where to apply for financial aid

- If you're still choosing between colleges, use our searchable rankings of *The Best 382 Colleges* to find out more information about your dream school

- Access a variety of printable resources, including bonus "could know" material and a "further reading" list for U.S. History

- Check to see if there have been any corrections or updates to this edition

- Get our take on any recent or pending updates to the AP U.S. History Exam

Introduction

What Is This Book and When Should I Use It?

Welcome to *ASAP U.S. History,* your quick-review study guide for the AP U.S. History Exam written by the staff of The Princeton Review. This is a brand-new series custom built for crammers, visual learners, and any student doing high-level AP concept review. As you read through this book, you will notice that there aren't any practice tests, end-of-chapter drills, or multiple-choice questions. There's also very little test-taking strategy presented in here. Both of those things (practice and strategy) can be found in The Princeton Review's other top-notch AP series—*Cracking.* So if you need a deep dive into AP U.S. History, check out *Cracking the AP U.S. History Exam* at your local bookstore.

ASAP U.S. History is our fast track to understanding the material—like a fantastic set of class notes. We present the most important information that you MUST know (or should know or could know—more on that later) in visually friendly formats such as charts, graphs, and maps, and we even threw a few jokes in there to keep things interesting.

Use this book anytime you want—it's never too late to do some studying (nor is it ever too early). It's small, so you can take it with you anywhere and crack it open while you're waiting for soccer practice to start or for your friend to meet you for a study date or for the library to open.* *ASAP U.S. History* is the perfect study guide for students who need high-level review in addition to their regular review and also for students who perhaps need to cram pre-Exam. Whatever you need it for, you'll find no judgment here!

Because you camp out in front of it like they are selling concert tickets in there, right? Only kidding.

Who Is This Book For?

This book is for YOU! No matter what kind of student you are, this book is the right one for you. How do you know what kind of student you are? Follow this handy chart to find out!

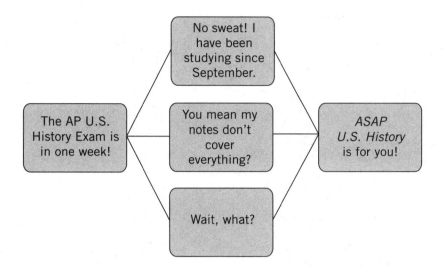

As you can see, this book is meant for every kind of student. Our quick lessons let you focus on the topics you must know, you should know, and you could know—that way, even if the test is tomorrow (!), you can get a little extra study time in, and learn only the material you need.

How Do I Use This Book?

This book is your study tool, so feel free to customize it in whatever way makes the most sense to you, given your available time to prepare. Here are some suggestions:

Target Practice
If you know what topics give you the most trouble, hone in on those chapters or sections.

ASK Away
Answer all of the Ask Yourself questions *first*. This will help you to identify any additional tough spots that may need special attention.

Three-Pass System
Start at the very beginning!* Read the book several times from cover to cover, focusing selectively on the MUST content for your first pass, the SHOULD content for your second pass, and finally, the COULD content.

 It's a very good place to start.

Why Are There Icons?

Your standard AP course is designed to be equivalent to a college-level class, and as such, the amount of material that's covered may seem overwhelming. It's certainly admirable to want to learn everything— these are, after all, fascinating subjects. But every student's course load, to say nothing of his or her life, is different, and there isn't always time to memorize every last fact.

To that end, *ASAP U.S. History* doesn't just distill the key information into bite-sized chunks and memorable tables and figures. This book also breaks down the material into three major types of content:

! This symbol calls out a section that has MUST KNOW information. This is the core content that is either the most likely to appear in some format on the test or is foundational knowledge that's needed to make sense of other highly tested topics.

••• This symbol refers to SHOULD KNOW material. This is either content that has been tested in some form before (but not as frequently) or which will help you to deepen your understanding of the surrounding topics. If you're pressed for time, you might just want to skim it, and read only those sections that you feel particularly unfamiliar with.

∾ This symbol indicates COULD KNOW material, but don't just write it off! This material is still within the AP's expansive curriculum, so if you're aiming for a perfect 5, you'll still want to know all of this. That said, this is the information that is least likely to be directly tested, so if the test is just around the corner, you should probably save this material for last.

As you work through the book, you'll also notice a few other types of icons.

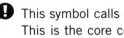 The Ask Yourself question is an opportunity to solidify your understanding of the material you've just read. It's also a great way to take these concepts outside of the book and make the sort of real-world connections that you'll need in order to answer the free-response questions on the AP Exam.

There's a reason why people still say that "all work and no play" is a bad thing. These jokes and fun facts help to shake your brain up a bit and keep it from just glazing over all of the content—they're a bit like mental speed bumps, there to keep you from going too fast for your own good.

Where Can I Find Other Resources?

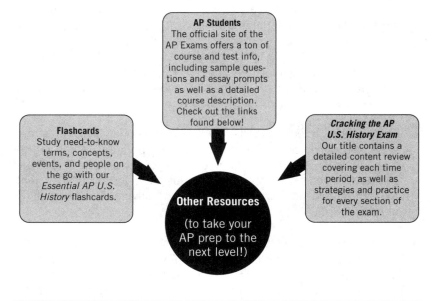

AP Students
The official site of the AP Exams offers a ton of course and test info, including sample questions and essay prompts as well as a detailed course description. Check out the links found below!

Flashcards
Study need-to-know terms, concepts, events, and people on the go with our *Essential AP U.S. History* flashcards.

Cracking the AP U.S. History Exam
Our title contains a detailed content review covering each time period, as well as strategies and practice for every section of the exam.

Other Resources
(to take your AP prep to the next level!)

Useful Links

- AP U.S. History Homepage: https://apstudent.collegeboard.org/apcourse/ap-united-states-history
- Your Student Tools: www.PrincetonReview.com/cracking
  See the "Get More (Free) Content" page at the beginning of this book for step-by-step instructions for registering your book and accessing more materials to boost your test prep.

PERIOD 1 (1491–1607):
Early Contact with the New World

United States history is traditionally thought to have begun when Christopher Columbus inadvertently discovered the Americas and claimed the land for Spain. This section examines the various cultures of the indigenous people living here at that time and the effects of the early contacts between Europeans and Native Americans.

Native Peoples of North America 🛑

When **Christopher Columbus** discovered the "New World" and set the stage for European colonization, there were already millions of indigenous people living there. These **Native Americans**, who are believed to be descendants of Asian migrants who traveled across the **Bering land bridge** thousands of years earlier, were scattered across modern-day North and South America. The name "Indian," which has been historically applied to these earliest Americans, comes from Columbus's mistaken belief that he had in fact reached his intended destination— the East Indies. During the **pre-Columbian** era, various tribes with widely divergent cultures and lifestyles were scattered throughout the region.

Tribes of the Pacific Northwest	• Typically lived in permanent shelters made of wood and tree bark and survived through hunting, foraging, and especially fishing • 🔊 Notable tribes include the Chinook (who would later famously encounter explorers Lewis and Clark in the 19th century).
Tribes of the Northeast	• Typically lived in permanent single-family shelters ("wigwams") or long multi-family wooden dwellings ("longhouses") and survived through farming and local hunting • 💬 Notable tribes include the Iroquois and the Algonquian.
Tribes of the Great Plains	• Typically lived a nomadic lifestyle, often hunting bison for survival and living in makeshift shelters made from animal skins ("teepees") • 💬 Notable tribes include the Lakota Sioux.
Tribes of the Southwest	• Typically lived in permanent stuctures made from clay and straw and survived through dry farming; maize cultivation, which spread northward from present-day Mexico, facilitated the establishment of these permanent settlements • 💬 Notable tribes include the Pueblo people of the desert, known for their impressive towns and elaborate multistory houses.

Tribes of the Southeast	• Typically lived in permanent single-family dwellings and survived through farming a variety of crops, as well as through hunting and gathering • 😎 Notable tribes include the Cherokee.
The Inuit	• Typically lived a nomadic lifestyle in extremely cold northern regions and survived through hunting, gathering, whaling, and fishing; they lived in "igloos" (houses built out of snow) in the winter and in makeshift (often wooden) shelters in the summer • 😎 Notable tribes include the Iñupiat people of Alaska (sometimes called "Eskimos").

Some Regional Lifestyle Differences Among Pre-Columbian Native Americans

---

The Native Americans of the Great Plains would later embrace the Spanish introduction of the horse to North America, which greatly facilitated their nomadic lifestyle. They would often travel on horseback and sleep in teepee tents that were easily constructed and disassembled. They fiercely resisted European occupation of their lands and were viewed as warlike, sometimes wearing war paint and the brightly colored "feathered war bonnet."

 Columbus's proposal to find a new sea passage to Asia was rejected by the rulers of Portugal, France, and England. Many experts at the time believed his calculations were way off and that he'd never make it. They were right.

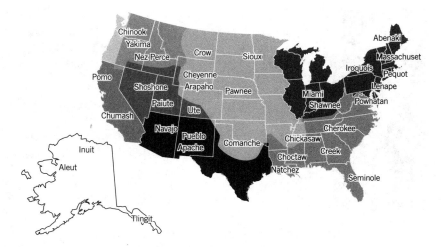

**Pre-Columbian Disbursement of Native American Tribes
Throughout the Modern-Day United States**

 Ask Yourself...

The Native Americans of the Great Plains are most closely associated with the iconic image of the "Indian" in popular culture. Accordingly, to what extent have Hollywood depictions (particularly those of the western genre) distorted our modern perceptions of what life was historically like for the majority of indigenous people?

Early Interactions Between Europeans and Native Americans ❗

Columbus's arrival in 1492 marked the beginning of the **Contact Period**, during which Europeans and Native Americans interacted. While in some places, such as the Roanoke Colony, initial relations could be characterized as friendly and mutually beneficial, conflict soon arose as the various foreign nations began to colonize the region and dominate the indigenous people. While the native population reaped the benefit of some European technologies and advances, their population was eventually decimated by the introduction of deadly disease.

First Contact with the Natives 🛑

When the Europeans first arrived in the Americas, the two races exchanged goods and information, creating new opportunities for both cultures. Unfortunately, however, there were substantial negative repercussions from this **Columbian exchange**, particularly for the native people.

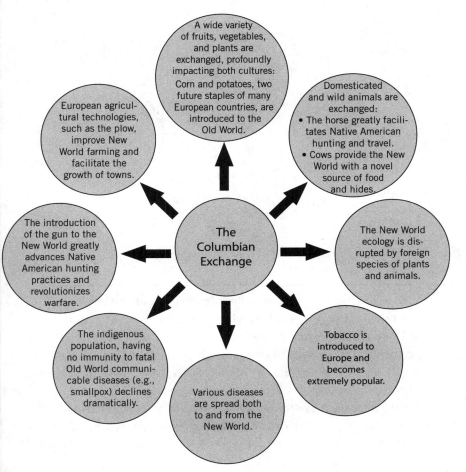

A wide variety of fruits, vegetables, and plants are exchanged, profoundly impacting both cultures: Corn and potatoes, two future staples of many European countries, are introduced to the Old World.

European agricultural technologies, such as the plow, improve New World farming and facilitate the growth of towns.

Domesticated and wild animals are exchanged:
• The horse greatly facilitates Native American hunting and travel.
• Cows provide the New World with a novel source of food and hides.

The introduction of the gun to the New World greatly advances Native American hunting practices and revolutionizes warfare.

The Columbian Exchange

The New World ecology is disrupted by foreign species of plants and animals.

The indigenous population, having no immunity to fatal Old World communicable diseases (e.g., smallpox) declines dramatically.

Various diseases are spread both to and from the New World.

Tobacco is introduced to Europe and becomes extremely popular.

The European Nations Race to Colonize ❗

Spain, the nation that sponsored Columbus and the superpower of the day, was the first to establish colonies in the Americas. Eventually other countries, such as France, England, and the Netherlands, followed suit in an eager effort to carve out their own valuable pieces of the vast New World. While the different nations interacted with the indigenous population with varying levels of acceptance, with some (such as the French) permitting intermarriage, the natives and their culture were almost invariably viewed as inferior. Colonization was seen as a civilizing force, particularly in the realm of religion.

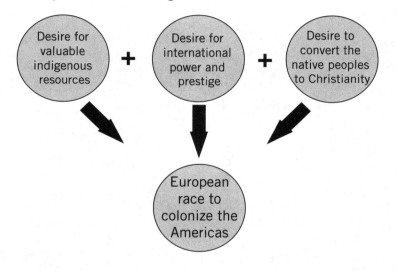

The establishment of a colony in the New World was an extremely expensive and risky venture! The likelihood of success was often slim, and the monetary losses involved could be catastrophic (even for the governments of Europe). The willingness of some nations (especially England) to gamble on colonization was largely due to the development of **joint stock companies,** which operate much like modern corporations. Stock in the company is sold to many different investors (or "shareholders"), who then reap the profits of a successful enterprise but risk only their own investment. **Jamestown,** the first permanent British colony in America, was founded through joint stock funding.

The Spanish Empire ❗

Spain was the ultimate colonial power in the Americas during the 16th and 17th centuries. While the European and Native American cultures did intermix freely, a racial caste system was established whereby whites were considered superior to those of color. Moreover, some of the Spanish labor practices amounted to little more than enslavement of the indigenous population.

Encomienda ❗

The **encomienda** system entailed a grant from the Spanish crown to certain colonists, usually to **conquistadors** ("conquerors"), giving them authority over a specified number of Native Americans. The colonists then had certain responsibilities toward these natives, such as providing religious instruction and protecting them from hostile tribes, in exchange for which the natives had to provide their labor. Unfortunately the indigenous people had little say in the matter.

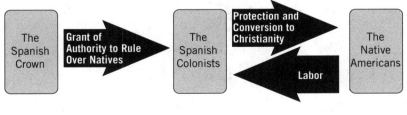

The Spanish Crown → Grant of Authority to Rule Over Natives → The Spanish Colonists → Protection and Conversion to Christianity / Labor → The Native Americans

The Encomienda System

> 💬 New World enterprises such as **sugar harvesting** and **silver mining** were very lucrative for the Spanish Empire. While the Native Americans were not technically considered slaves, the abundance of essentially free labor that the encomienda system provided was vital to the economic success of the colonial system.

The Caste System ❗

While Spanish and Portuguese colonization of North America was marked by a liberal mixing of cultures, and many colonists did marry Native American women, a racial hierarchy nonetheless developed. Intermingling did not create an egalitarian society.

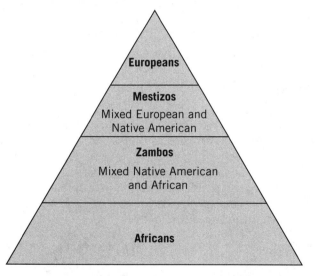

Europeans

Mestizos
Mixed European and Native American

Zambos
Mixed Native American and African

Africans

The Social Hierarchy in Spanish Colonial America

 Ask Yourself...

What might have been a more ethical labor program for the Spanish Empire to adopt than encomienda? Could the settlers have paid the Native Americans for their voluntary labor in the form of desired goods, and offered care and protection as well? Had they done so, might European and Native American relations have evolved differently?

PERIOD 2 (1607–1754):

Colonization of North America

The European colonization of North America laid the groundwork for the subsequent shaping of the United States. This section reviews the key characteristics of European influence on the continent and some of the major conflicts that arose in the 17th and 18th centuries in addition to providing an overview of slavery in the American colonies.

French, Dutch, and English Colonization 🔟

From the arrival of Christopher Columbus in the New World in 1492 until the English defeat of the **Spanish Armada** in 1588, Spain was the major colonial power in the Americas. After the decline of Spain's naval power in the Atlantic Ocean, other European nations seized the opportunity to do their own exploration and colonization in the Americas. Principal among these were France, the Netherlands, and Britain; each nation had its own motivations and goals, and each nation interacted with the Native Americans in its own unique way.

The French and the Dutch 🔟

The French and the Dutch arrived in the New World in relatively small numbers compared with the Spanish and the English. The colonists of both France and the Netherlands were primarily motivated by trading opportunities and therefore had many interactions with Native Americans.

Country	Major Colonial Outposts	Motivations	Interactions with Native Americans
France	Quebec City and other locations along the St. Lawrence River	• Trade alliances (fur) • Search for natural resources (gold) • Quest for religious converts	• Did not take a large amount of native land • Economic cooperation and intermarriage common • Few violent conflicts • Many natives killed by disease
The Netherlands	New Amsterdam (New York) and Albany	• Trade alliances (fur) • Slave trade • Creation of profit/merchant centers • Quest for geopolitical power and a passage west	• Took a large amount of native land • Intermarriage rare • Some toleration of native culture • Many natives killed by disease

The English ❗

The English moved to the New World in large numbers, often in full family units (as opposed to the French and Dutch settlers, who were usually single men). Unlike their counterparts from Spain, France, and the Netherlands, the English colonists largely tried to isolate themselves from the Native Americans.

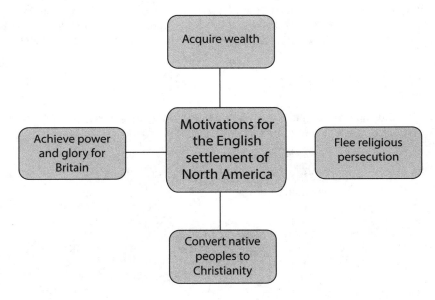

Acquire wealth

Achieve power and glory for Britain

Motivations for the English settlement of North America

Flee religious persecution

Convert native peoples to Christianity

 Ask Yourself...

What are the major similarities and differences among the various European colonization efforts in the Americas?

Early English Colonies 🔊

Compared with the other European powers, England didn't attempt to make significant settlements in North America until relatively late. England's first major settlement was on Roanoke Island, now in North Carolina, in the mid-1580s. This colony was extremely short-lived, however, and it had disappeared completely by 1590 (the Roanoke Island settlement is now known as the **Lost Colony**). It was nearly twenty years later, in 1607, when the English tried again and settled **Jamestown**.

The Chesapeake Colonies 🔊

The **Chesapeake Colonies** of Virginia and Maryland were among the earliest English settlements on the East Coast of North America.

Virginia	Both colonies:	Maryland
Most of the original inhabitants of Jamestown, the first major settlement, died of starvation or disease. The surrounding area became home to many settlements and Virginia eventually became one of the largest and most powerful of the colonies.	• Very rural, dependent on agriculture (tobacco in particular) • Rapid economic growth fueled by **indentured servitude,** later by slavery	This colony was founded in 1634 by **Lord Baltimore,** who settled the town of St. Mary's and wielded enormous power in the region.

The Virginia House of Burgesses 💬

In 1619, the year that slavery was introduced to the English colonies, Virginia established the **House of Burgesses**:

- the first elected assembly in the New World;
- a proto-democratic assembly that fostered debate and allowed any property-holding white male to vote;
- a legislative body that had the ability to create laws and levy taxes—but ultimately its power was restricted because it was beholden to the directors of the **Virginia Company** in London and the governor retained the power to veto laws passed by the assembly.

💬 Bacon's Rebellion

By the middle of the 17th century, most of the good land in the Virginia colony had been claimed. Newcomers who wished to settle in the area were forced to move farther and farther west from the coast, and that movement inevitably resulted in conflicts between English settlers and the Native Americans. Some of the settlers, led by **Nathaniel Bacon**, sought to attack and remove Native Americans from Virginia's western frontier in 1676. Bacon himself died soon after the uprising began, and the governor of Virginia, **William Berkeley**, refused to support the populist militias attacking the Native Americans. Nevertheless, Bacon's Rebellion remains one of the most important armed conflicts of the early colonial period.

Catholic Maryland 💬

The religious makeup of the Maryland colony was different from that of the colonies farther north. Whereas the New England colonies were a haven for Protestants who faced religious persecution of various types in Europe, Maryland was (initially) a haven for Catholics fleeing persecution in largely Protestant England.

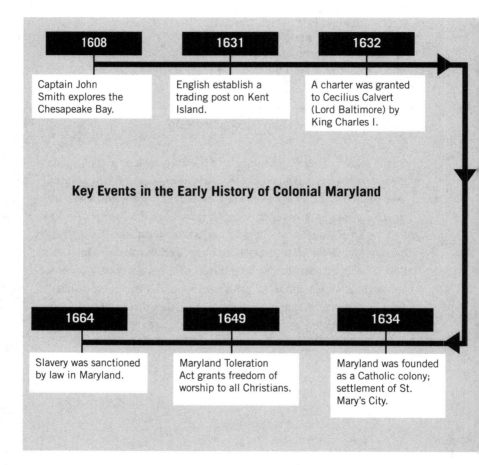

1608	1631	1632
Captain John Smith explores the Chesapeake Bay.	English establish a trading post on Kent Island.	A charter was granted to Cecilius Calvert (Lord Baltimore) by King Charles I.

Key Events in the Early History of Colonial Maryland

1664	1649	1634
Slavery was sanctioned by law in Maryland.	Maryland Toleration Act grants freedom of worship to all Christians.	Maryland was founded as a Catholic colony; settlement of St. Mary's City.

 Ask Yourself...

In what ways were the motivations for English settlement different across the earliest North American colonies?

New England ❗

At the beginning of the 17th century, a group of Protestants in England became disillusioned with the dominant **Anglican** Church (Church of England) and wished to purify it of Roman Catholic influence (hence the name **"Puritans"**). Within the Puritan movement, one faction—known as the **Separatists**—believed that the Church of England was so incapable of being reformed that they decided to travel to the New World in the early 1600s in the hope of establishing their ideal religious communities. Some of these settlers had intended to head to Virginia, but their boat, the **Mayflower**, went off course and landed farther north in New England. Because it was almost winter, these pilgrims decided to settle where they landed and called their colony **Plymouth**. Nearby colonies at Dover, Portsmouth, and Salem were also established.

The **Mayflower Compact** was an agreement that established a basic legal system in which power derived from the consent of the people and not from God.

Massachusetts Bay 💬

In 1629, the political situation in England changed and the non-Separatist Puritans began to feel a great deal of pressure from the authorities, who were cracking down on ministers with Puritan beliefs. The non-Separatists, also known as **Congregationalists**, maintained that they wanted to reform the Anglican Church from within but felt pressured to leave England. They ultimately received a royal charter from King Charles I and began to settle the **Massachusetts Bay Colony** (the area surrounding modern-day Boston).

A large number of Puritans moved to the Massachusetts Bay Colony between 1629 and 1642, and most of these were **Calvinists** who believed that God had predestined some people to be "saved" and others not to be "saved." They believed, furthermore, that "saved" individuals had an obligation to engage in hard work and to be a model for others.

Rhode Island

Ironically, despite the fact that the Puritans had fled England due to religious discrimination, they were not particularly tolerant of alternative points of view. One early victim of Puritan religious intolerance was a minister named **Roger Williams**, who believed in the separation of church and state and advocated for fair dealings with Native Americans.

Because of his outspoken and controversial views, Williams was banished from the Massachusetts Bay Colony and founded his own colony farther southwest: **Rhode Island**. In this new colony, voters were not required to be members of any particular church, and freedom of religion was more broadly granted than it had been in the stricter settlements of Massachusetts.

NOTABLE FIGURE:

Rhode Island became something of a haven for others who were not welcome in Massachusetts. **Anne Hutchinson,** an extremely well-educated woman who was the daughter of an Anglican clergyman, was banished from Massachusetts to Rhode Island in 1637 after she clashed with governor John Winthrop and others over the issue of what gave someone the right to be part of the "elect." Known as the **Antinomian Controversy,** this theological debate concerned the principle of salvation by grace as opposed to adherence to particular moral laws.

Ask Yourself...

How did religious ideology shape the early New England colonies? More specifically, in what ways did the banishment of individuals whose beliefs differed from those in positions of power within the Massachusetts Bay Colony lead to unity or factionalism?

The Middle Colonies 🔟

The so-called Middle Colonies—New York, New Jersey, Pennsylvania, and Delaware—were known as the "bread colonies" due to their excellent farmland and high-quality grain exports. There was less industry in these colonies than in the New England colonies, but more than in the Southern colonies (lumber production and shipbuilding, for example, were prominent economic activities). The population of the Middle Colonies was also more ethnically diverse than was that of the New England colonies, and as a result there was more tolerance of religious and cultural differences.

Characteristics of the Middle Colonies				
Settlers	Important People	Major Cities	Economics	Governance
Dutch, Swedish, English, Scots-Irish, Quakers, Catholics, Protestants, Jews	Peter Minuit, Peter Stuyvesant, John Berkeley, George Carteret, William Penn	New Amsterdam (New York City), Philadelphia	Farming (especially grain, fruits, and vegetables), livestock, timber, mining, trade	Proprietorship, royal charter

William Penn 💬

The founder of the Province of Pennsylvania (which included modern-day Delaware) was an English Quaker named William Penn. Penn was very progressive in his ideas about religious toleration, and as such was an important advocate for religious freedom and democratic ideals in the early colonies. Because he was a Quaker, Penn was also a pacifist and practiced friendly relations with the Native Americans. He also campaigned for peaceable solutions to various conflicts among the colonies and between the colonies and England.

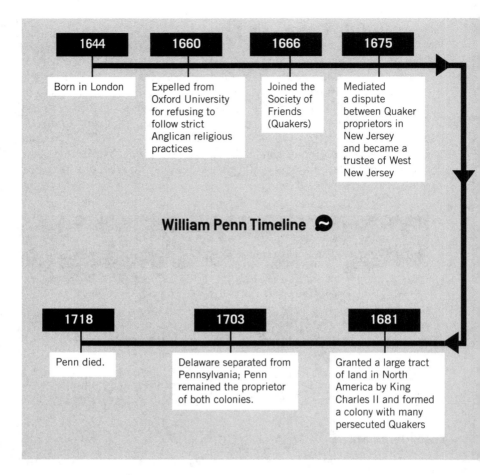

1644	1660	1666	1675
Born in London	Expelled from Oxford University for refusing to follow strict Anglican religious practices	Joined the Society of Friends (Quakers)	Mediated a dispute between Quaker proprietors in New Jersey and became a trustee of West New Jersey

William Penn Timeline

1718	1703	1681
Penn died.	Delaware separated from Pennsylvania; Penn remained the proprietor of both colonies.	Granted a large tract of land in North America by King Charles II and formed a colony with many persecuted Quakers

The Southern Colonies

Unlike the Northern and mid-Atlantic settlers, those who colonized the southern region of North America were primarily motivated by economic opportunities. The vast majority of the original settlers in the Carolinas and Georgia came from England, where they had struggled to prosper. In North America, these settlers found new opportunities in the form of lucrative cash crops, notably tobacco, indigo, and rice. The Southern colonies were largely rural, and the practicalities of growing large quantities of cash crops necessitated a large labor force.

The colony of Carolina split into North and South Carolina in 1729, and a large number of English settlers moved from Barbados in the Caribbean to South Carolina. Building on the economic model that they had seen in Barbados, these South Carolinians inaugurated the widespread use of slavery in the American south. Wealthy landowners developed huge plantations on which both slaves and indentured servants worked in miserable conditions.

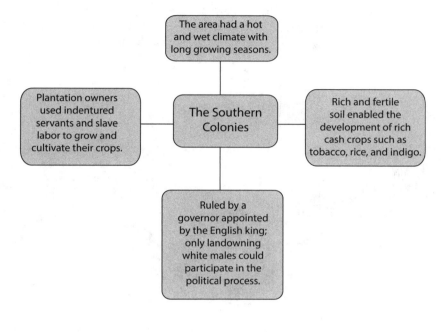

The area had a hot and wet climate with long growing seasons.

Plantation owners used indentured servants and slave labor to grow and cultivate their crops.

The Southern Colonies

Rich and fertile soil enabled the development of rich cash crops such as tobacco, rice, and indigo.

Ruled by a governor appointed by the English king; only landowning white males could participate in the political process.

Georgia

The first European settlers in Georgia were led by the Englishman **James Oglethorpe**, who arrived in the 1730s (Georgia was the last of the original thirteen colonies to be settled). As in the Carolinas, Georgia's economy was based primarily on agriculture. At the outset, Oglethorpe wanted Georgia to serve as a refuge for people who had been imprisoned in England due to debt, but the settlers came from many walks of life. Initially, Georgia did not allow slave labor, but slavery was legalized in 1749. Among other controversial decisions, Oglethorpe severely restricted land ownership and prohibited the use of alcohol.

Salutary Neglect !

The period between 1650 and the mid-1700s, especially the years immediately preceding the French and Indian War of 1754, is often known as the period of "Salutary Neglect" or "Benign Neglect." It was during this period that the English involved themselves in American colonial affairs as little as possible. England still regulated trade and other governmental activities in its North American territories, but it took a hands-off approach that enabled the Americans to develop a sense of autonomy as well as their own distinct culture.

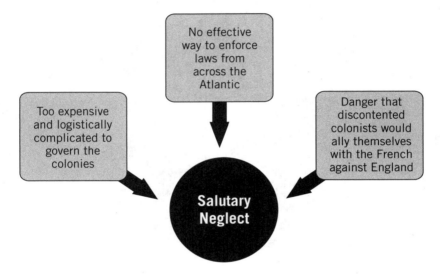

One of the distinctively American forms of democracy that arose during this period of Salutary Neglect was the New England town meeting. While the New England town meetings were not truly democratic in the modern sense of the word (they were restricted to white adult males), they were an important building block for later American political institutions.

New England Town Meetings

Free male citizens chose a group of people (selectmen) to govern the town the following year.	Free male citizens voted directly on public issues (direct, rather than representative democracy).	Free male citizens had the power to levy taxes and create laws.

During the age of Salutary Neglect, most of the political power in the Southern colonies was held by wealthy plantation owners. Because the southern economy was so intricately connected to the cultivation of rice, tobacco, and cotton, those plantation owners who used slaves amassed considerable wealth and influence. The Southern colonies were predominantly structured around colonial legislatures, and politically the planter class wielded the greatest influence in such assemblies.

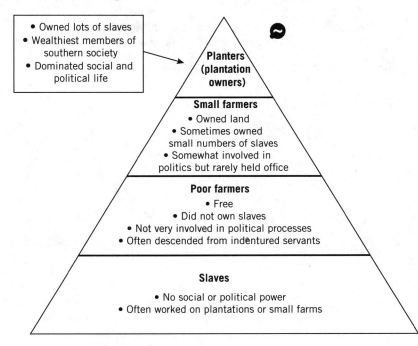

- Owned lots of slaves
- Wealthiest members of southern society
- Dominated social and political life

Planters (plantation owners)

Small farmers
- Owned land
- Sometimes owned small numbers of slaves
- Somewhat involved in politics but rarely held office

Poor farmers
- Free
- Did not own slaves
- Not very involved in political processes
- Often descended from indentured servants

Slaves
- No social or political power
- Often worked on plantations or small farms

Early Conflicts 🛈

Interactions with Native Americans 🛈

The early years of European colonization of the Americas were characterized by interaction with the native populations that often led to conflict.
The Europeans did establish friendly or mutually beneficial trading relationships with some Native Americans, but there was hostility between
the groups as well. Ultimately, huge numbers of Native Americans died
as a result of these early interactions with the Europeans, some through
warfare and other instances of physical violence but most through
epidemic disease. The Native Americans, who had not been exposed to
the same microbes that Europeans had been living with for centuries,
were highly susceptible to diseases such as smallpox, measles, influ-
enza, and diphtheria.

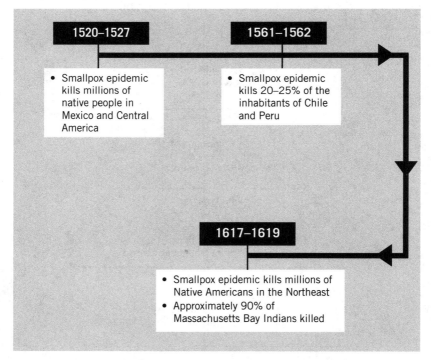

1520–1527

- Smallpox epidemic
  kills millions of
  native people in
  Mexico and Central
  America

1561–1562

- Smallpox epidemic
  kills 20–25% of the
  inhabitants of Chile
  and Peru

1617–1619

- Smallpox epidemic kills millions of
  Native Americans in the Northeast
- Approximately 90% of
  Massachusetts Bay Indians killed

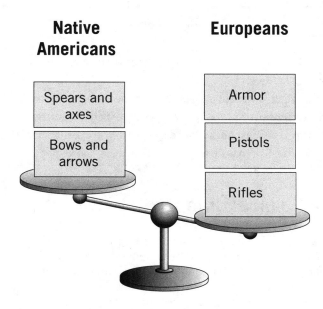

Native Americans

Europeans

Spears and axes

Bows and arrows

Armor

Pistols

Rifles

European Alliances with Native Americans 🛑

At the beginning of the 18th century, the French in North America were greatly outnumbered by the British. The French had a long history of settlement on the continent, particularly in regions that are now part of Canada. Because they were so few in number, and also because they had historically been more open to harmonious relations and inter-marriage with the Native Americans than were the British, the French allied themselves militarily with various Native American tribes in several major conflicts. The British also allied themselves with Native Americans, but were not as successful in doing so as were the French.

FRENCH	BRITISH
Allied with Huron, Algonquin, and Ottawa tribes as well as some members of the Iroquois League	Allied with some members of the Iroquois League
Alliances mainly in the Great Lakes region	Alliances mainly in upper New York
Generally more interested in trading (especially fur) than land	Generally more interested in land than trading

🔊 The Métis

- The Métis were descendants of indigenous North Americans and European settlers.
- Historically they were heavily involved in the Canadian fur trade.
- Some were involved as interpreters because they were often multilingual.
- They helped shape modern Canada, especially in expansion to the west.
- Many Métis children were exposed to French Catholicism.

British Colonial Unrest ❗

As late as the 1750s, very few colonists in North America could have imagined that they would ever be independent of Britain. The **Seven Years' War** (1754–1763) ignited the most intense period of conflict between the colonies and the European powers, but even prior to that there was evidence of unrest in North America.

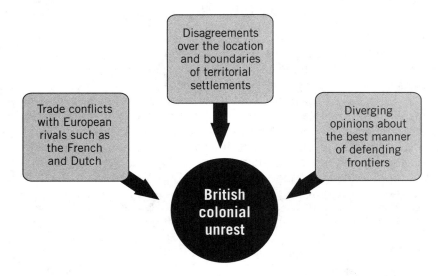

Smuggling

The British government was very concerned about trade relationships with its colonies and made every attempt to control the types of goods manufactured and shipped to other locations from North America. The colonists had to pay import taxes on goods that did not originate in Britain, and widespread smuggling resulted from the colonists' desire to avoid such restrictions.

Colonial smuggling techniques	Types of goods commonly smuggled in North American colonies
• Seeking to evade import and export taxes • Ignoring trade laws that prohibited particular goods • Bribing customs agents and other authorities • Sidestepping restrictions on geographical limits to trade	• Rum and molasses • Non-British manufactured and luxury goods • Enslaved Africans • Military equipment and weapons • Gold and silver bullion

Ask Yourself...

In what ways were colonists in North America able to resist pressures from Europe, and in what ways did they begin to form distinctively American identities in the 17th and 18th centuries?

The Salem Witch Trials

Throughout the early years of American history, there were numerous instances of mass hysteria. The most well-known of these is probably the notorious period during which there were multiple prosecutions and executions of individuals accused of witchcraft in Massachusetts in 1692 and 1693. Although these events are commonly known as the **Salem Witch Trials,** the legal hearings (such as they were) actually occurred in four or five different towns, including Danvers and Ipswich. Ultimately, about twenty people—mostly women—were hanged.

Causes

Long history of witchcraft trials in Europe

Biblical texts commanding capital punishment for "witches"

Suspicion of nontraditional or nonconformist viewpoints and behaviors

Gendered stereotypes about women and their bodies

Puritan religious fixation on the devil and the presence of evil in the world

Lack of knowledge about potential medical or psychological explanations for mysterious behavior

Legal proceedings centered around dubious evidence and forced confessions

Effects

Changing societal opinions about how to conduct fair trials

Increased suspicion of torture as a means of extracting confessions

Discontinuation of "spectral evidence" (witness testimony that the spirit of the accused appeared in a dream or vision)

Subsequent release of some of the accused; some executed individuals were posthumously exonerated

Continuation of the practice of "witch hunts" in the modern world (20th century "Red Scare," persecution of Arab Americans after 9/11, etc.)

King Philip's War ❗

There were, of course, many armed conflicts between the European colonists and various Native American tribes throughout the early centuries of American history. One of the most deadly occurred in 17th-century New England: **King Philip's War,** sometimes known as Metacom's War or Metacom's Rebellion. The war is named for the Wampanoag chief Metacom, who adopted the English name Philip.

The Wampanoag tribes had lived relatively peacefully alongside the English settlers for some time, but in the mid-17th century tensions increased over land disputes and English attempts to convert the natives to Christianity and European cultural practices. When Plymouth Colony controversially hanged three of Metacom's men for murder, the Native American tribes initiated a series of armed raids beginning in 1675, and in the several years that followed thousands of Native Americans and English settlers were killed. In the early conflicts, Metacom's forces gained a few victories, but ultimately the Native Americans were overpowered and decimated.

Effects of King Philip's War

* Over half of New England's towns were attacked; several were completely destroyed.
* New England's economy was devastated.
* About 1,000 English and 3,000 Native Americans were killed.
* Many surviving tribesmen were sold into slavery in the West Indies.
* The conflict helped lead to the development of a colonial British identity separate from those who lived in Britain.

The Pueblo Revolt ❗

At around the same time that the English colonists were clashing with Native Americans in the Northeast region, Spanish settlers in the Southwest had their own conflicts with local natives. By the late 16th century, the Spanish had seized hundreds of pueblos, or villages, in what is now New Mexico and Arizona. The Native Americans were frequently compelled into the Spanish encomienda system and were forbidden by Spanish priests from practicing their traditional religious rituals.

The Pueblo people eventually revolted. In 1680, led by a charismatic leader named Popé, more than 8,000 warriors engaged in coordinated attacks against the Spanish that left hundreds dead and forced the survivors to seek refuge in the governor's palace in Santa Fe. The Pueblos were independent for twelve years, during which time Catholicism was nearly eradicated and the use of the Spanish language was penalized. Popé died in 1688, and in 1692, the Spanish returned to the area with a superior military force and reconquered the Southwest for Spain.

1540: The Spanish conquistadors, led by Francisco Vásquez de Coronado, claim large swaths of land in the Southwest.

1598: Spanish soldiers and priests impose the *encomienda* system on the native populations.

1668: Popé first suggests a revolt against harsh Spanish domination but is unable to gather enough support.

1675: Popé is arrested by the Spanish and tortured, but refuses to convert to Christianity.

1680: Popé organizes and leads the Pueblo Revolt, killing many Spanish settlers and destroying their Catholic missions.

⊙	Other Important Conflicts and Alliances between Europeans and Native Americans
Powhatan Wars	Between 1610 and 1646, the Powhatan tribes fought the English settlers of the Virginia colony, resulting in a boundary established between English and Native American lands.
Beaver Wars (a.k.a. Iroquois Wars)	Between the 1640s and 1680s, the Iroquois fought the French and other Native Americans for control of the fur trade in the Great Lakes region.
Chickasaw Wars	Between 1721 and 1763, the Chickasaw tribes allied themselves with the British against the French and their allies in the southern Mississippi valley region, ending with France ceding much of its land to the British in the Treaty of Paris.
The Catawba People	The Catawba tribes of the Piedmont region (North and South Carolina) coexisted relatively peacefully with European settlers, fighting alongside the British during the Seven Years' War of 1756–1763 and alongside the Patriots during the American Revolution.
The Huron People	The Huron tribes of the Great Lakes and Quebec regions were enemies of the Iroquois and fought alongside the French during the Seven Years' War of 1756–1763.

 Ask Yourself...

What are some of the ways that Native Americans sought to maintain their cultural identity in the face of pressures from European colonists?

Later Evolution of British Colonies ❶

European Enlightenment ❶

The later generations of European colonists in North America were, generally speaking, less religiously fervent than were the original settlers who preceded them. In large measure this was a result of the influential ideas of the European **Enlightenment,** a major movement within western philosophy that had an enormous impact on attitudes toward traditional morality and religious beliefs. Enlightenment thinkers promoted the importance of human reason and argued that society could advance most effectively through rational, rather than supernatural, forces. Only the elite, well-educated colonists read the Enlightenment thinkers' works directly, but popularized versions of Enlightenment philosophy nevertheless had a major influence on the development of American identity.

Francis Bacon (1561–1626)	• Developed the "inductive method" of scientific investigation • Emphasized coming to conclusions through observation and reasoning
Thomas Hobbes (1588–1679)	• Argued that all humans are self-centered and prone to evil • Claimed that the best form of government was to have an all-powerful monarch
René Descartes (1596–1650)	• Made great advances in algebra and geometry • Developed a deductive approach to philosophy that emphasized math and logic
John Locke (1632–1704)	• Hypothesized that the human mind is a "tabula rasa," or blank slate, ultimately shaped by a person's environment • Believed that knowledge was gained by experience rather than supernatural or outside truth
Isaac Newton (1642–1727)	• Published important theories on gravity • Articulated a series of scientific laws describing the functioning of the natural world

The First Great Awakening ❗

Even though American society at large was experiencing the influence of European Enlightenment ideals during the 17th and 18th centuries, there was a wave of religious revivalism in the 1730s and 1740s that swept both Protestant parts of Europe and the American colonies. Led by Congregationalist minister Jonathan Edwards and Methodist minister George Whitefield, this evangelical movement was known as the **First Great Awakening.**

Jonathan Edwards
- Puritan/Calvinist roots
- Emphasized personal religious experience
- Not a believer in church hierarchy
- Famous sermon, "Sinners in the Hands of an Angry God," stressed emotional connection with God and deterministic beliefs about heaven and hell

George Whitefield
- Originally Anglican; one of the founders of the Methodist movement after he moved to North America
- Sermons attracted large crowds and mass "conversions"
- Emphasis on proselytization and gospel
- Preached an egalitarian message and was critical of slaveholders' harsh treatment of their slaves

First Great Awakening

Ask Yourself...

How were the ideals of the European Enlightenment reflected in the thinking of the founders of the United States as evidenced by the Declaration of Independence and the American Constitution?

Colonial Legislatures and Courts ❗

The colonists were fairly autonomous in their governing structures, with each colony headed by a governor who had been appointed either by the king of England or by the proprietor of the colony in question. These governors were dependent to some degree upon the consent of the colonists and relied upon the colonial legislatures for their financial resources. Except for Pennsylvania, the colonies were modeled after the British Parliament's bicameral system in which there was a "lower house" of members who were directly elected and an "upper house" of members who were appointed.

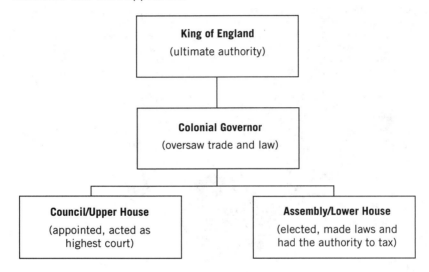

Mercantilism ❗

The broad economic theory that dominated throughout most of the colonial period in North America was known as **mercantilism.** The two main ideals of mercantilist economic theory were favorable balance of trade and control of specie (or currency). Balance of trade, from the British point of view, meant exporting more goods and raw materials from the colonies than importing. One means of achieving this balance was to impose tariffs on imports from other countries that might compete with British-owned goods.

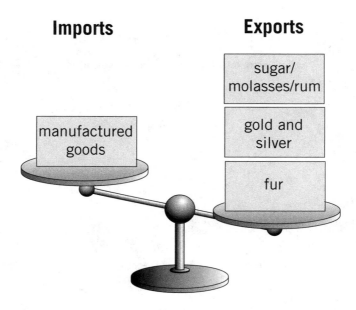

Imports

Exports

| manufactured goods |

| sugar/ molasses/rum |
| gold and silver |
| fur |

The Navigation Acts 💬

Several of the most important (and controversial) tariffs imposed by the British crown on the American colonies were known collectively as the **Navigation Acts,** passed between 1651 and 1673. Intended to shore up British control of trade to and from North America, the Navigation Acts required the colonists to buy British goods and to sell certain goods only to England. These restrictive laws ultimately fueled colonial dissent and resistance to British rule.

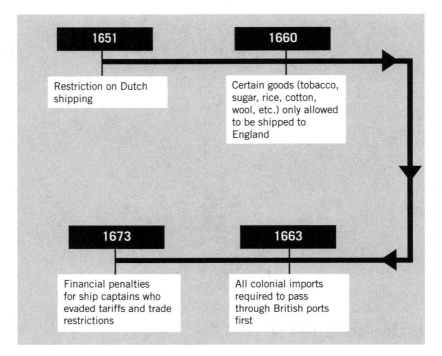

1651

Restriction on Dutch shipping

1660

Certain goods (tobacco, sugar, rice, cotton, wool, etc.) only allowed to be shipped to England

1673

Financial penalties for ship captains who evaded tariffs and trade restrictions

1663

All colonial imports required to pass through British ports first

Ask Yourself...

How did British economic policies ultimately backfire and help stoke the flames of dissent and revolution in the colonies?

Slavery 🛑

The widespread use of slavery in England's North American colonies began as early as the settling of the Carolinas by Europeans in the mid-1600s. In the centuries before the American Revolution, the vast majority of slaves taken from Africa ended up in the Caribbean and South America. There were, however, more than 300,000 slaves brought against their will from Africa (and the Caribbean) to North America. According to some estimates, by 1790 the number of enslaved blacks in England's North American colonies reached as high as 750,000.

Number of Slaves Embarked from Slave Ships				
Region	1651 to 1700	1701 to 1750	1751 to 1800	1801 to 1850	*Total*
North America	15,047	145,973	149,509	77,704	388,233
Europe	2,896	4,126	1,113	0	8,135
British Caribbean	283,270	637,620	1,175,703	194,452	2,291,045
French Caribbean	38,140	294,471	700,662	86,397	1,119,670
Dutch Americas	124,158	126,464	168,751	25,355	444,728
Spanish Americas	46,313	55,291	90,242	588,558	780,404
Brazil	464,050	891,851	1,097,166	2,054,726	4,507,793
Total	973,874	2,155,796	3,383,146	3,027,192	9,540,008

Source: The Trans-Atlantic Slave Trade Database, www.slavevoyages.org/assessment/estimates

Transition from Indentured Servitude 🔱

Prior to the influx of massive numbers of African slaves to North America, the European colonists used Native American slaves in very small numbers and indentured servants in larger numbers. As agriculture grew exponentially in the colonies, especially in the South, labor needs were more intensive than indentured servants could meet. Engaging white laborers, furthermore, had proved problematic for landowners, as evidenced by the unrest and violence of events such as Bacon's Rebellion in 1676. While both indentured servants and slaves endured terrible living and working conditions, indentured servants enjoyed several important advantages.

Indentured Servants
- European origin
- Voluntary
- Contractual "employees" with legal rights
- Typically 4–7 years of labor

Slaves
- African origin (usually)
- Involuntary
- No legal rights
- Typically lifelong labor

Triangular Trade and the Middle Passage 🔱

Slaves were brought from Africa to North America via the so-called **Middle Passage,** the middle portion of the triangular trade route among the colonies, Africa, and Europe. The conditions aboard the slave ships were horrendous, with slaves packed as tightly as physically possible into the hulls of the ships. Many slaves died en route, and some even committed suicide because of the misery they were forced to endure.

European slave traders sold African slaves at auctions and used the profits to buy sugar, cotton, tobacco, and other raw goods to take back to Europe.

Slave ships left Europe for West and Central Africa carrying cloth, guns, and other manufactured goods.

European slave traders bought slaves from African slave traders and packed their ships before heading to the Americas and the Caribbean.

Ask Yourself...

What were some of the primary reasons for the increase in slave labor in the British colonies in the 17th century?

Racial Segregation and the Law 🛑

Slavery in the American colonies cannot be separated from the colonists' attitudes about race. In addition to the obvious fact that African slaves had a different skin tone than the majority-white population of the colonies and were thus easily identified, Europeans had a long history of rationalizing the inferior treatment of dark-skinned people. The intersection of racial attitudes and the law is seen best in a series of laws passed in Virginia between 1640 and 1705, a critical period during which slave labor began to take hold in the North American colonies.

Virginia Race and Slave Laws

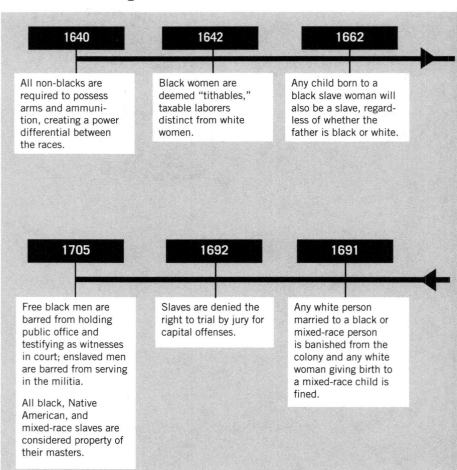

1640	1642	1662
All non-blacks are required to possess arms and ammunition, creating a power differential between the races.	Black women are deemed "tithables," taxable laborers distinct from white women.	Any child born to a black slave woman will also be a slave, regardless of whether the father is black or white.

1705	1692	1691
Free black men are barred from holding public office and testifying as witnesses in court; enslaved men are barred from serving in the militia. All black, Native American, and mixed-race slaves are considered property of their masters.	Slaves are denied the right to trial by jury for capital offenses.	Any white person married to a black or mixed-race person is banished from the colony and any white woman giving birth to a mixed-race child is fined.

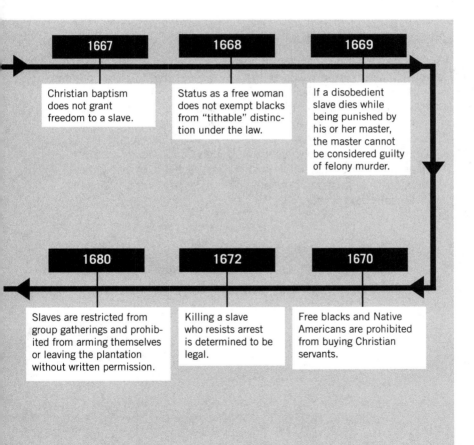

1667

Christian baptism does not grant freedom to a slave.

1668

Status as a free woman does not exempt blacks from "tithable" distinction under the law.

1669

If a disobedient slave dies while being punished by his or her master, the master cannot be considered guilty of felony murder.

1680

Slaves are restricted from group gatherings and prohibited from arming themselves or leaving the plantation without written permission.

1672

Killing a slave who resists arrest is determined to be legal.

1670

Free blacks and Native Americans are prohibited from buying Christian servants.

The Development of Slave Culture ❗

As colonization spread in the Americas and in the Caribbean, and as slave labor became entrenched in colonial societies, distinct slave cultures began to develop. These cultures took on various characteristics that were regionally distinctive, but the blending of African and European linguistic and religious influences was commonplace. Religions such as voodoo, for example, developed in the Caribbean with a blending of African animist and European Christian beliefs and rituals. Enslaved blacks often sang songs from their African homelands as they worked in the fields and developed art that was heavily influenced by African tribal traditions.

Elements of Slave Culture

- **Folktales:** Building on the oral traditions common in African societies, slaves told folktales and fables that reflected African themes and characters, such as the trickster Br'er Rabbit.
- **Music:** Using instruments (many of which were similar to those found in Africa), song, and dance, slaves developed a unique musical culture.
- **Religion:** White slaveowners were strongly encouraged to convert their slaves to Christianity; most slaves practiced an evangelical form of Protestantism, but some held on to their African animist or Muslim traditions.

 Ask Yourself...

In what ways did African slaves in the Americas and the Caribbean seek to preserve their cultural heritage as distinct from the dominant white European culture?

PERIOD 3 (1754–1800):
Conflict and American Independence

The early United States was shaped through conflict—conflict both with British and among the colonists themselves. Even after navigating the difficult waters of the Revolutionary War, Americans were challenged by figuring out what they wanted the country to be—and what they wanted it to *not* be.

Seven Years' War (1754–1763) ❗

The British and French had been feuding with each other for years, and by the mid-18th century, American colonists found themselves stuck in the middle of it. Westward bound English settlers clashed with the French fur trappers, who feared the English were encroaching on their territory. Soon an all-out war between the two nations began—the colonists siding with the British, and the Indians siding with the French, the European power with which they had the best relations. The English and colonists referred to this conflict as the **French and Indian War.**

Albany Plan of Union (1754) 💬

At the start of the French and Indian War, the colonists toyed with the idea of a unified government.

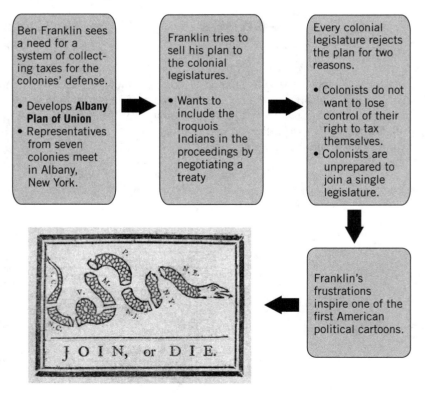

Ben Franklin sees a need for a system of collecting taxes for the colonies' defense.

- Develops **Albany Plan of Union**
- Representatives from seven colonies meet in Albany, New York.

➡️

Franklin tries to sell his plan to the colonial legislatures.

- Wants to include the Iroquois Indians in the proceedings by negotiating a treaty

➡️

Every colonial legislature rejects the plan for two reasons.

- Colonists do not want to lose control of their right to tax themselves.
- Colonists are unprepared to join a single legislature.

⬇️

Franklin's frustrations inspire one of the first American political cartoons.

⬅️

JOIN, or DIE.

Outcome of the Seven Years' War ❗

The British eventually won this long, drawn-out war. They gained control of Canada and the land east of the Mississippi Valley.

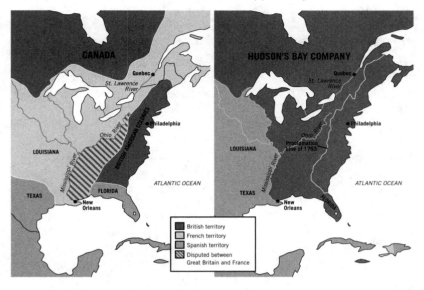

Prewar Boundaries, 1754   **Postwar Boundaries, 1763**

Crown and Indian Resistance to Westward Expansion 💬

Any hopes that colonists had to move westward in the immediate after-math of the Seven Years' War were quickly stymied by two challenges.

Pontiac's Rebellion 〰	Proclamation of 1763 💬
Background: After the war, the British raised prices on goods sold to the Native Americans, as well as stopped paying for use of Indian land.	**Background**: Chief Pontiac attacked colonial outposts in the Ohio Valley.
What happened: Ottawa war chief Pontiac led attacks on colonial outposts in the Ohio Valley.	**What happened**: To prevent further conflicts with Native Americans, the British issued this proclamation to stop colonists from settling west of the rivers running through the Appalachians. It did not stop settlers from moving westward, but it did foster colonial resentment toward the British crown.

Fallout of the Seven Years' War ❗

Britain's victory also signaled a turning point in its relationship with the colonists.

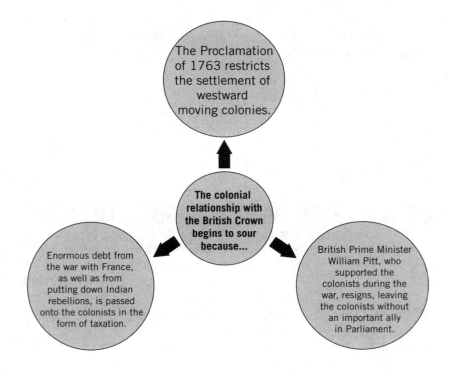

The Proclamation of 1763 restricts the settlement of westward moving colonies.

The colonial relationship with the British Crown begins to sour because...

Enormous debt from the war with France, as well as from putting down Indian rebellions, is passed onto the colonists in the form of taxation.

British Prime Minister William Pitt, who supported the colonists during the war, resigns, leaving the colonists without an important ally in Parliament.

 Ask Yourself...

In what ways did the French and Indian War and its aftermath signal a change for British colonial rule?

The Revolutionary War 🔵

In the decades leading up to the Revolutionary War, American colonists began to develop a sense of identity separate from their British colonizers. The British responded to this separation by implementing new draconian laws. The combination of these two elements was enough to jumpstart an eight-year war.

Declaratory Act 🔵

A major point of contention between the colonists and the British government was over the right to tax the colonists. Since they had no say in the British Parliament, American colonists were at the whim of a government body that had no accountability to them.

Colonists	British
Colonists wanted the right to determine their own taxes.	The British insisted that the colonists were already represented in Parliament, whether they had a vote or not (a concept known as virtual representation).
James Otis wrote a pamphlet entitled *The Rights of the British Colonies Asserted and Proved* coining the phrase "No taxation without representation."	The British passed the **Declaratory Act,** asserting the British government's ability to tax and legislate in all cases anywhere in its colonies.

The Priority of Self-Rule 🛈

The colonists developed a taste for self-rule for two reasons, one practical (salutary neglect) and one theoretical (Enlightenment ideals).

Practical Reason

- Due to the distance between the colonies and Great Britain, the British were not able to enforce every trade rule, arbitrate every dispute, and oversee economic violation in the New World.

- While England established absentee customs officials, the colonies were mostly left to self-govern.

- This salutary neglect (or benign neglect) allowed for the development of an independent American culture and identity, as opposed to a transplanted English culture.

Theoretical Reason

- At the time of this salutary neglect, European philosophers were describing the ideals of what historians refer to as the Enlightenment Period.

- These include principles such as liberty, equality, and popular sovereignty.

- Thomas Hobbes and John Locke were two Enlightenment philosophers whose ideas of the social contract inspired America's Founding Fathers to seek self-rule.

Colonists prioritize self-rule over colonial protection.

Colonial Resistance

The Navigation Acts proved to be highly unpopular among the American colonists and eventually led to widespread smuggling and other forms of resistance to British trade policies. The so-called Dominion of New England, in particular, generated a lot of hostility among the colonists. The short-lived Dominion, 1686–1689, was an administrative experiment designed to centralize and unify the New England and mid-Atlantic colonies such that the British crown could more easily control them and clamp down on the colonists, who frequently ignored laws such as those enumerated in the various Navigation Acts.

Hobbes and Locke ❗

Both Thomas Hobbes, in his book *Leviathan* (1651), and John Locke, in *Second Treatise of Government* (1689) arrived at the importance of self-rule through the understanding of a **social contract**. How they got to that common idea is quite different, and stems from each philosopher's view of human nature.

John Locke

People are not inherently evil, but it is nonetheless important to create a social contract so that the government could act as a neutral party to settle disputes and provide for our communal defense.

Thomas Hobbes

Humans are inherently evil and will kill each other if left without laws. Humans escape this state of nature by using a social contract—giving up total freedom in order to have safety and security.

Both philosophers agree that the social contract consists of sacrificing certain liberties for the common good. Therefore, according to each, government is by the people and exists with the consent of the governed (although Hobbes did maintain that an absolute authority figure would best benefit a society). The belief in the consent of the governed, which is at the heart of self-rule, animated the American Revolution.

Founding Fathers ❗

Inspired by the Enlightenment-era philosophers, the men who became known as the **Founding Fathers** emerged in leadership roles as the colonies approached the Revolutionary War. They were all wealthy elites, and some even owned slaves—an attribute at odds with some of the Enlightenment ideals, such as equality and the consent of the governed.

The following are some of the Founding Fathers you should know.

	Founding Father	State	Education	Occupation (pre-Constitutional Convention	Fun fact
	John Adams	Massachusetts	Harvard College	Lawyer	Mr. Adams became the first president to live in the White House.
	Benjamin Franklin	Pennsylvania	Self-educated	News Publisher, Inventor, Scientist, All-Around Fascinating Guy	The French, both men and women, took fashion inspiration from Ben Franklin.
	Alexander Hamilton	New York	Kings College	Army Officer	Hamilton was raised in the Caribbean and orphaned there as a youth—humble beginnings for the subject of a major Broadway hit!
	Thomas Jefferson	Virginia	College of William and Mary	Lawyer	Jefferson founded the University of Virginia.
	George Washington	Virginia	Primary education through tutors	Surveyor, Army General	Washington never had wooden teeth—his dentures were actually made from ivory, and sometimes, human teeth.

> 〰 Charles Beard, an early 20th-century historian, provides a cynical theory about the Founding Fathers. In his 1913 book, *An Economic Interpretation of the Constitution of the United States*, Beard argues that the Founding Fathers participated in the Constitutional Convention for personal gain, constructing the Constitution in a way that would protect the interests of wealthy elites.

Quartering of Soldiers ❗

The British passed **Quartering Acts** in 1765 and 1774. Under these laws, the colonies were required to house and feed British soldiers. Most colonies refused to accommodate, which only heightened tensions between Great Britain and its colonies. Colonists saw the 1774 Quartering Act as an example of the **Intolerable Acts**, laws that were intended to punish the colonists.

Townshend Acts 〰

In 1767, the British minister to the exchequer (basically a treasury minister), Charles Townshend, penned a series of laws for Prime Minister William Pitt to enact. The Townshend Acts greatly antagonized the colonists. Some of the measures included the following:

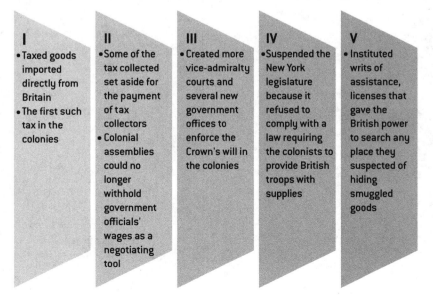

I	II	III	IV	V
• Taxed goods imported directly from Britain • The first such tax in the colonies	• Some of the tax collected set aside for the payment of tax collectors • Colonial assemblies could no longer withhold government officials' wages as a negotiating tool	• Created more vice-admiralty courts and several new government offices to enforce the Crown's will in the colonies	• Suspended the New York legislature because it refused to comply with a law requiring the colonists to provide British troops with supplies	• Instituted writs of assistance, licenses that gave the British power to search any place they suspected of hiding smuggled goods

Boston Massacre 💬

Colonists' frustration with the quartering of soldiers and other British demands came to a head on March 5, 1770, with the infamous **Boston Massacre**.

The Quartering Act of 1765 stationed large numbers of troops in America and made the colonists responsible for the cost of feeding and housing them.

The soldiers sought off-hour employment and so competed with colonists for jobs.

A mob pelted a group of soldiers with rock-lined snowballs.

- 💥 British soldiers responded by firing on the crowd, killing five colonists.
- 💥 Colonial propaganda suggested that the soldiers fired into a crowd of innocent bystanders.
- 💥 In a forerunner to an important protection that would appear in the Constitution—the rights of the accused—John Adams defended the soldiers in court.

I'm the Tax Man

The British had accumulated significant debts following the Seven Years' War. Incoming king, **George III**, and British Prime Minister **George Grenville** decided that the burden for this debt should fall, in part, on the colonists, who had benefited from the war. The colonists, on the other hand, felt that they had contributed many soldiers toward the war effort, which represented their share of the sacrifice. In order to attempt to make ends meet, Grenville's parliament passed a number of taxes. The **Sugar Act** and **Stamp Act** were two of the most significant ones.

Sugar Act

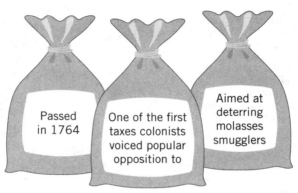

Passed in 1764

One of the first taxes colonists voiced popular opposition to

Aimed at deterring molasses smugglers

Stamp Act

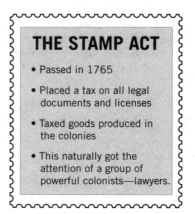

THE STAMP ACT

- Passed in 1765

- Placed a tax on all legal documents and licenses

- Taxed goods produced in the colonies

- This naturally got the attention of a group of powerful colonists—lawyers.

Sons of Liberty 💬

Opponents of these acts united around the colonies to protest the implementation of new taxes.

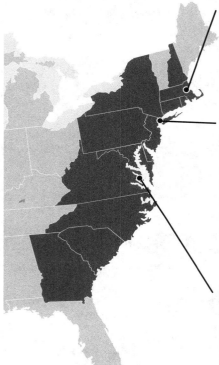

Boston, Massachusetts (1765)
Mobs burn the customs officers in effigy, tear down a customs house, and nearly destroy the governor's mansion.

New York City, New York (1773)
Sons of Liberty write a pamphlet known as the "Association of the Sons of Liberty in New York" that declares that any agent who supports carrying out the Tea Act is an enemy to the colonies and will be barred from employment or business transactions.

Williamsburg, Virginia (1765)
Patrick Henry drafts the Virginia Stamp Act Resolves, protesting the tax and asserting the colonists' right to a large measure of self-government.

As a result of the widespread opposition, duty collectors refused to do their jobs. The Stamp Act was repealed in 1766, and King George replaced Prime Minister Grenville with Lord Rockingham, an opponent of the Stamp Act. Rockingham stopped short of denying the British Crown the ability to legislate and collect taxes from the colonies.

Boston Tea Party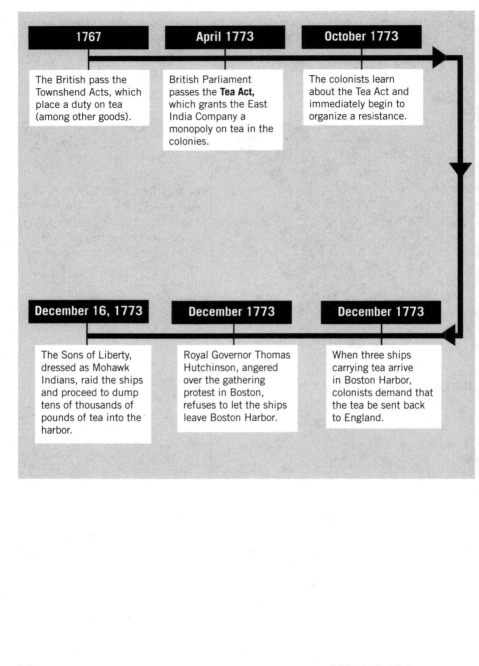

1767	April 1773	October 1773
The British pass the Townshend Acts, which place a duty on tea (among other goods).	British Parliament passes the **Tea Act,** which grants the East India Company a monopoly on tea in the colonies.	The colonists learn about the Tea Act and immediately begin to organize a resistance.

December 16, 1773	December 1773	December 1773
The Sons of Liberty, dressed as Mohawk Indians, raid the ships and proceed to dump tens of thousands of pounds of tea into the harbor.	Royal Governor Thomas Hutchinson, angered over the gathering protest in Boston, refuses to let the ships leave Boston Harbor.	When three ships carrying tea arrive in Boston Harbor, colonists demand that the tea be sent back to England.

Boycotts 💬

The colonists organized themselves to protest the news taxes and, in particular, the Townshend Acts. In 1768, Samuel Adams wrote the **Massachusetts Circular Letter** to the various colonial assemblies advocating a resistance to the new taxes.

> The [Massachusetts] House, therefore, hope[s] that this letter will be candidly considered...as expressing a...common concern, in the same manner as they would be glad to receive the sentiments of your or any other House of Assembly on the continent.
>
> ...it is an essential, unalterable right, in nature, engrafted into the British constitution, as a fundamental law, and ever held sacred and irrevocable by the subjects within the realm, that what a man has honestly acquired is absolutely his own, which he may freely give, but cannot be taken from him without his consent; that the American subjects may, therefore, exclusive of any consideration of charter rights, with a decent firmness, adapted to the character of free men and subjects, assert this natural and constitutional right.

Effects of the Massachusetts Circular Letter:

- The British ordered the assemblies *not* to address the Massachusetts letter (which obviously made the letter the primary thing the assemblies wanted to discuss).

- Governors of colonies where legislatures discussed the letter dissolved those legislatures, which of course, further infuriated colonists.

- Colonists held rallies and organized boycotts, which were larger than any previous demonstration due to the inclusion of commoners (previously only aristocrats participated in such demonstrations).

- British merchants, directly impacted by the protests, joined the colonists in calling for a repeal of the Townshend Acts.

- After two years of protest, Parliament repealed the Townshend duties, although not the other statutes of the Townshend Acts, and not the duty on tea.

Committees of Correspondence ⊘

Following the passage of the Townshend Acts, the colonists set up groups known as **Committees of Correspondence** throughout the colonies to organize plans for resistance to their British occupiers and inform one another of the political mood.

The success of the anti-Townshend Acts demonstrations began to inspire colonists that they could resist the British Empire in a variety of ways. Some colonists were even openly calling for a revolution. Writer **Mercy Otis Warren**, a friend of Abigail Adams and Martha Washington, produced pamphlets to rally support for such an action. John Dickenson wrote a series of essays known as *Letters from a Farmer in Pennsylvania* to garner further opposition to the Townshend Acts.

First Continental Congress 💬

The First Continental Congress convened in 1774.

All colonies except for Georgia sent representatives to discuss what should be the appropriate arrangement between the colonies and the British Parliament.

The colonies set up a Continental Association, and towns created committees of observation to enforce the boycotts.

Committees of observation replaced British-appointed assemblies and began to act as local governments.

Committees of observation collected taxes, interrupted court proceedings, organized militias, and stock-piled weapons.

Loyalists vs. Patriots ❗

With war on the horizon, the battle lines were drawn. Colonists identified as either **Loyalists** or **Patriots**. Some, particularly the pacifist Quakers in Pennsylvania, did not take a side and hoped the whole thing would blow over.

Loyalists	Patriots
Loyal to the British Crown	Advocates of complete independence from Great Britain
Anglican (members of the Church of England)	White and Protestant
Merchants dependent on trade with England	Property holders
Religious and ethnic minorities	Urban artisans
Many slaves who felt they had a better chance of freedom under the British than under the Patriots	New Englanders (Puritans had long opposed Anglicans.)

Timeline of the Revolutionary War 🛑

The following is a brief overview of the parts of the war you must know for the AP test. Remember, the test writers do not care much about military history, so the scope of what you need to know is not terribly overwhelming.

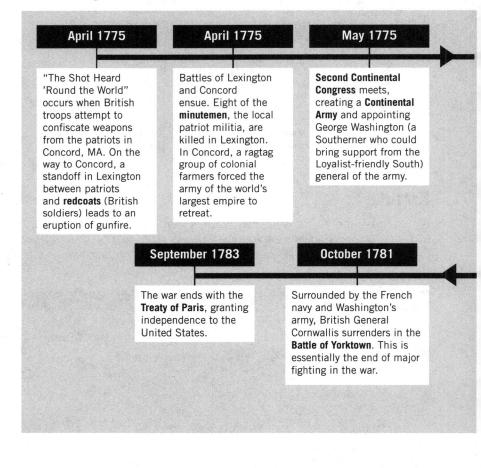

April 1775

"The Shot Heard 'Round the World" occurs when British troops attempt to confiscate weapons from the patriots in Concord, MA. On the way to Concord, a standoff in Lexington between patriots and **redcoats** (British soldiers) leads to an eruption of gunfire.

April 1775

Battles of Lexington and Concord ensue. Eight of the **minutemen**, the local patriot militia, are killed in Lexington. In Concord, a ragtag group of colonial farmers forced the army of the world's largest empire to retreat.

May 1775

Second Continental Congress meets, creating a **Continental Army** and appointing George Washington (a Southerner who could bring support from the Loyalist-friendly South) general of the army.

September 1783

The war ends with the **Treaty of Paris**, granting independence to the United States.

October 1781

Surrounded by the French navy and Washington's army, British General Cornwallis surrenders in the **Battle of Yorktown**. This is essentially the end of major fighting in the war.

July 1775	January 1776
Colonists create the **Olive Branch Petition**, hoping to avoid war with the British Empire. Given the colonists' recent rebellious behavior, King George III rejects the proposal.	**Thomas Paine** inspires colonists to fight for independence when he lays out the benefits of republicanism over monarchy in his pamphlet *Common Sense.*

October 1777	July 1776
After many defeats to the British, the colonists experienced a reversal of fortune with the **Battle of Saratoga**. The colonists' decisive victory in upstate New York allowed the patriots to recruit more volunteers. It also got the attention of the French, whose government agreed to an alliance with the Continental Congress. The French send military advisers, weapons, and financial assistance.	The Second Continental Congress approves the **Declaration of Independence**, a document outlining the general grievances that the colonists hold regarding King George III.

 Ask Yourself...

1. What factors inspired the colonists to seek independence?
2. Were all actions by the colonists against the British Empire just? Which were and which were not? Why?

Conflict and American Independence

Revolutionary Politics 🔔

As the Revolution went on, more and more colonists began to reject policies associated with the monarchy. These policies included anything that had to do with the preservation of the aristocracy or laws that were held over from the English feudal era. The politics of the Revolutionary period strongly favored ideals of the European Enlightenment: namely, individual liberty and God-given rights.

🔁 Few customs held over from the English feudal period can be seen in more stark contrast to the ideals of the Revolution than the primogeniture laws. These were inheritance laws that guaranteed a father's land would be given to his eldest son. These kinds of inheritance laws contradicted the spirit of fairness and equality promised by the Declaration of Independence. Within fourteen years of Georgia becoming the first state to outlaw primogeniture in 1777, all states had banned the practice.

Natural Rights 🔔

In reaction to the oppressive rule of the English monarchy, the Founding Fathers touted the importance of **republicanism**, or representative government. This argument was rooted in appeals to natural rights— ideals explored by Enlightenment philosophers. Central to these ideals was the Consent of the Governed. Two documents that articulated the importance of natural rights were Thomas Paine's *Common Sense* and the Declaration of Independence, authored by Thomas Jefferson.

Common Sense

A popular pamphlet in pre-Revolutionary America due to its use of plain language, Thomas Paine's famous text called for independence from England and a new, republican form of government.

Declaration of Independence

Using less of the plain language of Paine and more of the lofty language of Enlightenment thinkers, Thomas Jefferson nonetheless memorably captured the scope of natural rights by writing "We hold these truths to be self-evident, that all men are created equal, that they are endowed by their Creator with certain unalienable Rights, that among these are Life, Liberty and the Pursuit of Happiness."

Push for Representative Democracy ❶

Post-Revolutionary War America had to confront new challenges. If the Revolution was based on the doctrine that "all men are created equal," where would this leave blacks and women? The number of free blacks in the colonies grew during and after the war, but their increased presence among whites was also accompanied by a growth of racist publications and legislation. Further, women were denied the vote in the early Republic, and the country was home to 700,000 enslaved people at the end of the war.

Pennsylvania Gradual Emancipation Law 〰

Abolitionists in northern states searched for legal ways to rid their states of slavery. In 1780, Pennsylvania created a model for accomplishing such a task. While it did not outright prohibit slavery, and adults who were born into slavery before 1780 remained slaves for the rest of the lives, it went a long way in limiting the ability to own slaves in the state. There were three key components of the law:

All child slaves are freed (become indentured servants).

Importation of slaves is prohibited.

All slaves must be registered on a yearly basis. Slaves are freed if owners neglect to register.

Pennsylvania Gradual Emancipation Law (1780)

"Remember the Ladies" 🗨

In March 1776, Abigail Adams wrote a letter to her husband, John Adams, pleading with him to include the rights of women in the movement toward American independence.

"I long to hear that you have declared an independency. And, by the way, in the new code of laws which I suppose it will be necessary for you to make, I desire you would remember the ladies and be more generous and favorable to them than your ancestors. Do not put such unlimited power into the hands of the husbands. Remember, all men would be tyrants if they could. If particular care and attention is not paid to the ladies, we are determined to foment a rebellion, and will not hold ourselves bound by any laws in which we have no voice or representation."

—Abigail Adams, March 31, 1776

Republican Motherhood 🚨

Following the Revolutionary War, the young nation reconsidered the position of women in American society. While the term "Republican Motherhood" was not actually created until the the late 20th century, the concept described the benefits and drawbacks of womanhood in the late 18th century.

Pros
- Women were seen as essential to civic life.
- Women were depended upon for the education of male citizens.
- Motherhood was appreciated as something central to American culture.

Cons
- Women were still excluded from political activity.
- For the most part, girls were still not offered education beyond learning how to be in service to their families.
- Due to the prominence of motherhood, career options for women, outside of teaching and child-rearing, were practically nil.

Broad Impact of the American Revolution 🚨

The Revolutionary War inspired similar rebellions around the world.

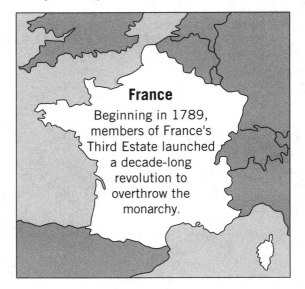

France

Beginning in 1789, members of France's Third Estate launched a decade-long revolution to overthrow the monarchy.

Haiti (1804) Slaves revolted against the French colonial powers.

Venezuela (1821)

Columbia (1820)

Ecuador (1822)

Many South American nations fought for and gained independence from Spain in the early 19th century.

Peru (1820)

Bolivia (1824)

Paraguay (1811)

Argentina (1816)

Chile (1810)

Uruguay (1811)

Ask Yourself...

How well did the American nation that emerged from the Revolutionary Period live up to the Enlightenment ideals that inspired it?

Creation of the Constitution ❗

Long before the United States declared independence, the colonies had their own governments. Many of these governments were modeled after the British parliament—all states had bicameral (two-house) legislatures except for Pennsylvania, which had only one house. Some colonies even tried to experiment with a centralized government. The New England Confederation was one such example, though the organization mostly just exercised an advisory role. In nearly all of the colonial governments, voting rights were reserved for male landowners.

Articles of Confederation ❗

By 1781, the thirteen states had ratified the Articles of Confederation, a document that established the new government of the United States of America. The document attempted to strike a balance between cooperation between the states and state autonomy. The experiment was not without its problems.

Pros:
- States organized under a common govt.
- Congress given power to negotiate internationally
- Helped create a national identity
- States kept independence

Cons:
- Federal govt. cannot enforce taxation
- No military draft
- Federal govt. cannot regulate international trade or trade among the states
- No executive or judicial branches
- Large and small states had equal representation
- 9/13 of states needed to agree to pass a law

Effect of Articles of Confederation

The weaknesses of the Articles of Confederation were quickly made apparent. Many who were frustrated by the inaction of the Confederation, including leaders in the underrepresented large states, called for a stronger central government.

Constitutional Convention 🛇

The new Constitution was written in Philadelphia in 1787. The final document was largely a result of several compromises made by states and parties with vastly differing viewpoints and interests.

Issue	Major arguments	Compromise
How to delegate representatives	• Small states wanted an equal number of representatives in the federal legislature. This was called the **New Jersey Plan.** • Large states wanted representation to be allocated proportionally based on a state's population. This was called the **Virginia Plan.**	The Great Compromise, also known as the Connecticut Compromise, established two legislative houses—the upper house, known as the Senate, would grant two seats to each state, while the lower house, the House of Representatives, would grant representation based on population.
Citizenship of slaves	• Southern states wanted to count slaves in the census, as this would allocate the Southern states with more representatives in the federal government. • Northern states argued that slaves should not be counted in the census if they were not to be given rights of citizenship. More cynically, northern states wanted to limit the power of southern states.	The **Three-Fifths Compromise** of the Constitution stipulates that slaves were to be counted as 3/5 of a person.

Issue	Major arguments	Compromise
Separation of powers	• The legislature would have too much power. • The executive of the federal government would have too much power.	Three branches were created—a legislative branch to create laws, an executive branch to carry out laws, and a judicial branch to decide disputes. Each branch limits one another through checks and balances.
State autonomy	• **Anti-Federalists** wanted to ensure states did not give up their self-rule in favor of sweeping federal power. • Following the failures of the Articles of Confederation, **Federalists** sought to ensure the stability of the union through a stronger central government.	While the powers of the federal government increased substantially, the new Constitution explicitly listed all powers delegated to the federal government and left the states all powers not directly expressed in the Constitution.

⬯ The delegates at the Constitutional Convention agreed that the international slave trade could not be ended until at least 1808. There was a debate about allowing Congress to place tariffs on exported goods, but the Southern states opposed this because they depended so much on foreign trade. A tax on imports was allowed to be passed (this would later cause much controversy over states' rights).

The Federalist Papers ❶

The framers of the Constitution still had to convince the states to ratify the new document. In order to convince the anti-Federalists (namely New York) to agree to a government with stronger central power, Alexander Hamilton, James Madison, and John Jay published a series of articles known as the **Federalist Papers** to make the pro-Constitution argument.

James Madison

Federalist Paper #51: The national government will need checks and balances as well as a separation of powers.

Alexander Hamilton

Federalist Paper #68: An Electoral College will be necessary to keep people from electing a president who is unfit for office.

John Jay

Federalist Paper #2: An undivided country will protect the United States against foreign threats.

The Bill of Rights ❗

The Constitution was officially ratified in 1788 when the ninth state, New Hampshire, signed it. Perhaps the most effective way that the Framers convinced the hold-out states to ratify the document (as well as eased concerns about an overly powerful federal government) was the inclusion of a **Bill of Rights,** the first ten amendments to the Constitution.

1st Amendment	Freedom of religion, speech, press, assembly, and petition
2nd Amendment	Right to bear arms
3rd Amendment	No quartering of soldiers in private homes during peacetime without consent
4th Amendment	Freedom from unreasonable search and seizure
5th Amendment	Right to due process of law, freedom from self-incrimination, and freedom from double jeopardy (being tried twice for the same crime)
6th Amendment	Rights of accused persons in criminal cases; for example, the right to a speedy and public trial
7th Amendment	Right of trial by jury in civil cases
8th Amendment	Freedom from excessive bail and from cruel and unusual punishment
9th Amendment	Rights not listed are kept by the people
10th Amendment	Powers not listed are kept by the states or the people

A Tale of Two Rebellions 💬

The new Constitution provided the nation with the ability to maintain a certain stability despite the competing interests of the various states. This is perhaps best illustrated by the outcomes of two different rebellions, one before the Constitutional Convention and one after it.

	Shays' Rebellion 1786–1787	Both	Whiskey Rebellion 1791–1794

Shays' Rebellion 1786–1787

- A Revolutionary War veteran, Daniel Shays, had not received pay for his service and was burdened with taxes to cover the war debt.
- Banks were foreclosing on his home.
- Shays and his men seized the courthouse that ruled on his foreclosure since he lacked any formal way to petition the government.
- Massachusetts government was unequipped to put down the rebellion.
- Private citizens put down the rebellion.

Both

- Backcountry farmers held resentment for the coastal elites.
- Farmers felt singled out to support the war debt through taxes.
- Rebels felt "taxation without local representation" was contrary to the principles of the Revolutionary War.

Whiskey Rebellion 1791–1794

- Congress created a tax on spirits in order to lower the national debt.
- Western Pennsylvanian corn farmers who produced whiskey felt the tax particularly hard.
- Farmers violently prevented federal officials from collecting the tax.
- President Washington brought an army to Western Pennsylvania to end the rebellion.
- Rebels had the power to elect different representatives under the new Constitution.

Ask Yourself...

Were the compromises of the Constitutional Convention sufficient to smooth over the tensions between the different states and parties? Why or why not?

The Early Republic

Following the ratification of the Constitution, the nation had many challenges ahead. Saddled with war debt, the United States spent its first decade defining the presidency, dealing with fights among political parties, and negotiating the fine balance between federal and state powers. Throughout this time period, a unique American culture began to develop.

George Washington 🔊

The choice of George Washington as the nation's first president was a no-brainer. The Electoral College unanimously chose Washington, who was arguably the most well-known man in the United States following the Revolutionary War. Though Washington did not actively seek the position, he did more than perhaps any of his successors to define the presidency. Each day that he held the office, Washington was keenly aware of his responsibility to set precedent for future office holders. In fact, even though the Constitution does not mention anything about a presidential cabinet, Washington formed such a group of advisors in order to delegate responsibilities. Every president since has followed this example. Notably, Washington appointed rivals to his team: Democratic-Republican Thomas Jefferson was named Secretary of State, while Federalist Alexander Hamilton became the Secretary of the Treasury.

Timeline of the Washington Presidency	
1789	President Washington is inaugurated with John Adams as his vice president.
1791	Whiskey Rebellion
1792	President Washington wins second term; John Adams had the second most Electoral College votes, continuing his role as vice president.
1794	The **Battle of Fallen Timbers** occurs between the United States government and Native American tribes over control of the Northwest Territory.
1796	President Washington establishes **executive privilege** when he refuses to turn over documents relating to Jay's Treaty to a Congressional investigation, citing national security as his reason.
1796	President Washington declines to seek office for a third term.

John Adams 🔴

The second president of the United States, John Adams, was a Northern elite, encompassing much of what Democratic-Republicans disliked about Federalists. Due to the rules of the Electoral College pre-12th Amendment, political rival Thomas Jefferson ended up as Adams's vice president.

Timeline of the Adams Presidency	
1796	Vice President Adams wins the presidency, and Democratic-Republican Thomas Jefferson becomes vice president by receiving the second most Electoral College votes.
1797	John Adams is inaugurated as the second president of the United States.
1798	President Adams creates the Department of the United States Navy.
1798	XYZ Affair (more on this on page 88)
1798	President Adams signs the **Alien and Sedition Acts.**
1800	President Adams loses his reelection bid when the Electoral College chooses Thomas Jefferson.

Federalists vs. Democratic-Republicans ❗

The two prominent parties in the early days of the republic were the Federalists and the Democratic-Republicans.

The First Party System		
	Federalists	**Democratic-Republicans**
Leaders	Hamilton, Washington, Adams, Jay, Marshall	Jefferson, Madison
Vision	Economy based on commerce	Economy based on agriculture
Governmental Power	Strong federal government	Stronger state governments
Supporters	Wealthy, Northeast	Yeoman farmers, Southerners
Constitution	Loose construction	Strict construction
National Bank	Believed it was "necessary"	Believed it was merely "desirable"
Foreign Affairs	More sympathetic toward Great Britain	More sympathetic toward France

Note: The Federalist party would die out after the Hartford Convention, following the War of 1812. Hamilton's vision and programs would be carried out by the nationalist program and Henry Clay's American System during the Era of Good Feelings. The Second Party System would emerge during the presidency of Andrew Jackson and would consist of the Whigs, who embraced many Federalist principles and policies, and the Jacksonian Democrats, who saw themselves as the heirs of the Jeffersonian Republicans.

Controversies over key policies in the early United States highlighted the animosity between the two parties.

Alien and Sedition Acts 💬

Policy	Controversy	Outcome
The **Alien and Sedition Acts,** passed by the Adams Administration, allowed the government to forcibly expel foreigners and to jail newspaper editors for "scandalous and malicious writing."	The Democratic-Republicans claimed that the acts were purely political, aimed at destroying new immigrants'—especially French immigrants'—support for the Democratic-Republicans. Further, the Sedition Act, which strictly regulated anti-government speech, was a clear violation of the First Amendment.	Adams's own vice president, Thomas Jefferson, led the opposition to the Alien and Sedition Acts. He and James Madison wrote the **Virginia** and **Kentucky Resolutions.**

Virginia and Kentucky Resolutions 💬

Policy	Controversy	Outcome
The Virginia and Kentucky Resolutions argued that the states had the right to judge the constitutionality of federal laws.	Under the Virginia and Kentucky Resolutions, states declared the Alien and Sedition Acts void, a process known as nullification. Federalists, who believed in the supremecy of the federal government, strongly disagreed that states reserved this right.	The Virginia and Kentucky Resolutions never prevented the enforcement of the laws. Jefferson went on to use the Alien and Sedition Acts, as well as the Resolutions, to strategically create a wedge issue for his 1800 presidential campaign.

First Bank of the United States 💬

Policy

As Secretary of the Treasury, Alexander Hamilton proposed a **National Bank** with the intention of regulating banking and strengthening the economy.

⮕

Controversy

Strict constructionists, such as Jefferson and Madison, claimed that the Constitution does not allow the federal government to create a bank, because it is not "necessary and proper" to carrying out its **enumerated powers**.

⮕

Outcome

Hamiton, a **broad (loose) constructionist**, argued that the creation of a bank was an **implied power** because the government already had the ability to coin money, borrow money, and collect taxes.

Washington agreed with Hamilton and signed the bill, creating the **First Bank of the United States.**

Perhaps Hamilton's greatest achievement as Secretary of the Treasury was his successful handling of the **national debt** accrued during the war. The First Bank of the United States was driven by a Federalist agenda. By taking on the states' war debts, the bank gave the federal government further power over the states. Hamilton's plan benefited the Northern states for a couple of reasons: (1) Northern banks had purchased debt certificates and would be repaid by the national bank, and (2) Northern states had a larger share of war debt than did the Southern states.

Hamilton faced accusations of favoritism toward Northern elites. As a compromise, he was able to offer the South a new location for the nation's capital: **Washington D.C.**, a city created to house the federal government.

Regional Disagreements over Slavery ❗

The banking controversy was not the only issue over which Americans were largely divided by region. By the end of the Adams Presidency, nearly every Northern state had abolished slavery. The tension created between the North and South over this issue would only get stronger in the coming decades.

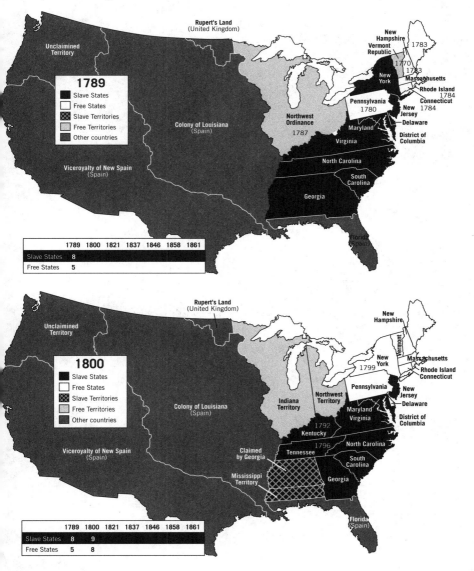

	1789	1800	1821	1837	1846	1858	1861
Slave States	8						
Free States	5						

	1789	1800	1821	1837	1846	1858	1861
Slave States	8	9					
Free States	5	8					

Rise of American Art, Literature, and Architecture ❗

Despite the regional tensions, the post-Revolution years were characterized by a sense of pride in the emerging American culture. Artists and writers began to define American culture through their media.

Novels	• The first American novelists emerged following the Revolutionary War. • Best sellers: Tragic stories of abuse and forbidden love • Two female authors prominent among the canon of authors • Popular titles: Susanna Rowson's *Charlotte Temple*, Hannah Webster Foster's *The Coquette: Or, the History of Eliza Wharton*, and William Hill Brown's *The Power of Sympathy*
Art	• American artists celebrated the young nation, paying respect to the people and events responsible for the creation of the U.S. • Typical works: John Singleton Copely's *Portrait of Paul Revere* and Benjamin West's *The Treaty of Penn with the Indians*
Architecture	• American architects created their own style: Federal Style. • Distinctly neoclassical as a nod to the democracies of Ancient Greece and the republicanism of Ancient Rome • Offered its own take on traditional architecture by including conspicuously American symbols, such as the eagle, on buildings

 Ask Yourself...

What conflicts were created in the early years of the republic that could have been avoided had the Constitution been more specific?

Expanded Migration and Interaction with Indians ❗

During and following the Revolution, the American movement toward the westernmost reaches of the states brought the young nation into even more contentious contact with Indian tribes.

Increased Alliances Between the British and Indians ❗

Fearing further American settlements, many Indian tribes formed alliances with the British.

Some notable events of the British and Indian relationship:

While most tribes sided with the French in the Seven Years' War, the British formed an alliance with the Iroquois Confederacy. Primarily, this was because the tribes allied with the French were enemies of the Iroquois.

The Royal Proclamation of 1763 saw the British protect Indian land west of the Appalachians in order to prevent colonists from settling farther west. In 1779, after the colonists broke the Treaty of Fort Pitt by killing Delaware Indians, the Ohio tribes allied with the British.

Unfortunately for the Indians, following the treaty of Paris, they were left high and dry by the British. Without British protection, Indians on United States land were at the mercy of the Americans. The United States continued westward and used treaties and military force to cede land from Native American tribes—both tribes who allied with the British and those who allied with the colonists.

The Iroquois 💬

The **Iroquois** was a trade and defense alliance of Indian tribes. Historians trace the origins of this confederacy to the 15th century, though some trace it as far back as the 12th century. However, conflicts with the colonists (including the Seven Years' War) brought about tensions within the confederacy. The Iroquois eventually divided during the Revolutionary War.

Tribes allied with the united colonies
- Oneida
- Tuscarora

Tribes allied with Great Britain
- Cayuga
- Mohawk
- Onondaga
- Seneca

Early Westward Expansion and Territorial Disputes ❗

The movement of American settlers to the Northwest Territory (modern-day Ohio, Michigan, Indiana, Illinois, and Wisconsin) was not welcomed by the Indian tribes who had already been pushed west. Chiefs such as Miami tribal leader **Little Turtle** clashed with frontiersmen, in particular the **Scots-Irish**, a large group of recent immigrants that included the infamous **Paxton Boys**.

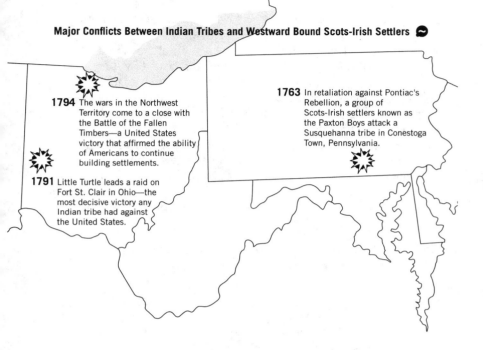

Major Conflicts Between Indian Tribes and Westward Bound Scots-Irish Settlers

1794 The wars in the Northwest Territory come to a close with the Battle of the Fallen Timbers—a United States victory that affirmed the ability of Americans to continue building settlements.

1791 Little Turtle leads a raid on Fort St. Clair in Ohio—the most decisive victory any Indian tribe had against the United States.

1763 In retaliation against Pontiac's Rebellion, a group of Scots-Irish settlers known as the Paxton Boys attack a Susquehanna tribe in Conestoga Town, Pennsylvania.

Northwest Ordinance (1787) ❗

Due to the westward movement of settlers, ongoing violent confrontations with Native Americans, and tensions with the British, the Congress established under the Articles of Confederacy created the **Northwest Ordinance** in 1787 to create the United States' first territories.

What the ordinance included

- Specific regulations concerning the conditions under which territories could apply for statehood
- Abolishment of slavery in the Northwest territories
- A bill of rights guaranteeing trial by jury, freedom of religion, and freedom from excessive punishment
- Claims on Native American land without Native American consent

Impact of the ordinance

- Remained important long after the Northwest territories were settled because of its pertinence to
  - the statehood process
  - the issue of slavery
- It was a forerunner to the Bill of Rights and other progressive government policies.
- War ensued; peace did not come until 1795 when the United States gained a military advantage over the Miami Confederacy, its chief Native American opponent in the area.

The territories were defined as the areas northwest of the Ohio River and east of the Mississippi River, up to the Canadian border.

Early Beginnings of Sectional Conflict 💬

The Northwest Territory presented issues that would foreshadow a sectional conflict that culminated in the Civil War.

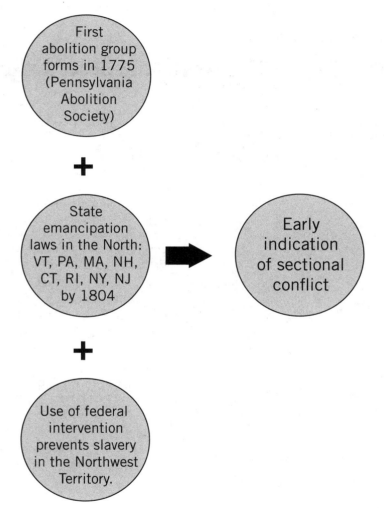

None of these issues pressed the United States enough to lead to war, but the seeds of conflict were clearly planted from the very beginning of America's nationhood.

Treaty with the Indians 🛑

Following the Declaration of Independence, the United States signed multiple treaties with Native American tribes. The U.S. government saw these treaties as strategic ways to expand territories, protect settlers, and form alliances. Unfortunately, the U.S. government reneged on many of these treaties over years.

Year	Treaty	Description
1778	Treaty with the Delaware	Peace treaty
1784	Treaty with the Six Nations	Peace in exchange for hostage release; clarified borders of the Iroquois (Six Nations) land
1786	Treaty with the Shawnee	The Shawnee are required to cede all land that the British lost to the United States in the Revolutionary War (the British had previously promised land to the Shawnee and other tribes in the Royal Proclamation of 1763).
1791	Treaty with the Cherokee	Peace treaty; clarified borders of Cherokee nation; called for release of prisoners taken by the Cherokee
1795	Treaty of Greenville	Followed the Battle of Fallen Timbers; ended the Northwest Indian War; drew a line to demarcate Indian land in the Northwest Territory

Spanish Mission Settlements ❗

In the western and southwestern portions of the continental United States, Spanish missionaries converted many Indians to Christianity.

Spain had previously been particularly successful in converting much of Mesoamerica to Catholicism through the **Spanish mission system.**

➡️

Spanish missionaries turned their attention to the regions that would one day become the states of Texas, New Mexico, Arizona, and California.

➡️

Explorers, such as **Juan de Oñate,** swept through the American Southwest, determined to create Christian converts by any means necessary— including violence.

〰️ The missionary expeditions that arrived from Mexico were largely comprised of **vaqueros,** Spanish cowboys. These vaqueros brought new traditions to their northern missions including **corridos,** songs and poems that depict the memories of history and the struggles of daily life.

 Ask Yourself...

1. What challenges did westbound settlers face?
2. What lasting impact did the conflicts with Native Americans cause?

Relations with Europe ❗

By the end of the 18th century, the United States was only decades removed from wars with both the French and the British. Maintaining diplomatic and economic relationships with European countries was both necessary and something of a tightrope walk.

Attempts at Diplomacy 🔔

Americans Debate Support for France 🔔

The Washington Presidency largely sought to maintain strong relationships with foreign nations, but to avoid involvement with conflicts abroad. The major conflicts abroad during his presidency typically involved France.

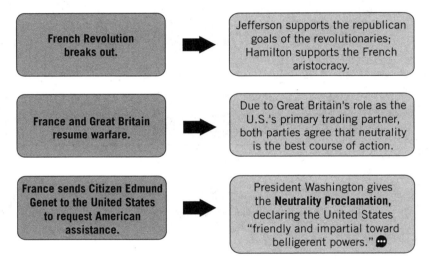

European Event	American Reaction
French Revolution breaks out.	Jefferson supports the republican goals of the revolutionaries; Hamilton supports the French aristocracy.
France and Great Britain resume warfare.	Due to Great Britain's role as the U.S.'s primary trading partner, both parties agree that neutrality is the best course of action.
France sends Citizen Edmund Genet to the United States to request American assistance.	President Washington gives the **Neutrality Proclamation,** declaring the United States "friendly and impartial toward belligerent powers." 💬

Washington's Farewell Address 🔔

George Washington reinforced his feelings on the importance of American neutrality in the final lines of his farewell address in 1796.

"The great rule of conduct for us, in regard to foreign Nations, is, in extending our commercial relations, to have with them as little Political connection as possible....

It is our true policy to steer clear of permanent alliances, with any portion of the foreign world...."

—George Washington

Jay's Treaty 〰

In 1794, President Washington sent Chief Justice John Jay to Great Britain to enforce various concessions the British made after the Revolutionary War (such as evacuating the Northwest Territory) and to discuss the British's apparent violations of free trade. Jay avoided war with Great Britain but was widely criticized for giving too many concessions to the British.

Pinckney's Treaty 〰

In a much more successful endeavor, President Washington sent Thomas Pinckney on a similar mission to Spain to discuss use of the Mississippi River, expanded access to international trade, and the removal of Spanish forts that remained on U.S. soil. After fruitful negotiations, Pinckney even got the Spanish to promise to defend American settlers from attacks by Native Americans.

Parties Further Divide over Foreign Policy ❗

While President Washington may have declared the United States neutral in the conflict between Great Britain and France, the political parties took sides.

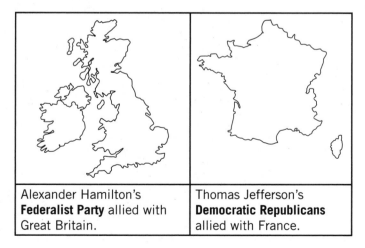

| Alexander Hamilton's **Federalist Party** allied with Great Britain. | Thomas Jefferson's **Democratic Republicans** allied with France. |

During the Adams Administration, just three years after Jay's and Pinckney's treaties, France began seizing American merchant ships on the open sea. An angry President Adams sent diplomats to France, who were immediately denied a meeting with French officials unless they paid a bribe. When the diplomats returned home and gave Adams their report, he sent it to be published in newspapers around the country. The names of the French officials were changed to X, Y, and Z. Upon reading the report, Americans lost whatever sympathy they had for France, and the **XYZ Affair** nearly propelled the U.S. into war on the tide of popular anger. Adhering to Washington's foreign policy, Adams avoided war and negotiated a settlement with France.

 Ask Yourself...

1. What factors challenged Washington's commitment to neutrality?
2. Why was Washington so committed to neutrality?

PERIOD 4 (1800–1848):

Beginnings of Modern American Democracy

The early to mid-19th century was a formative period for the United States. This section examines how the young nation struggled to establish itself internationally, fine-tune its democratic political system, and develop a uniquely American cultural identity. It also explores how regional tensions evolved and worsened, setting the stage for the Civil War.

The Defining Political Issues of the Era ❗

The first half of the 19th century presented many novel challenges for the newly formed nation as it struggled to refine its own political system and establish itself on an international stage. Achieving a delicate balance between state and federal power was a highly contentious defining task of the era, as reasonable minds differed about how to interpret the United States Constitution. The new republic was also forced to prove itself diplomatically and militarily as conflicts arose with the much stronger European states.

Jefferson, Hamilton, and Party Politics in the Early Republic ❗

Ideological disputes among the Founding Fathers were the source of much political strife during this era.

Federalist Party
- Alexander Hamilton
- Strong federal government
- Loose interpretation of the Constitution, enabling a centralized government to acquire more power in relation to the states

Democratic-Republican Party
- Thomas Jefferson
- Weak central government
- Strict interpretation of the Constitution, allowing for state autonomy

Jefferson Wins the Presidency 💬

The Federalists dominated the 18th-century republic, with both George Washington and John Adams adhering to its principles, but by the turn of the century, the party was severely fractured. When Jefferson defeated Adams in the presidential election of 1800, and the governing Federalist party relinquished power without a fight, it was a momentous transition. At that time, changes from one political regime to another were almost always effected through bloodshed.

Both John Adams and Thomas Jefferson died on July 4, 1826—exactly fifty years after the Declaration of Independence!

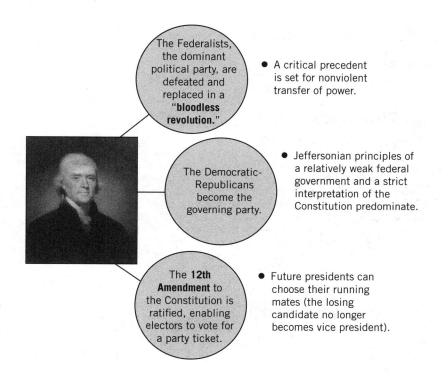

The Federalists, the dominant political party, are defeated and replaced in a **"bloodless revolution."**

- A critical precedent is set for nonviolent transfer of power.

The Democratic-Republicans become the governing party.

- Jeffersonian principles of a relatively weak federal government and a strict interpretation of the Constitution predominate.

The **12th Amendment** to the Constitution is ratified, enabling electors to vote for a party ticket.

- Future presidents can choose their running mates (the losing candidate no longer becomes vice president).

Effects of Jefferson's 1800 Presidential Victory

◑ Not Completely Bloodless

Despite the laudable "bloodless revolution," political rivalries between Federalists and Jeffersonian Democrats were not entirely free of violence. After years of fierce rivalry and intense personal animosity, Vice President Aaron Burr challenged Alexander Hamilton to a duel. Hamilton was killed in the infamous showdown (under circumstances that are unclear), and the resulting public condemnation of Burr virtually ended his political career.

The Marshall Court ❗

NOTABLE FIGURE:

The Supreme Court under **Chief Justice John Marshall** (1801–1835) laid the foundations for modern U.S. constitutional law. During his thirty-four year tenure Marshall, a staunch Federalist, led the Court in rendering landmark decisions that expanded the power of the national government. He also elevated the judiciary to the level of the executive and legislative branches, effectively completing our system of political checks and balances. The Marshall Court established one of the most critical doctrines in the American court system—that of **judicial review**—by which the judicial branch can deem executive and legislative acts unconstitutional.

Marbury v. Madison (1803) 💬

Judicial review was established in this seminal case involving "lame duck" president John Adams, who had controversially made many last-minute judicial appointments before Jefferson took office. William Marbury, one of these **"midnight judges,"** later sued Jefferson's Secretary of State James Madison in order to force him to certify the appointment. The Marshall Court ruled that, while Marbury had in fact been rightfully appointed, the Court could not compel Madison. It held that the Judiciary Act of 1789, which had authorized the Supreme Court to enforce judicial appointments, was unconstitutional. In declaring an act of Congress invalid on such grounds, the Court established its fundamental role as arbiter of the constitutionality of laws and other governmental actions.

~ In *McCulloch v. Maryland* (1819), the Marshall Court increased exponentially the power of the federal government in relation to that of the states. The Court unanimously held that the "Necessary and Proper" clause of the Constitution granted Congress the authority to charter a national bank, and that federal supremacy precluded the states from taxing any U.S. government institution.

Increased	Decreased
• Federal power in relation to the states • The reach of the enumerated powers granted to Congress, with the recognition of implied Congressional power • The power of the judicial branch of government in relation to the legislative and executive branches	• State power in relation to the federal government • The reach of the 10th Amendment as a basis for state power and autonomy • Congressional and presidential autonomy in terms of the power to act unscrutinized by the judiciary

The Marshall Court

 Ask Yourself...

1. Why is the doctrine of judicial review so important to our system of checks and balances? What kinds of abuses of power might occur if the courts could not declare laws or executive actions unconstitutional?
2. How might the United States be different today if the individual states had retained their pre-Marshall levels of power and autonomy?

The War of 1812 ❶

Jefferson's second term was plagued by hostilities between England and France. With the two nations at war, the United States was caught in the middle of a mutual blockade, with both sides harassing American ships and impeding U.S. foreign trade. Despite a British frigate attack on an American vessel, Jefferson knew that the U.S. navy was no match for Great Britain's Royal Navy at the time and did not declare war. He responded with economic sanctions instead.

	Embargo Act of 1807 ●●●	Non-Intercourse Act of 1809 ➰
Purpose	• Prohibited U.S. trade in foreign ports • Designed to punish France and England for violating U.S. neutrality	• Resumed trade with most nations other than France and England • Intended as a continued punishment for both France and England by exclusion
Outcome	• Brought all legal American import and export business to a halt • Had devastating consequences for the national economy	• Caused the economy to continue to suffer under the restrictions • Brought the nation closer to war as the result of the ongoing tensions

Early 19th-Century U.S. Economic Sanctions Against England and France

---

Impressment (forced entry into military or public service) of American seamen was a pivotal issue that eventually led to the War of 1812. The British would seize American ships and impress their sailors, claiming (almost always falsely) that the men were deserters from the Royal Navy.

Madison Takes Over ❗

Jefferson's successor, James Madison, reopened trade with both England and France. However, he made the strategic error of proclaiming that, if either nation would promise to stop interfering with American trade, he would cut off the other one. Napoleon agreed and Madison followed through (although French harassment ultimately continued), and relations with England worsened. Many Americans wished to avoid armed conflict, but a powerful faction exerted increasing pressure on Madison to declare war on England, which he ultimately did in 1812.

Federalists	War Hawks
• Favored friendly relations with England in order to preserve lucrative trade links • Originated mostly from the Eastern and Northeastern states • Desired a strong U.S. international presence based largely on economic power	• Favored war with England in order to avenge national insults involving U.S. seamen and British support of Native Americans • Originated mostly from the Southern and Western states • Desired U.S. territorial expansion by means of land acquired through warfare

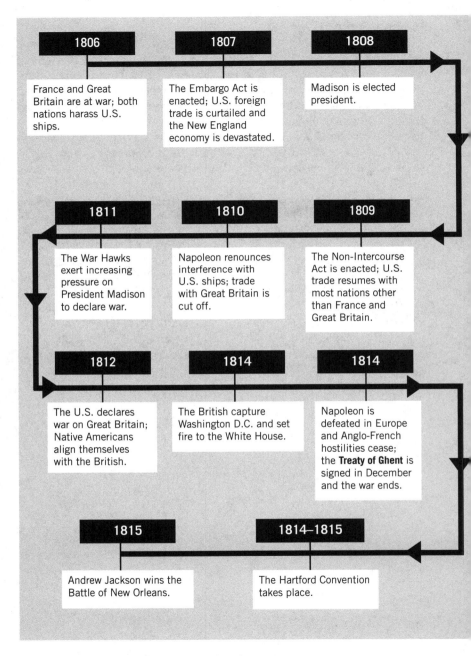

1806

France and Great Britain are at war; both nations harass U.S. ships.

1807

The Embargo Act is enacted; U.S. foreign trade is curtailed and the New England economy is devastated.

1808

Madison is elected president.

1811

The War Hawks exert increasing pressure on President Madison to declare war.

1810

Napoleon renounces interference with U.S. ships; trade with Great Britain is cut off.

1809

The Non-Intercourse Act is enacted; U.S. trade resumes with most nations other than France and Great Britain.

1812

The U.S. declares war on Great Britain; Native Americans align themselves with the British.

1814

The British capture Washington D.C. and set fire to the White House.

1814

Napoleon is defeated in Europe and Anglo-French hostilities cease; the **Treaty of Ghent** is signed in December and the war ends.

1815

Andrew Jackson wins the Battle of New Orleans.

1814–1815

The Hartford Convention takes place.

War of 1812 Timeline of Events

NOTABLE FIGURE:

The only clear U.S. military victory in the War of 1812 occurred after the war was over! Unaware that the Treaty of Ghent had been signed two weeks earlier officially ending hostilities, General **Andrew Jackson** defeated British forces at the **Battle of New Orleans.** His victory made him a national hero.

The Hartford Convention

Also unaware that the war was drawing to an end at the close of 1815 were the Federalists, who took part in the **Hartford Convention.** There they advocated for either a major revision of the Constitution or secession from the union. They consequently received a great backlash after the war ended and were generally viewed as traitors. This led to the general dissolution of the party, with Federalism exerting only a very limited influence over the course of the next decade.

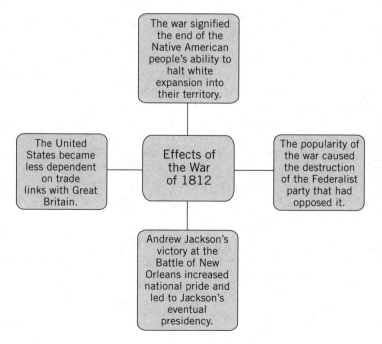

Francis Scott Key wrote "The Star Spangled Banner," the American national anthem, after witnessing the British bombardment of Fort McHenry during the War of 1812.

Beginnings of Modern American Democracy   **97**

The Postwar Madison Years 💬

After the War of 1812 ended, Madison focused on promoting national growth. In keeping with his Democratic-Republican beliefs, however, he remained cautious in expanding federal power while supporting several programs designed to strengthen the young nation. Despite the fact that the rival Federalist party traditionally championed the use of tariffs and the Democratic-Republicans opposed them, Madison approved of such tariffs in order to protect American economic interests. Speaker of the House **Henry Clay** was so vocal in his support for the tariffs and other programs that they were often referred to as **"Henry Clay's American system."**

Henry Clay's American System

- Protective tariffs on imports
- Improvements to interstate roads
- Rechartering of the National Bank

Monroe and the "Era of Good Feelings" 💬

The demise of the Federalists led to a brief period in which the Democratic-Republicans were basically the only political party in the United States. This was known as the "era of good feelings" because of the apparent lack of warring factions. When **James Monroe** ran for president in 1816, he therefore faced no formidable opposition and easily won. Despite this appearance of national unity, however, escalating sectionalism and economic instability were actually increasing tensions within the country. The "good feelings" ended abruptly in 1819 when the National Bank called in its loans and the country was thrust into devastating financial turmoil. Without organized political opposition, however, Monroe won reelection in 1820 by a landslide!

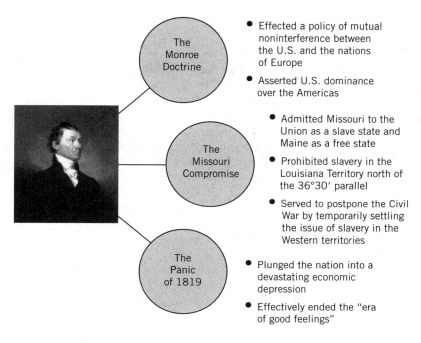

Highlights of the Monroe Administration

The **election of 1824** marked a turning point in the way that states choose their electors in presidential elections. Previously groups of congressmen known as **congressional caucuses** often chose their respective parties' nominees. Since these congressmen (or their friends) were also likely to have chosen the electors themselves, these choices were rarely challenged. When the Democratic-Republican caucus nominated William H. Crawford in 1824, candidates John Quincy Adams, Henry Clay, and Andrew Jackson challenged the nomination on the grounds that the caucuses were undemocratic. Adams ultimately won the presidency, and the candidates' defiance led to the end of the caucus system in U.S. elections.

A Dirty Deal?
Some have alleged that John Quincy
Adams and Henry Clay conspired to rob
Andrew Jackson of the presidency in 1824 (with
Jackson himself being among the chief proponents
of this idea)! Jackson had received more electoral (and
popular) votes than any of the four candiates but, since
nobody had received a majority, the Constitution dictated
that the House of Representatives choose the president
from among the three candidates who received the most
votes. Speaker Henry Clay, who had come in fourth,
advocated for Adams and thus secured the latter's
victory. Adams then appointed Clay Secretary of
State, the position regarded as a gateway to the
presidency. Jackson and others denounced
this apparent collusion as a **"corrupt
bargain."** What do you think?

Jacksonian Democracy ❗

The extremely popular Jackson campaigned against John Quincy Adams with a vengeance in 1828 and finally won the presidency. While previous presidents had come from the genteel upper class, Jackson was seen as the epitome of the self-made man who championed the cause of the common people. By 1834, Jackson faced strong opposition from Henry Clay's **Whig party** which, although it resembed the defunct Federalist party in many respects, was essentially made up of a variety of people who were opposed to Jackson's administration for whatever reason. Jackson's policies laid the foundation for the modern Democatic party.

	Jackson	The Whigs
Favored	• States' rights (although not to the point of nullification) • Increased presidential power through the use of the veto • Universal suffrage for white males • Western interests, as opposed to those of the North and South	• A strong federal government • Increased congressional power • The manufacturing industry • Protective tariffs • National banking
Opposed	• A strong federal government • Governmental activism on social issues • Big banks and the Northeastern power brokers • State nullification of federal law	• One or more of Jackson's various policies • Immigration

Jackson was not afraid to wield his presidential power and veto acts of Congress that violated his democratic principles. Believing the **Second Bank of the United States** to be an unconstitutional monopoly, Jackson vetoed it; he withdrew the federal funds and deposited them into various state **"pet banks"** instead .

Jackson Draws the Line at Nullification ❗

Jackson's firm belief in states' rights and the dangers of federal power had its limits. He strongly opposed the hotly contested doctrine of **nullification**, which asserted that states have the right to disobey federal laws if they consider them unconstitutional. The highly contentious **"Tariff of 1828"** (or "Tariff of Abominations") adversely affected the South's critical trade links with England, and when the Tariff of 1832 failed to sufficiently lower the rates, South Carolina nullified the tariffs. Jackson wisely viewed nullification as a serious threat to the Union and had Congress authorize a **Force Bill** by which troops would enforce these tariffs. A compromise tariff was agreed upon and the issue was basically moot, but South Carolina still nullified the Force Bill as an assertion of states' rights. The ongoing battle about the limits of state autonomy would escalate sharply over the next thirty years as regional interests conflicted with federal ones, particularly in the case of slavery and other economic issues concerning the South. This ongoing political and ideological question would ultimately be settled militarily when federal supremacy was permanently established by four bloody years of civil war.

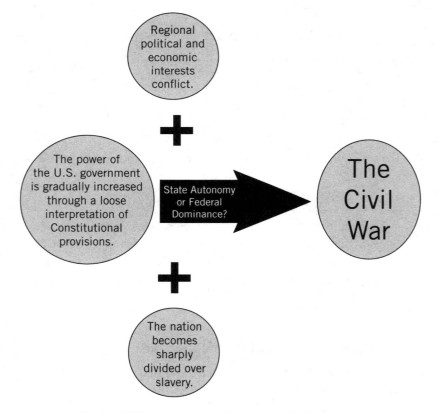

Regional Disputes and the Question of Federal Power

1. Who was right—Jefferson or Hamilton—in terms of how loosely the Constitution should be interpreted?
2. Should the Supreme Court have the right to contemplate constitutionally based governmental powers or, for that matter, individual liberties, that were never mentioned in the document itself (e.g., the right to privacy)? Does the intent of the Founding Fathers who wrote the Constitution matter in this regard, or does modern necessity outweigh any 18th-century ideological objectives or design?

Social and Cultural Movements of the Period ❶

During the early to mid-1800s, the United States also struggled to form a national identity in terms of its collective morality, philosophical and spiritual values, and even artistic expression. New religious and reform movements exerted a strong influence on the developing culture, and Americans sought to understand 19th-century issues within the existing constitutional framework developed by the Founding Fathers. Disputes once again tended to fall along regional lines, particularly regarding the critical issue of slavery.

The Second Great Awakening and the Quest for Utopia ❶

The modern image of the United States as a religious people (compared to many of its European cousins) has its roots in the revivalist movements that took place during the nation's infancy. The **Second Great Awakening** involved a 19th-century large-scale religious revival and newfound commitment to fundamentalist Protestant teachings. Millions of Americans (most of whom were women) rejected the secularist philosophies of the previous century and sought lives grounded in fervent Christian faith.

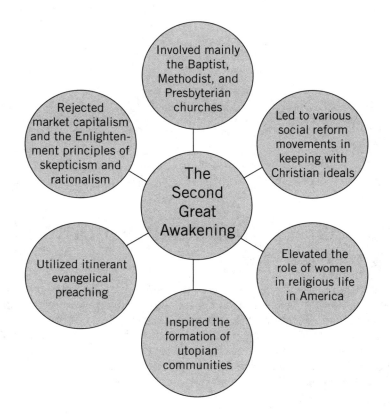

The Second Great Awakening

- Involved mainly the Baptist, Methodist, and Presbyterian churches
- Led to various social reform movements in keeping with Christian ideals
- Rejected market capitalism and the Enlightenment principles of skepticism and rationalism
- Elevated the role of women in religious life in America
- Utilized itinerant evangelical preaching
- Inspired the formation of utopian communities

Christian Revival Sparks Reform 💬

The great 19th-century reform movements in America were inextricably linked to the resurgence of religious fervor. Grounded in the teachings of Christian charity, social reformers (many of whom were women) fought to establish institutions to care for those who could not care for themselves. Social activists also fought against various forms of vice, including gambling, prostitution, and, most notably, alcohol consumption. Prison reformers, focusing upon the Christian idea of redemption, sought humane treatment for criminals and created the basis for the modern American prison system.

> 〜 The word *penitentiary* stems from this period in history when reformers applied Christian principles to the penal system. Incarceration had historically been used to keep the accused from escaping eventual punishment (which, for serious crimes, was usually corporal punishment or death)—it was not the punishment itself. In contrast, reformers like Dorothea Dix built huge prisons wherein "penitents" would be forced to reflect upon their misdeeds all day long in silence and seclusion. This severe regimen, so the theory goes, would inevitably lead to enlightenment, repentence, and redemption

A Very Romantic Era ❗

The ideals of staunch individualism and reliance upon emotion that enabled the Protestant religious revival stemmed in part from the **Romanticism** of early 19th-century America. In contrast to the rational views of the Enlightenment, the Romantics valued intuition and imagination above reason and tended to glorify nature. Hallmarks of the movement can be seen in the art, literature, philosophy, and architecture of the period. The **transcendentalists**, a group of nonconformists who were heavily influenced by Romantic ideals, believed that human beings harbor elements of the divine within them and can ultimately attain perfection. Among the transcendentalists, you will find some of the most famous names in American literature.

Ralph Waldo Emerson 1803–1882)	Henry David Thoreau (1817–1862)	Nathaniel Hawthorne (1804–1864)
• Essayist, poet, philosopher, lecturer • Was a leader of the transcendentalist movement • Dealt with themes of nature, individualism, and freedom • Best known works: *Nature*, "The American Scholar"	• Essayist, poet, philosopher, political protester • Was a leader of the transcendentalist movement • Dealt with themes of the individual's relationship to the state and perfection through nature/simple living • Best known works: *Walden*, "Civil Disobedience"	• Novelist, short-story writer • Was heavily influenced by transcendentalism, but later sharply criticized the movement • Dealt with "dark romantic" themes of guilt, sin, and evil as inherent human qualities • Best known works: *The Scarlet Letter*, *The House of the Seven Gables*

The Nation Remains Divided ❗

Despite the uniquely American multifaceted national identity that was emerging, the country remained sharply divided, usually along regional lines. The most contentious issue was still slavery, with moral, spiritual, and philosophical positions on the matter hardening with time. The spirit of freedom and individualism that was prevalent in the nation prompted many blacks, both free and slave, to unite in taking up the abolitionist cause. Moreover, white outrage and antagonism toward the practice increased exponentially in the North as the first half of the century neared its close.

Ask Yourself...

To what extent is the United States still a divided nation today? Is it basically a unified people with a firmly ingrained American identity, or do divisions, regional or otherwise, still predominate?

Major Political Organizations ⚠️

The wave of reformist sentiment in the first half of the century led to the emergence of powerful political organizations to lead the fight for their respective social causes. Groups that espoused the abolitionist, temperance, and women's suffrage movements were the most prominent and contentious. However, efforts to aid the poor and ill and to remedy long-standing social inequities were also controversial and divisive.

The Temperance Societies ⚠️

The turn of the century brought about the temperance movement in America, which was largely fueled by the efforts of women. The American Temperance Society and other temperance groups originally endeavored to have members voluntarily abstain from the use of alcohol by means of a personal oath. However, members were soon fighting for total prohibition at the national level.

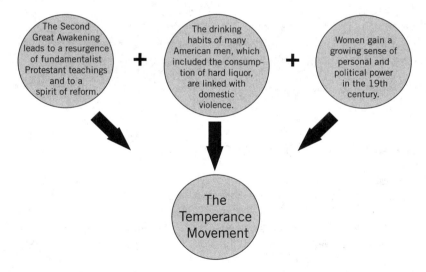

Abolitionism ❗

While the temperance movement was the more popular and prominent political cause of the day, the abolitionist movement is undeni-
ably the more historically important. Anyone espousing the abolitionist
cause was seen as radical at the time, although abolitionists were not
all of like mind. In fact, the various groups and organizations often had
substantially different agendas.

The Moderates	The Immediatists
• Wanted emancipation of slaves to occur gradually and peacefully over an extended period • Believed that slaveowners' property rights should be considered when formulating a plan for emancipation • Considered the repatriation of slaves back to Africa to be a viable option • Focused predominantly upon the issue of slavery • Constituted the vast majority of abolitionists	• Wanted immediate and total emancipation for all slaves • Believed that slaveowners had no legitimate property rights to their slaves • Considered the idea of repatriation to be racist and unacceptable • Focused upon full and equal rights for black Americans • Constituted a highly radical minority of abolitionists

The American Anti-Slavery Society 💬

One of the most influential and effective organizations espousing
immediatist doctrine was the **American Anti-Slavery Society**, which was
founded in 1833. The Society, whose members included such notable
persons as Frederick Douglass and Susan B. Anthony, was viewed as
so radical and dangerous that its meetings were sometimes met with
violence. Its policy not only to include women as members but also to
place them in positions of authority within the organization, was highly
controversial and led many to leave and join other abolitionist societies.

Women's Suffrage 🔵

With the spirit of justice and reform in America leading to progressive ideas about the established social hierarchy, a minority of women began to demand the right to vote. Many of those women were ardent abolitionists who, willing to fight for the rights and suffrage of black men, could not resign themselves to the reality that they themselves lacked such rights. The two movements are often seen as inextricably linked.

NOTABLE FIGURE: 💬

In 1840, a group of women, including the indomitable **Elizabeth Cady Stanton,** was barred from an abolitionist conference in London because of their gender. This injustice prompted Stanton and others to hold a meeting of their own a few years later. At **The Seneca Falls Convention** in 1848, which took place in the same "burned-over district" that had hosted the Second Great Awakening, they drafted the "Declaration of the Rights and Sentiments of Women." This document, which became a cornerstone of women's suffrage, boldly asserted that all men and women are created equal.

NOTABLE FIGURE: 〰️

Sojourner Truth was a slave who escaped to freedom and then fought for the rights and suffrage of both blacks and women. She was an eloquent orator in support of these causes, although some dispute remains about the exact content of her most famous speech. While addressing the audience at a women's rights convention she reportedly spoke of her harsh life as a slave and asked, "Ain't I a woman?" several times in rhetorical fashion.

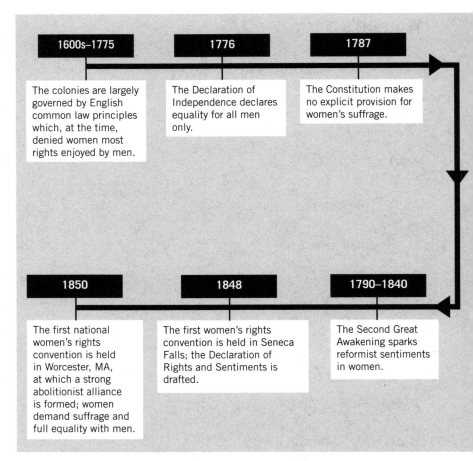

1600s–1775	1776	1787
The colonies are largely governed by English common law principles which, at the time, denied women most rights enjoyed by men.	The Declaration of Independence declares equality for all men only.	The Constitution makes no explicit provision for women's suffrage.

1850	1848	1790–1840
The first national women's rights convention is held in Worcester, MA, at which a strong abolitionist alliance is formed; women demand suffrage and full equality with men.	The first women's rights convention is held in Seneca Falls; the Declaration of Rights and Sentiments is drafted.	The Second Great Awakening sparks reformist sentiments in women.

Timeline of the American Women's Suffrage Movement Through 1850

Other Reform Movements ❗

Political organizations seeking reform in the early to mid-19th century also focused on other groups who had been traditionally disenfranchised, downtrodden, reviled, or neglected. These activist organizations had to overcome the age-old view that those on the lowest rung of society usually deserved to be there. Gradually a spirit of compassion and social conscience replaced the harsher attitudes of the past.

	Criminals	The Mentally Ill	Education	Orphans and the Poor
Traditional View	Criminals are morally deficient and sinful; those who break the law should be executed, otherwise punished severely, or ostracized.	Care of the "mad" is primarily the responsibility of the family; those who behave oddly must be separated from society at large.	A good education is the privilege of those who can afford to pay for it; typically only white affluent males should receive higher education.	Those who are destitute are generally inferior (and often lazy) persons who deserve their plight; they should usually be punished or imprisoned.
Reformers Wanted	Humane treatment of prisoners; rehabilitation and eventual reintegration into society	Compassionate medical treatment for all mentally ill persons with a focus upon curing them	Free quality public education for everyone	An end to punitive attitudes toward the needy; adequate food, shelter, and necessities
Methods	The penitentiary system encouraged thoughtful reflection and repentance through a strict regimen of silence and seclusion.	"Insane asylums" offered care and shelter (although inadequate by modern standards) for the mentally ill.	The number of government-supported public schools was greatly increased; textbooks were standardized, and the school year was lengthened.	Orphanages and houses of refuge for the poor (although often unpleasant) provided for individuals' basic needs and served as an alternative to homelessness or prison.

Other Reform Movements in America (1800–1850)

Ask Yourself...

Was the moderate abolitionist approach to emancipation, which sought to gradually eliminate slavery with as little disruption to southern society as possible, ever a morally sound one? Could its successful implementation have avoided the trauma experienced by millions of slaves who were suddenly freed, and thus suddenly displaced, by a decisive edict?

The Market Revolution ❗

Prior to the Revolutionary War, most colonists were self-sufficient farmers who grew their own food and provided for most of their own needs. In the 19th century, however, a monumental national shift ocurred from subsistence living to a **market economy**, in which individuals exchange their labor or goods for cash. The endless possibilities for lucrative dealings gave rise to "big business" and powerful corporations. This societal transformation was made possible by the many revolutionary technological innovations that characterize this pivotal era.

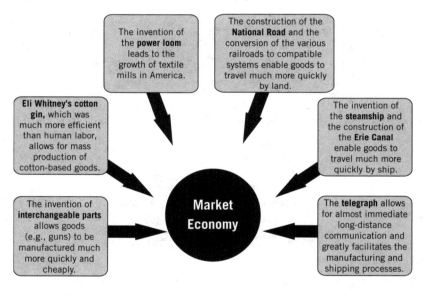

The invention of the **power loom** leads to the growth of textile mills in America.

The construction of the **National Road** and the conversion of the various railroads to compatible systems enable goods to travel much more quickly by land.

Eli Whitney's cotton gin, which was much more efficient than human labor, allows for mass production of cotton-based goods.

The invention of the **steamship** and the construction of the **Erie Canal** enable goods to travel much more quickly by ship.

Market Economy

The invention of **interchangeable parts** allows goods (e.g., guns) to be manufactured much more quickly and cheaply.

The **telegraph** allows for almost immediate long-distance communication and greatly facilitates the manufacturing and shipping processes.

The sudden high demand for labor caused by the market revolution did have its advantages for some workers. Lowell mills (named after the Massachusetts town in which they operated) were designed to lure girls and women from their family farms to work in the textile industry. Although life in the mills was hard, these workers were offered cash wages, housing in respectable quarters (equipped with a proper chaperone, of course!), and the benefit of various social and cultural events during leisure hours.

Ask Yourself...

In what ways has the quality of life in America improved since the market revolution? In what ways, if any, has it worsened?

Shifts in the Labor Market and Class Structure ❗

The market revolution made factories central to the economy, which provided a dramatic increase in jobs for the working class. It also loosened the boundaries of the traditional class system, as a successful business venture offered a chance for wealth and advancement that would have been elusive under the old regime. While greater opportunities for work for women did further gender equality, some attitudes that evolved during this period about proper male and female roles have proven difficult to overcome.

In some ways, the market economy actually thwarted the movement for women's equality. Despite the greater opportunities for females created by an industrialized society, the notion that men worked outside the home (in the newly built factories, offices, etc.), while the woman's place was in the home (at least for families who could afford to have only one wage-earner), became firmly established. A **cult of domesticity** emerged, which glorified life within the home as the ultimate ideal for women and strongly discouraged female education and personal autonomy.

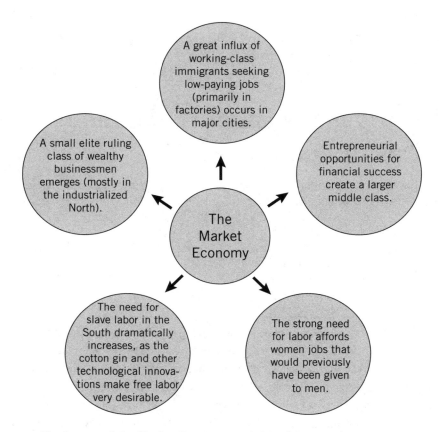

The following text appears within the diagram:

A great influx of working-class immigrants seeking low-paying jobs (primarily in factories) occurs in major cities.

A small elite ruling class of wealthy businessmen emerges (mostly in the industrialized North).

Entrepreneurial opportunities for financial success create a larger middle class.

The Market Economy

The need for slave labor in the South dramatically increases, as the cotton gin and other technological innovations make free labor very desirable.

The strong need for labor affords women jobs that would previously have been given to men.

The Impact of the Market Economy on the Socioeconomic Structure

 Ask Yourself...

How closely does the 19th-century socioeconomic structure that resulted from market economy forces resemble the one the U.S. has today? Apart from the obvious abolition of slave labor, in what ways has this class system changed?

Regionalism 🔊

The changes brought about by industrialization, which affected the three main sections of the country quite differently, only served to heighten regional tensions. Economic needs often conflicted, as did divergent values and lifestyles. The divisive issue of slavery continued to be a major source of animosity and contention.

The North	• Had a highly industrialized economy based largely on manufacturing, banking, and shipping • Had little need of slaves; disapproved of slavery and wanted to stop its expansion into the territories • Permitted some upward socioeconomic mobility through industry, although there remained an established social hierarchy • Was heavily populated, with a steady influx of immigrants • Resented the South for utilizing and promoting slavery; resented the West for its growing prominence and for western migration by Northerners
The South	• Had an agrarian economy based largely on plantation-grown tobacco and cotton • Had a critical need for slave labor, viewed slavery as an integral part of southern society, and strongly desired its expansion into the territories • Permitted very little upward mobility owing to an extremely rigid hierarchical class system and little opportunity for the lower classes to attain wealth • Was sparsely populated, with little immigration; slaves constituted a substantial portion of the comparatively small population • Resented the North for its wealth and power and for its interference in southern society in terms of slavery; resented the West for its egalitarian practices; developed its own distinct regional identity, typically viewing both western and northern customs as less genteel than southern rules of conduct

| The West | • Had a varied economy based largely on commercial farming, fur trapping, and real estate speculation
• Had little interest in the issue of slavery and sought to avoid the conflict
• Permitted a great deal of upward mobility in a comparatively egalitarian society; embraced the idea of the "self-made man"
• Was sparsely populated, but with numbers steadily increasing through western migration
• Resented the South for its desire to expand slavery into the territories and for its aristocratic ideals; resented the North for its power and because its bankers controlled western land |

Regional Differences in America (1800–1850)

 Ask Yourself...

1. What could have been done to ease regional tensions in the first half of the 19th century? Was permanent compromise a viable possibility?
2. Do regional differences still exist in America today? If so, what are they?

Territorialism

A combination of bold political moves, wise decision making, and downright lucky circumstances during this period led to enormous territorial gains and vast increases in power for the United States. The nation acquired its Western and Southwestern regions through purchase and military conquest and managed to increase its northern border while avoiding war with England. Hard-line policies put an end to European colonization in the Americas, but also, in procuring Western and Southeastern lands from indigenous peoples, resulted in Native American displacement.

ASAP U.S. History

The Monroe Doctrine	• Involved a policy of mutual noninterference between the U.S. and the nations of Europe • Initiated by Monroe in 1823 • Resulted in an end to European colonization in the Americas and in undisputed U.S. dominance in the region • Inspired controversy internationally because its largely successful implementation greatly increased U.S. power and prestige
The Louisiana Purchase	• Involved the purchase of the **Louisiana Territory** from Napoleon for $15 million • Initiated by Jefferson in 1803 • Resulted in vast territorial gains for the U.S., but also led to conflict with Native Americans as the result of westward expansion by whites • Inspired controversy because of land disputes with indigenous people and also because Jefferson increased established levels of presidential power in order to purchase land without congressional approval
The Indian Removal Act	• Involved the removal of Native Americans in existing states to federal lands in the Western territories • Initiated by Jackson in 1830 • Resulted in the near total translocation of Southeastern Native American tribes to the West and in greater land opportunities for the white population • Inspired controversy because thousands of Native Americans were displaced

Instruments of 19th-Century U.S. Territorialism

When Jefferson purchased the Louisiana Territory, which doubled the size of the young republic, nobody knew exactly what was out there in this mysterious uncharted land. To find out, he engaged Captain Meriwether Lewis and Lieutenant William Clark, (the legendary **"Lewis & Clark"**) to explore the unknown region and establish relations with the native peoples. Reports of what Lewis and Clark discovered out west inspired hundreds of bold pioneers to risk grave danger and hardship in the pursuit of wealth, personal advancement, and adventure. This migration laid the foundation for the creation of the Western and Midwestern United States.

A Trail of Tears ⓘ

While some of the indigenous tribes fought the relocation policies and some did not, resistance largely proved futile and thousands of Native Americans moved westward. These migrations, which were orchestrated by the military, were often brutal and many died along the way from disease, exposure, and starvation. Several tribes were affected, but the **"trail of tears"** refers specifically to a depiction of the hardships endured by the Cherokee nation as its people walked all the way from Georgia to Oklahoma.

Many argued at the time that relocation was actually in the best interests of Native American people, who were in clear danger of being eclipsed by the white population. Proponents of the policy asserted that relocation would serve to protect and preserve indigenous culture and traditions and prevent the loss of identity that comes from assimilation into a dominant society. Assuming that the transition could be accomplished humanely (which was often not the case), a move out west was deemed the most compassionate way to deal with a minority group residing in a potentially hostile environment. What do you think?

The presidency of **James K. Polk** (1845–1849) was of critical importance in acquiring the territories that make up the present-day United States. Polk not only peacefully negotiated the American-Canadian border with Great Britain, thus acquiring the future states of Oregon, Washington, and parts of Idaho, but also gained the entire Southwest through victory in the Mexican-American war.

 Ask Yourself...

Without the vast territorial gains and ambitious national and international policies of the 19th century, how likely is it that the United States would still enjoy superpower status today? How might the course of history have been different had the United States become a relatively weak nation?

Conflict over Slavery Increases ❗

The nation's large territorial acquisitions greatly exacerbated regional tensions, as the delicate balance between "free" and "slave" states was threatened as slavery slowly moved west. The abolitionist sentiments of the North were increasingly pitted against the economic needs and cultural predilections of the Southern plantation owners, as both sides became firmly entrenched in their positions. Political compromise managed to forestall armed conflict for a short period, while abolitionists, some committed to peace and some to violence, continued to fight for emancipation.

Frederick Douglass 💬	Nat Turner 💬	David Walker 💬
• Was an escaped slave, author, and orator • Advocated emancipation through peaceful means • Best known for his abolitionist newspaper *The North Star* and for his autobiography *Narrative of the Life of Frederick Douglass, an American Slave*	• Was an escaped slave, preacher, and self-professed visionary • Advocated emancipation through violence • Best known for his 1831 Virginia slave rebellion in which nearly 60 whites were randomly murdered in their homes, leading to large-scale retaliation against the black population	• Was a free black Bostonian and author • Advocated emancipation through both peaceful and violent means • Best known for his pamphlet *Appeal to the Coloured Citizens of the World*, which encouraged all free blacks to work to end slavery

Some Notable Abolitionists

NOTABLE FIGURE: 💬

Abolitionists had a formidable opponent in the form of **John C. Calhoun,** an eloquent politician who served as secretary of war, secretary of state, and vice president of the United States. A native South Carolinian and senator from his home state, Calhoun became the champion of the Southern slave-owning plantation system. Calhoun argued for states' rights in the face of federal interference. He also asserted that slavery was a natural manifestation of black inferiority and was thus inherently beneficial for all.

The Missouri Compromise—A Quick Fix! ❗

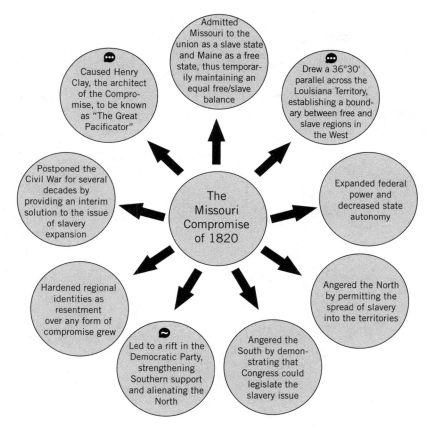

Effects of the Missouri Compromise

 Ask Yourself...

What good, if any, did the Missouri Compromise do for the nation? Some may liken its enactment to putting a band-aid on a bullet wound. Is it fair, however, to judge the wisdom of the Compromise from a 21st-century perspective, knowing that the attempt at conciliation would ultimately fail?

PERIOD 5 (1844–1877):
Toward the Civil War and Reconstruction

The mid-19th century brought about a number of seismic changes in the American story. This section reviews the exploration and settlement of the American west, immigration, and the conflicts over slavery and other tensions that ultimately led to the Civil War and Reconstruction.

Westward Expansion 🔵

After the Louisiana Purchase in 1803, the land holdings of the continental United States had almost doubled, and throughout the 19th century more and more Americans moved westward, settling new frontiers and establishing trading posts, farms, mines, and towns in areas that had previously been uninhabited or inhabited only by Native Americans. During this period, Native Americans were often removed from their ancestral lands and moved onto reservations. Law enforcement was not always particularly effective, and, as a result, settlers occasionally fought over land ownership. This period of westward expansion is often romanticized in books and movies and spawned such epic characters as Jesse James, Billy the Kid, and Wyatt Earp.

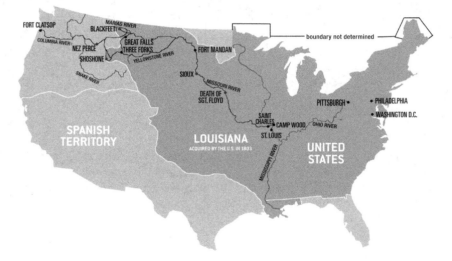

Lewis and Clark Expedition, 1804–1806

The Gold Rush 🔵

Beginning in 1803, when President Thomas Jefferson instructed Meriwether Lewis to explore the Northwest territories, fur traders and other adventurers began to map and settle areas that are now Kansas, Nebraska, Wyoming, Idaho, and Oregon along the so-called Oregon Trail. Some explorers also ventured south into California, and in 1848 one lucky individual found gold in the California mountains. This discovery precipitated a huge boom of settlers traveling to California from 1848 to 1855 in what was known as the **Gold Rush.** Because many of the settlers moved to California in 1849, they are sometimes referred to as **Forty-Niners.** Most of these gold prospectors didn't get rich from their findings, but urban centers in California—such as San Francisco—developed rather quickly and California's path to statehood took only a few short years. The prospectors were around 90 percent male, but contrary to popular imagination, they made up a fairly diverse lot.

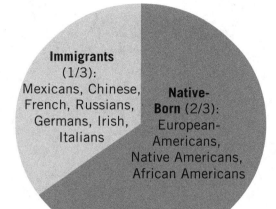

Immigrants (1/3): Mexicans, Chinese, French, Russians, Germans, Irish, Italians

Native-Born (2/3): European-Americans, Native Americans, African Americans

Demographics of the California Gold Rush

Silver and Copper Mining 🛑

In addition to the numerous valuable gold deposits discovered after 1848, prospectors found many types of valuable metals and minerals. Among the most important of these were silver and copper. Two particularly large finds were mined at Pike's Peak in Colorado and Comstock Lode in Nevada. The resources mined from these western frontiers were extremely valuable in the booming Industrial Revolution, as factories in the East needed raw materials for their manufactured products. Prior to the advent of mining regulations in the 20th century, the mining techniques in the American West also had a number of deleterious effects on the natural environment.

Poisonous sulfurous gases were released into the atmosphere.

Rock dust from drilling polluted the rivers and caused silt deposits that flooded towns.

Strip mining caused erosion and deforestation.

Harmful Environmental Impact of Western Mining

Ranching

While many of the frontiersmen and women who headed west during the 19th century did so in search of riches from the gold, silver, and copper mines, others sought to achieve better lives through agriculture and ranching. Cattle had been introduced to North America in the 1400s, and were commonly kept in vast open ranges tended by cowboys or vaqueros, as they were called in areas such as Texas that were once controlled by Mexico. Life in these ranching communities was very difficult, but nevertheless many settlers were attracted to the frontier lifestyle as it offered opportunities to gain freedom and social advancement that were not available in the urban centers of the East. The image of American cowboys has become legendary in books, films, and television, but the reality was somewhat less glamorous.

- Cowboys often wore wide-brimmed hats and bandanas to protect themselves against the sun, wind, and dust.
- Cowboys wore chaps and high boots to protect their legs from briars and cactus needles.
- Almost half of all cowboys were African American, Mexican, or mixed-race.
- Cowboys didn't typically work alone, but in groups of drovers.
- Cowboys typically demonstrated their expertise with ropes and lassos rather than guns.
- Workdays typically consisted of spending most of the time on horseback, rounding, sorting, and counting cattle.

 Ask Yourself...

What are some of the primary differences between the mythic image of the American West and the harsh realities of mining and ranching?

The Homestead Act

As agriculture and ranching began to become more profitable on the American frontiers, especially in the Great Plains states, the U.S. government passed a series of legislation designed to attract more settlers to the West and to provide incentives to those families and individuals willing to undertake what was often a difficult and dangerous venture.

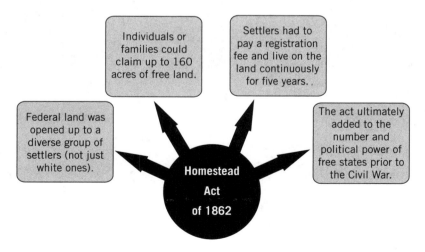

Individuals or families could claim up to 160 acres of free land.

Settlers had to pay a registration fee and live on the land continuously for five years.

Federal land was opened up to a diverse group of settlers (not just white ones).

The act ultimately added to the number and political power of free states prior to the Civil War.

Homestead Act of 1862

Manifest Destiny ❗

The amalgam of political, religious, and cultural ideology that was the foundation of American westward expansion in the 19th century is commonly known as Manifest Destiny. Broadly speaking, Manifest Destiny refers to the idea that Americans had a God-given right to settle the western part of continental North America.

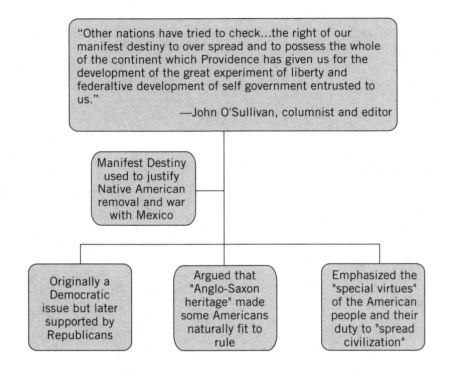

"Other nations have tried to check...the right of our manifest destiny to over spread and to possess the whole of the continent which Providence has given us for the development of the great experiment of liberty and federaltive development of self government entrusted to us."
—John O'Sullivan, columnist and editor

Manifest Destiny used to justify Native American removal and war with Mexico

Originally a Democratic issue but later supported by Republicans

Argued that "Anglo-Saxon heritage" made some Americans naturally fit to rule

Emphasized the "special virtues" of the American people and their duty to "spread civilization"

Texas 💬

Mexico had gained independence from Spain in 1821, and its territorial holdings included much of what is now the American Southwest (including California). American settlers who moved into this territory during the early 1800s were supposed to become Mexican citizens and follow Mexican laws, but they often did not comply with the wishes of the Mexican government. One particular point of contention was that many of the Americans who settled Texas refused to give up their slaves. Texas ultimately fought to gain independence from Mexico, and during that conflict occurred the famous battle at the Alamo (in modern-day San Antonio). The Texans suffered heavy losses but ultimately won their independence in 1836.

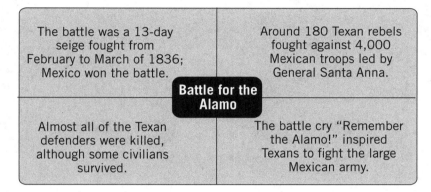

The battle was a 13-day seige fought from February to March of 1836; Mexico won the battle.	Around 180 Texan rebels fought against 4,000 Mexican troops led by General Santa Anna.
Battle for the Alamo	
Almost all of the Texan defenders were killed, although some civilians survived.	The battle cry "Remember the Alamo!" inspired Texans to fight the large Mexican army.

The Mexican-American War ❗

One of the more controversial military engagements of 19th-century America was the Mexican-American War, fought from 1846 to 1848. Tension already existed between Mexico and the United States as a result of the American annexation of Texas in 1836, and several skirmishes and larger battles had occurred prior to the 1840s.

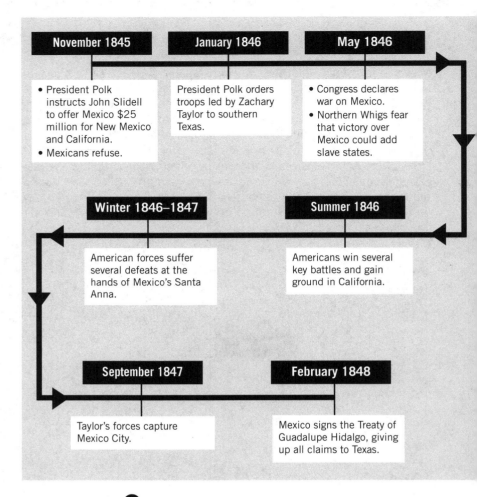

November 1845	January 1846	May 1846
• President Polk instructs John Slidell to offer Mexico $25 million for New Mexico and California. • Mexicans refuse.	President Polk orders troops led by Zachary Taylor to southern Texas.	• Congress declares war on Mexico. • Northern Whigs fear that victory over Mexico could add slave states.

Winter 1846–1847	Summer 1846
American forces suffer several defeats at the hands of Mexico's Santa Anna.	Americans win several key battles and gain ground in California.

September 1847	February 1848
Taylor's forces capture Mexico City.	Mexico signs the Treaty of Guadalupe Hidalgo, giving up all claims to Texas.

NOTABLE FIGURE: ~

December 1847: Future president **Abraham Lincoln** (then a Whig congressman) protested the Mexican-American War by offering a series of "spot resolutions," requesting that President Polk provide details of the exact locations where blood had been spilt on American soil. This action was seen as a challenge to Polk's veracity in asking Congress to declare war on Mexico.

The Transcontinental Railroad ❗

The events of the 19th century and the American expansion westward were inextricably linked to the development of American industrial prowess and the quickly burgeoning railroad companies. None other than Abraham Lincoln, in fact, issued a call for Americans to build a great transcontinental railroad that could transport people and goods from the East Coast to the West Coast and back again. In the years during and after the Civil War, Americans from all ethnic backgrounds and walks of life worked to implement Lincoln's dream, and by 1876 Americans could travel by train from New York City to San Francisco in 83 hours.

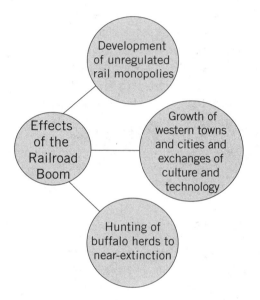

American Connections with Asia ❗

Throughout the 19th century, Americans had more and more contact with Asia, both in terms of Americans' own travels and the increasing flow of Asian immigrants to the United States. One key technological development that facilitated American contact with Asia was the **clipper ship,** a narrow and fast three-masted vessel that Americans and Europeans alike used on long voyages.

Missionaries 💬

One important player in this dynamic of American-Asian exchange was the island of Hawaii, where missionaries had first settled in the early 1800s. The American Board of Commissioners for Foreign Missions sent several waves of ships to Hawaii with the intention of converting the native population to Christianity. Within fewer than 80 years, Hawaii was in effect a colony of the United States. In addition to Hawaii, American missionaries (primarily Protestant) ventured to many places in Asia, taking Christianity and Western culture to societies that had previously had little contact with Americans.

💬 An important but often overlooked figure in the history of American-Asian relations is **Commodore Matthew Perry,** a naval officer who served in the Mexican-American War and the War of 1812 before embarking upon an ambitious mission to open Japanese ports to American trade in the 1850s. Prior to Perry's work in Japan, the country had held strictly to a policy of isolationism and seclusion for several hundred years and the Americans were not universally welcomed.

The Mormons 💬

There were several religious groups that formed in the aftermath of the Second Great Awakening. The one that remains most prominent today is the Mormons, otherwise known as the Church of Jesus Christ of Latter-Day Saints, founded by Joseph Smith in 1830. Smith's successor, Brigham Young, led the Mormons from the Midwest to the Salt Lake Valley of Utah in order to practice their new faith freely. The Mormons were able to survive and eventually thrive in the harsh landscape of Utah by building a robust irrigation network and using their strong sense of family and community to support one another.

Joseph Smith (1805–1844) 😐	Brigham Young (1801–1877) 😐
• Claimed to have experienced visions in which an angel showed him golden plates detailing a Judeo-Christian history in North America • At age 24, published the Book of Mormon, allegedly a translation of these golden plates • Smith's followers were called Latter-Day Saints, or Mormons. • Clashed with non-Mormons over his theological views and promotion of polygamy • Killed by an armed mob while he was held in jail	• Ordained President of the Mormon church three years after Joseph Smith's death • Led Mormon pioneers to relocate in the West, eventually settling in the Salt Lake Valley of Utah • Became Governor of the Utah Territory and established what eventually became Brigham Young University • Built many Mormon temples throughout Utah • Embraced several controversial views, such as the validity of polygamy and the barring of African Americans from the priesthood

Immigration 😮

One of the driving factors in the shift from an agricultural to an industrial economy in the United States was the implementation of new technologies and the subsequent shift in population from rural to urban centers in the 19th century. In the Northeast, in particular, massive waves of immigration boosted the number of people living in cities, but immigrants moved in large numbers to the West and Midwest as well. These immigrants were typically poor, working-class families who encountered resistance and hostility from other working-class Americans concerned that the new immigrants would take their jobs.

Irish, German, and Scandinavian Immigration ❶

Irish	German	Scandinavian
• Some Irish immigrants arrived during the colonial period.	• Some German immigrants arrived during the colonial period.	• Evidence of Scandinavian explorers in North America dates back to the 10th century.
• The largest influx arrived during the mid-1800s, due to overpopulation and poor harvests in Ireland.	• The largest influx arrived between 1820 and WWI.	• The largest influx arrived in the mid-1800s, due to economic difficulties and political strife.
• 1820s: Large numbers arrived to work on labor-intensive jobs (such as canal building) in the Northeast.	• They began to outnumber the Irish in 1854.	• The Homestead Act of 1862 offered agricultural opportunities in the Midwest and Upper Plains states. Settlers had to commit to their land for lengthy periods of time.
• 1845–1852: Huge numbers settled in East Coast cities (NYC, Philadelphia, Boston, Baltimore, etc.)	• They tended to be better educated than the Irish.	
	• A large number of professionals, politicians, and intellectuals left for the U.S. following political turmoil.	
• Approx. 10% of current American population can trace their lineage back to 1 or more Irish ancestors.	• Some settled on the East Coast (NYC); more settled in the Midwest and West (Chicago, Cincinnati, Milwaukee, St. Louis, Texas).	• They lacked the numbers of the Irish and Germans but still significantly impacted the history and development of the American landscape.

Decade	Number of Irish Immigrants	Number of German Immigrants
1820–1830	54,000	160,000
1831–1840	207,000	
1841–1850	781,000	435,000
1851–1860	914,000	952,000
1861–1870	436,000	787,000
1871–1880	437,000	718,000

Irish and German Immigration to the United States

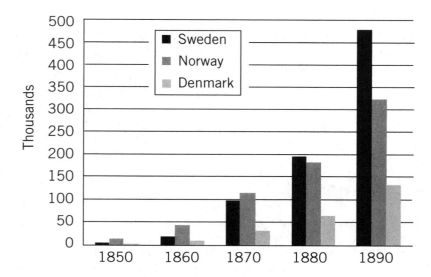

Birth Country of Foreign-Born Scandinavian-Americans

Nativism and Anti-Catholic Sentiment ❗

One unfortunate trend that occurred during the various waves of European immigration to the United States was a rising attitude of nativism, much of it fueled by religious strife (in particular, anti-Catholic sentiment). Almost all of the Irish and many of the German immigrants were Catholic, while the majority of Americans prior to the 19th century were Protestant. Anti-Catholic rioting occurred in many American cities, some of it violent in nature. Nativist political parties such as the "American Party," or **Know-Nothing Party,** emerged in the 1840s, and these parties actively campaigned to prevent foreign-born people from becoming citizens and to prevent them from holding public office. Riding upon the anti-immigrant mentality and anxiety that many Americans felt about the United States' changing demographics, Nativist parties won elections in several states in the 1850s. After the Republicans gained dominance in the 1860s, the Nativist parties largely fell into decline, but their suspicion of foreigners can still be seen today.

Anti-Irish sentiment was so commonplace during the mid-19th century that there was even a popular song that decried the anti-Irish discrimination found in many cities, where "NINA," or "No Irish Need Apply," was regularly affixed to job postings.

Mexican-Americans in the Southwest ❗

While they were not immigrants per se, another group of new Americans that emerged in the mid-19th century was the Mexican-Americans, primarily located in the southwestern part of the United States. Spain had ceded control of a large swath of land to Mexico in 1820, and many of the Mexicans who lived in the northern part of that territory became de facto American citizens after the United States defeated Mexico in the Mexican-American War of 1846–1848. Immigrants from other parts of the United States and from Europe (mainly Germans) settled in the American Southwest in large numbers during the entire 19th century. As in other parts of the United States, the Southwest experienced racial and religious tensions that occasionally flared into violence. Nevertheless, the Mexican-American influence on the United States is evident in a wide variety of realms, including language, architecture, religion, and cuisine.

Conflict over Slavery

The first half of the 19th century in the United States was marked by strong regional differences, many of which were economic, that led to what historians refer to as sectional strife. The Northern states, in particular, experienced the changes brought about by industrialization more rapidly than did the Southern and Western states.

Geographic Variations in Labor

As a result of the Industrial Revolution and the technological changes that it brought, Northern states became more urbanized and less agrarian in the late 18th and early 19th centuries. As a corollary to the increased availability of factory work, the dynamics of the labor market shifted in these Northern states: Paid labor became more common and slave labor became less common as the 19th century progressed. By contrast, the Southern economy remained heavily agricultural and thus heavily reliant upon unpaid slave labor.

	North	South
Geography	Lots of rivers and bays ideal for building cities with trading ports	Lots of fertile land ideal for developing agriculture
Demographics	Mainly of European descent, with a large influx due to recent immigrants from Ireland, Germany, and Scandinavia	About 2/3 of European descent (mostly England/Scotland) and 1/3 enslaved Africans
Urban vs. Rural	Ever increasing percentage of people living in cities	Very few large cities; most lived on farms
Economics	Based on manufacturing goods (esp. textiles) and trade	Based on agriculture (esp. cotton, sugar cane, tobacco, indigo, and rice)

Differences Between North and South (Early/Mid-19th Century)

The Free-Soil Movement ❶

In addition to the regional differences listed above, the mid-19th century brought about some important political changes that, largely due to differences in opinion about slavery, also caused regional splits. One of these splits was a political fight about the so-called **Wilmot Proviso,** a proposal by Congressman David Wilmot in 1846 that would ban slavery in all of the territory newly acquired by the United States during the Mexican-American War. The Northern states voted largely in favor of the Wilmot Proviso while the Southern states voted largely against it, but ultimately the proposal was defeated. As a response to the defeat of the Wilmot Proviso, a new political movement called the **Free-Soil Party** emerged. Active in the 1848 and 1852 presidential elections, the movement was ultimately short-lived and its members were eventually absorbed into the Republican Party.

ASAP U.S. History

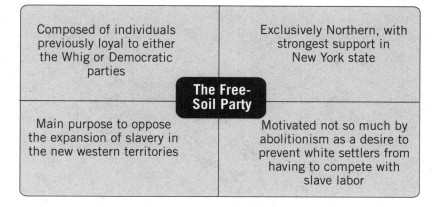

Composed of individuals previously loyal to either the Whig or Democratic parties	Exclusively Northern, with strongest support in New York state
The Free-Soil Party	
Main purpose to oppose the expansion of slavery in the new western territories	Motivated not so much by abolitionism as a desire to prevent white settlers from having to compete with slave labor

The Underground Railroad ❗

The discord over slavery in the early and mid-19th century facilitated the rise of another important social movement: abolitionism. While some groups, such as the Quakers, had opposed slavery for many years, prior to the 1830s very few white Americans actively campaigned to eliminate slavery. After the Second Great Awakening, an increasing number of whites were persuaded for religious and moral reasons that slavery was inherently evil and began to work toward its eradication. Free blacks, of course, had always been prominent advocates for the abolition of slavery. Among many well-known abolitionists was **Harriet Tubman,** who herself had escaped slavery but then returned south in order to help hundreds of slaves escape to the North via the **Underground Railroad,** a network of safe houses and travel routes organized by abolitionists and those sympathetic to the abolitionist cause.

 During the Civil War, Harriet Tubman was a Union spy, venturing into Confederate territory to gather information from other slaves about Confederate plans. She also became the first woman in U.S. history to lead a military expedition, the Combahee River Raid, which liberated more than 750 slaves from nearby plantations.

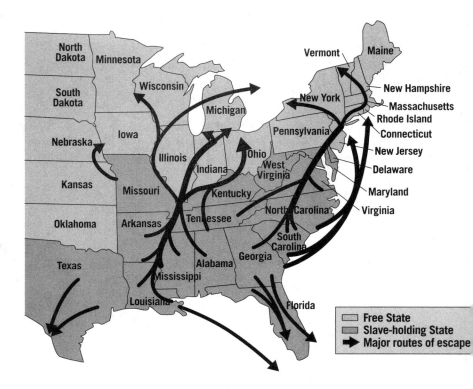

Routes of the Underground Railroad

 Uncle Tom's Cabin

One particular literary work had an immense impact upon Northern Americans' awareness of slavery and helped to propel the abolitionist movement: Harriet Beecher Stowe's *Uncle Tom's Cabin*, published in 1852. Hated by some and loved by others, the book undoubtedly acted as a powerful piece of literary propaganda, as it personalized the arguments for and against slavery. Legend has it that Abraham Lincoln even attributed part of the impetus for the Civil War to the widespread influence of *Uncle Tom's Cabin* on the American psyche.

John Brown 💬

While the majority of abolitionists did not embrace violence as a means to achieving their goals, occasionally pro and anti-slavery camps engaged in hostilities that led to injuries and deaths. Much of the tension arose after the passage of the **Kansas-Nebraska Act** of 1854, which left the decision about the legality of slavery in the western territories to the settlers of those territories themselves. Kansas, in particular, saw a lot of confrontations between those wishing to make Kansas a slave state and those wishing it to be a free state. John Brown, a radical white abolitionist, was instrumental in those confrontations disgusted by what he perceived as the lack of action among pacifists within the abolitionist movement, Brown proclaimed that armed resistance was the only way to combat the pro-slavery forces.

1855: John Brown and his sons move to Kansas in support of the Free-Soil movement.

1856: Brown's followers kill five pro-slavery settlers at Pottwatomie Creek, Kansas.

1859: Brown leads 16 white and 5 black men in a raid on Harpers Ferry, West Virginia, in an attempt to incite a slave rebellion. Almost all are killed or captured, including Brown, who was convicted of treason and murder and hanged.

Arguments for and Against Slavery ❗

In the years leading up to the American Civil War, both pro- and anti-slavery campaigners mustered all the arguments they could in an attempt either to defend the status quo or to abolish the institution. While there were many factors that led to the Civil War, these battles over slavery escalated matters to the extent that the state of the union was in danger.

Pro-Slavery Arguments

- Certain passages in the Bible seemed to justify slavery.
- Many historical examples of slavery exist, including ancient Greece and Rome.
- The Constitution recognized slavery as legitimate.
- The Constitution guaranteed states the right to govern themselves.
- Slavery had a "civilizing" influence and was good for the slaves.
- Racialists defended the idea of blacks' inherent inferiority.

Anti-Slavery Arguments

- It was morally wrong to own and control another human being.
- Harsh conditions for slaves violated Christian principles.
- The Declaration of Independence declared that "all men are created equal."
- Slavery had a destabilizing influence and thus was harmful to the unity of the states.
- Slavery limited the South's ability to grow and compete economically.

The American Colonization Society 💬

One lesser-known aspect of the abolitionist movement was the proposition, advocated for by white (and some prominent black) Americans, to return freed slaves and free-born black Americans to Africa. One group influenced by this ideology was the American Colonization Society, founded in 1816 with the expressed purpose of "repatriating" black Americans to Liberia (on the coast of West Africa).

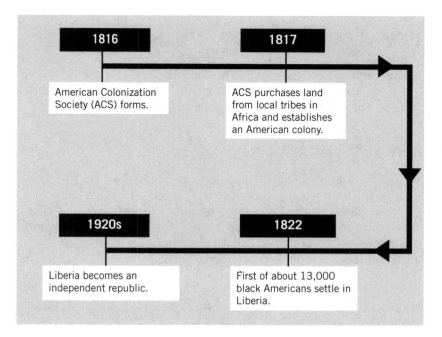

1816

American Colonization Society (ACS) forms.

1817

ACS purchases land from local tribes in Africa and establishes an American colony.

1920s

Liberia becomes an independent republic.

1822

First of about 13,000 black Americans settle in Liberia.

Liberia

Ask Yourself...

What were some of the principal divisions in American society in the early and mid-19th century? How did conflicts over slavery and economic differences between Northern and Southern states lead to tensions in the years before the Civil War?

Pre–Civil War Tensions 📙

Despite several compromises between Northern and Southern factions, the years leading up to the Civil War were characterized by sectional strife and insurmountable economic and political differences.

Mexican Cession 📙

American forces dominated during the Mexican-American War of 1846–1848. While the United States did suffer several setbacks, the American army gained territory quickly and had little difficulty vanquishing the ill-prepared Mexican forces; after the American troops entered Mexico City, the war was effectively over. Much of the American Southwest—including the states of New Mexico, Arizona, California, Nevada, and Utah—was territory that Mexico ceded to the United States in 1848 as part of the Treaty of Guadalupe Hidalgo. As part of this deal, the United States paid $15 million: The land transfer is known as the **Mexican Cession.**

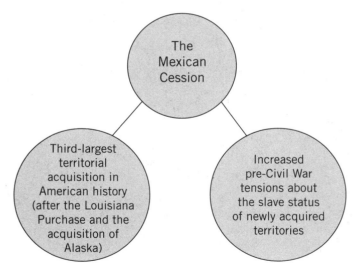

The Compromise of 1850 ❗

The American territories of the West and Southwest complicated the national debates about slavery, especially as those newer territories began to seek statehood. Southern states generally opposed admitting territories such as California into the Union, since California's constitution prohibited slavery and thus threatened the balance of free vs. slave states in the nation as a whole. The **Compromise of 1850,** negotiated between the Democrat Stephen Douglas and the Whig Henry Clay, aimed to ease these tensions by creating conditions favorable to both pro- and anti-slavery camps. While the Compromise as a whole was rejected by Congress, Douglas was able to extract elements of the Compromise into separate bills that were eventually passed into law.

The Compromise of 1850

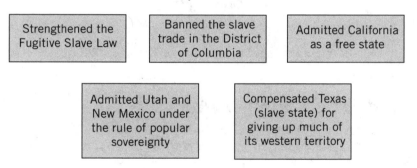

| Strengthened the Fugitive Slave Law | Banned the slave trade in the District of Columbia | Admitted California as a free state |

| Admitted Utah and New Mexico under the rule of popular sovereignty | Compensated Texas (slave state) for giving up much of its western territory |

The Fugitive Slave Act of 1850 💬

One of the most controversial aspects of the Compromise of 1850 was the enactment of a much-strengthened fugitive slave law, sometimes referred to as the **Fugitive Slave Act of 1850.** The law ruled that fugitive slaves, if caught, had to be returned to their masters in the South; moreover, the law required that whites living in Northern (free) states had to comply with this law, meaning that even if slaves escaped to freedom in the North, they were still in danger of being sent back south.

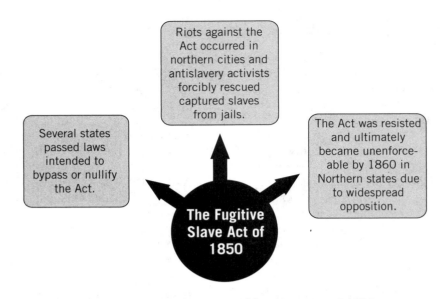

Northern Response to the Fugitive Slave Act of 1850

Dred Scott v. Sandford 🔟

Democrat James Buchanan had been elected president in 1856. He did not press for major changes regarding the issue of slavery: He enforced the Fugitive Slave Act and opposed abolitionists seeking to uproot the status quo. Soon after Buchanan took office, the Supreme Court ruled against a slave named **Dred Scott** who had sued the federal government for his freedom. The landmark decision, known as *Dred Scott v. Sandford,* determined that Scott, as a black slave, was not a citizen of the United States and therefore had no right to sue in court. In addition to the ruling about citizenship, the Supreme Court ruled that Congress could not regulate slavery in the territories, effectively nullifying the Missouri Compromise, the Kansas-Nebraska Act, and the Wilmot Proviso.

The Emergence of the Republican Party ❶

After the debate about and ultimate passage of the Kansas-Nebraska Act in 1854, the dynamics of American political parties changed considerably. The anti-slavery Whigs joined forces with northern Democrats and members of the Free-Soil movement to create a new party, the **Republicans.** While the new party was not strictly an abolitionist party, it was determined to keep Northern states and Western territories free of slavery.

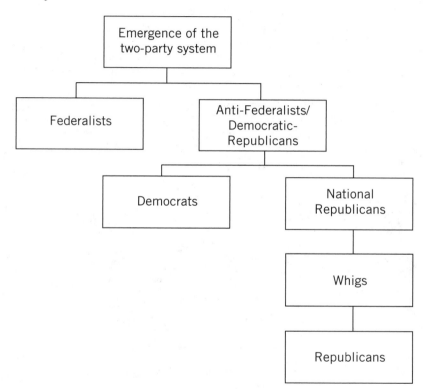

Major American Political Parties, 1776–1860

The Election of 1860 🛑

The 1858 off-year Senate election in Illinois was one that would ultimately have enormous consequences for the nation as a whole. The sitting senator at the time was Democrat Stephen Douglas, known as a powerful force in Congress. His opponent was Abraham Lincoln, a Republican lawyer-turned-politician who had gained attention due to his opposition to the Mexican-American War and the Kansas-Nebraska Act. Although Lincoln lost the Senate election, his debates with Douglas propelled him into national political stardom and laid the groundwork for his later stance on slavery.

In the run-up to the 1860 presidential election, the Democrats split into two different factions, northern Democrats backing Douglas and southern Democrats backing John Breckinridge, President James Buchanan's vice president. A minor third-party candidate from the Constitutional Union Party, John Bell, was also a candidate. Although Lincoln didn't even appear on the ballots of many Southern states, he won the election due to his widespread support in the North, which had a huge population advantage in the Electoral College.

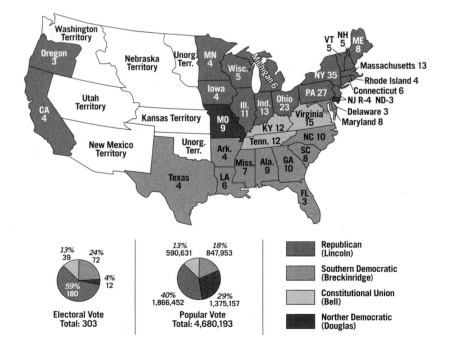

Electoral Vote Total: 303	13% 39 · 24% 72 · 59% 180 · 4% 12
Popular Vote Total: 4,680,193	13% 590,631 · 18% 847,953 · 40% 1,866,452 · 29% 1,375,157

Republican (Lincoln)
Southern Democratic (Breckinridge)
Constitutional Union (Bell)
Norther Democratic (Douglas)

Southern Secession ❗

The regional divisions between Northern and Southern states had become insurmountable by the time Lincoln was elected president in 1860. Before he even took office, in December 1860, South Carolina seceded from the Union, soon to be followed by six other states. The events that followed led to the nation's most deadly war, in which more American soldiers were killed than in any other war in history.

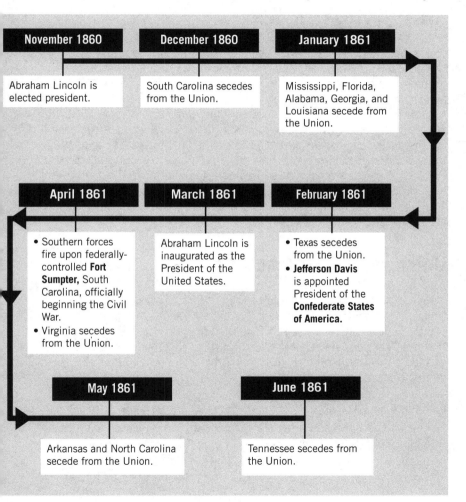

November 1860

Abraham Lincoln is elected president.

December 1860

South Carolina secedes from the Union.

January 1861

Mississippi, Florida, Alabama, Georgia, and Louisiana secede from the Union.

April 1861

- Southern forces fire upon federally-controlled **Fort Sumpter,** South Carolina, officially beginning the Civil War.
- Virginia secedes from the Union.

March 1861

Abraham Lincoln is inaugurated as the President of the United States.

February 1861

- Texas secedes from the Union.
- **Jefferson Davis** is appointed President of the **Confederate States of America.**

May 1861

Arkansas and North Carolina secede from the Union.

June 1861

Tennessee secedes from the Union.

Ask Yourself...

What major laws were passed in the years prior to the Civil War that exemplified and/or exacerbated regional tensions and discord about the issue of slavery? How did the major American political parties redefine themselves along sectional lines?

The Civil War ❗

The American Civil War was one of the most momentous events in United States history, not just in terms of the warfare itself but also in terms of the economic, political, and social upheaval it caused. Debates about slavery, of course, escalated the conflict between Northern and Southern states, but it is an oversimplification to view the Civil War solely in terms of slavery. Missouri, Kentucky, Maryland, and Delaware, for instance, were slave states that fought on the side of the Union. Most Southerners, moreover, argue that the primary issue at stake in the Civil War was states' rights. President Lincoln himself asserted that his primary goal was not to abolish slavery, but to preserve the union, and that any action he took to free the slaves was done in the interest of national unity.

Union vs. Confederacy ❗

Newly appointed Confederate President Jefferson Davis realized that the Northern states enjoyed considerable advantages in terms of economic power, population, and ease of long-distance transportation, and knew that the Southern states would need to band together. Therefore, Davis created a vast bureaucracy that many of his fellow Southerners vehemently opposed.

Union (Abraham Lincoln)
- larger population and army
- widespread railroad network
- telegraph system
- advanced industrialization

Confederacy (Jefferson Davis)
- better military leadership
- fighting mostly on own soil
- motivated to repel what they perceived to be a "foreign invasion" of their homeland

Battle of Gettysburg 💬	Sherman's "March to the Sea" 💬
• July 1–3, 1863 in Gettysburg, Pennsylvania • Union General Meade defeated Confederate General Lee, ending Lee's attempt to invade the North. • Considered a major turning point in the Civil War and a morale boost for Union troops • Bloodiest battle of the Civil War, with more than 45,000 people killed in three days	• November 15–December 21, 1864 in Georgia • Union General Sherman captured Atlanta and fought his way southeast to Savannah. • Union troops destroyed military targets and bridges, but also civilian property. • Aimed to frighten the Georgian population and weaken civilian support for the Confederacy

The Emancipation Proclamation ❗

Because Southern slaves were indirectly supporting the Confederate cause, President Lincoln had to determine what to do with slaves who were captured by the Union army as the troops made their way south. There were several good reasons, apart from the obvious moral imperative, for Lincoln to free the slaves: First, freeing the slaves would enable the federal government to avoid the logistical problems of holding them captive; second, freed slaves would be able to fight for the Union side; and third, because European nations such as Britain and France opposed slavery, Lincoln's decision to free the slaves meant that Europe would support the Union over the Confederacy.

Lincoln decided to make an official pronouncement about freeing the slaves after the Union army's 1862 success at the Battle of Antietam, near Sharpsburg, Maryland.

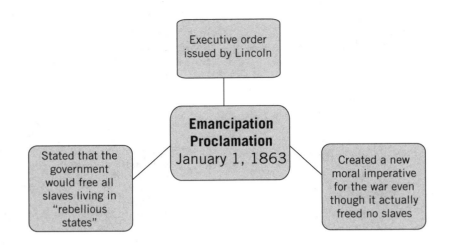

Executive order issued by Lincoln

Emancipation Proclamation January 1, 1863

Stated that the government would free all slaves living in "rebellious states"

Created a new moral imperative for the war even though it actually freed no slaves

Black Soldiers in the Civil War ❗

Approximately 200,000 black soldiers fought on the side of the Union during the Civil War, both free men and former slaves who had escaped from the South (a tiny number also fought on the Confederate side). Typically these soldiers were separated into their own units, often with white officers in charge. Although black soldiers performed many of the same duties as did white soldiers, they faced discrimination within the Union army and navy due to racial prejudice and were treated especially badly when captured by Confederate troops.

The Gettysburg Address ❗

One of the most well-known American political speeches of all time was delivered at the site of the Battle of Gettysburg by Abraham Lincoln in November 1863, several months after the Union victory there the previous summer. Interpreted as a reiteration of the principles inherent in the Declaration of Independence, the Gettysburg Address both advocated the ideals of equality and concisely summarized Lincoln's belief that at the core of the Civil War was a battle for the preservation of the United States.

"... from these honored dead we take increased devotion to that cause for which they gave the last full measure of devotion—that we here highly resolve that these dead shall not have died in vain—that this nation, under God, shall have a new birth of freedom—and that government of the people, by the people, for the people, shall not perish from the earth."

—Abraham Lincoln

The End of the Civil War

At times during 1863 and 1864, it seemed as if the Civil War would never end. By 1865, the Union forces had overcome numerous obstacles and the war turned in the Union's favor. The official end of the war is generally thought to be the moment that Confederate General Lee surrendered the Army of Northern Virginia in April 1865. Several small-scale skirmishes were fought after that date, but in essence the South had been defeated. Tragically, John Wilkes Booth assassinated President Lincoln only five days after Lee's surrender, and the period of Reconstruction had begun.

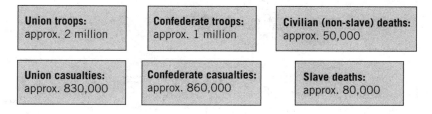

| Union troops: | Confederate troops: | Civilian (non-slave) deaths: |
| approx. 2 million | approx. 1 million | approx. 50,000 |

| Union casualties: | Confederate casualties: | Slave deaths: |
| approx. 830,000 | approx. 860,000 | approx. 80,000 |

The Civil War in Numbers

Ask Yourself...

Was the Civil War inevitable? What are some of the major reasons that the North eventually emerged victorious?

Reconstruction ⚠

At the end of the Civil War, Americans faced three crucial questions:

1. Under what conditions would southern states be readmitted to the Union?
2. What would be the status of blacks in the postwar era?
3. What would happen to the states (and people) that had rebelled against the Union?

The period that historians refer to as **Reconstruction** spans the years from 1865 (the end of the Civil War) to 1877 (when the Union army withdrew from the South). In addition to reconciling people who had just finished killing each other in massive numbers, those in charge of Reconstruction had a very tough task: rebuilding the infrastructure and property that had been destroyed during the war. Most of the devastated areas were in Southern states, where much of the fighting took place. The most difficult aspect of Reconstruction was the process of integrating free blacks into the broader American society.

Radical Republicans vs. Moderate Republicans ⚠

In the mid-1850s, the Republican party had effectively broken apart into two different factions: the Radical Republicans and the Moderate Republicans. Abraham Lincoln, who had argued for a gradual emancipation process when he was a presidential candidate, belonged to the latter camp. After the Southern states seceded, many of the Moderate Republicans left Congress, and the Radical Republicans—who wanted immediate emancipation—dominated the legislative branch. In the years following the Civil War, it was the Radical Republican wing that championed the more progressive legislation dealing with racial equity.

Radical Republicans	Moderate Republicans
• Wanted to punish the South • Wanted to see the South dramatically reconstructed • Wanted civil rights (such as voting) for freedmen • Wanted limited political rights for former Confederate officials and military officers	• Wanted to reintegrate the South into the Union • Wanted to see the South restored • Most supported Lincoln's "Ten Percent Plan," which would allow Southern states readmittance into the Union if 10% of its voters swore an oath of allegiance

The Reconstruction Amendments ❗

Several important Constitutional Amendments that dealt directly with issues of race and equality were passed in the years surrounding the Civil War. Although Abraham Lincoln had declared slaves free in his Emancipation Proclamation in 1863, the issue wasn't formally resolved until the passage of the 13th Amendment by the Senate in April 1864, and then by the House in January 1865. The 14th Amendment was passed in 1868, and the 15th was passed in 1870. Together, the three are known as the Reconstruction Amendments.

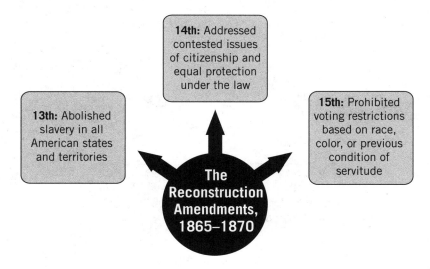

14th: Addressed contested issues of citizenship and equal protection under the law

13th: Abolished slavery in all American states and territories

15th: Prohibited voting restrictions based on race, color, or previous condition of servitude

The Reconstruction Amendments, 1865–1870

The 15th Amendment and Women's Suffrage ❗

One of the ironies of the Reconstruction Amendments is that while they created new opportunities for black men, suffrage for women of all races was not to become a reality until the passage of the 19th Amendment in 1920. Some women's suffrage advocates, such as Susan B. Anthony and Elizabeth Cady Stanton, refused to support the 15th Amendment because it did not include women's enfranchisement. Others, such as Julia Ward Howe and Lucy Stone, argued that those who favored women's suffrage should also support efforts to enable the enfranchisement of black men.

The Impeachment of Andrew Johnson 💬

President Andrew Johnson, Abraham Lincoln's Democratic vice president, assumed the office after Lincoln was assassinated in 1865. Johnson had an extremely contentious relationship with the Republican-dominated Congress. Johnson favored a quick restoration of Southern states into the Union and did not believe that former slaves should be given the new rights advocated by Republicans. In 1868, the conflict between Johnson and the Congress came to a head when he was formally accused of "high crimes and misdemeanors," becoming the first American president to be impeached. The official charges against Johnson dealt with a violation of the Tenure of Office Act, but it is widely believed that the deeper reason behind his impeachment was that he was standing in the way of Reconstruction.

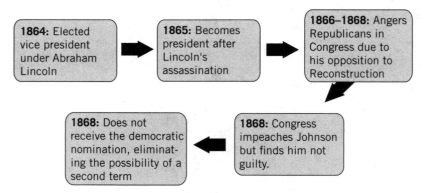

1864: Elected vice president under Abraham Lincoln ➡ **1865:** Becomes president after Lincoln's assassination ➡ **1866–1868:** Angers Republicans in Congress due to his opposition to Reconstruction

1868: Does not receive the democratic nomination, eliminating the possibility of a second term ⬅ **1868:** Congress impeaches Johnson but finds him not guilty.

Andrew Johnson Timeline

Successes and Failures of Reconstruction ❗

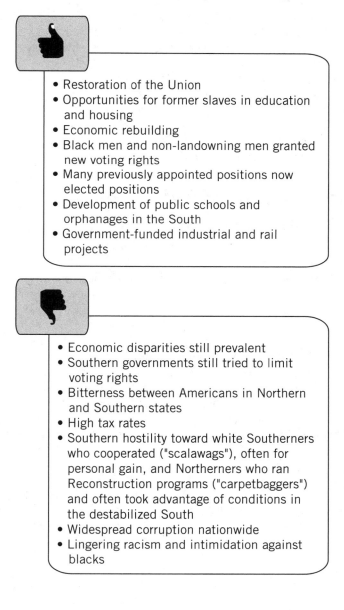

- Restoration of the Union
- Opportunities for former slaves in education and housing
- Economic rebuilding
- Black men and non-landowning men granted new voting rights
- Many previously appointed positions now elected positions
- Development of public schools and orphanages in the South
- Government-funded industrial and rail projects

- Economic disparities still prevalent
- Southern governments still tried to limit voting rights
- Bitterness between Americans in Northern and Southern states
- High tax rates
- Southern hostility toward white Southerners who cooperated ("scalawags"), often for personal gain, and Northerners who ran Reconstruction programs ("carpetbaggers") and often took advantage of conditions in the destabilized South
- Widespread corruption nationwide
- Lingering racism and intimidation against blacks

Sharecropping 🗨

During the Reconstruction period, many slaves (especially those who had endured the torments of cruel masters) fled the South. Others, however, stayed in the South and worked on farms as sharecroppers, trading part of their crop yields in exchange for the right to work land owned by someone else. In some cases the sharecropping arrangement worked well for Southern blacks, but often the conditions in which they worked were little better than they had experienced as slaves. It is worth noting that by the 1880s sharecropping was practiced by white farmers as well as black farmers, and by the middle of the 20th century, share-cropping was in fact predominantly practiced by poor whites.

Discrimination and Segregation During Reconstruction 🗨

The Reconstruction period brought many advances to the Southern states, but industrialization was slow to catch on and the South remained primarily rural and agricultural in the decades following the Civil War. Because of the prevalence of the sharecropping system, many farmers sold their land to wealthy owners, who consolidated the land into large farms and kept those who farmed the land in a state of constant debt. Many of the so-called black codes that had been enacted in the years prior to the Civil War remained in effect, and new racially motivated laws were enacted that were designed to reinforce the segregation and discrimination that were already deeply entrenched into the fabric of American society. Collectively, these racially discriminatory laws are known as **Jim Crow laws** (after a popular character from minstrel shows, in which white entertainers performed blackface caricatures of African Americans).

Many of the Jim Crow laws were specifically designed to prevent African Americans from voting:

Literacy Tests	Poll Taxes	"Grandfather" Clauses
• Administered by officials in charge of voter registration • Arbitrary and difficult questions asked in order to prohibit blacks and poor whites from voting • Results did not accurately reflect intelligence or education (designed to ensure failure).	• Payment of a poll tax was required in some states as a prerequisite for voter registration. • Adversely affected poor people, both black and white • Not outlawed until the passage of the 24th Amendment in 1962	• Allowed old rules to continue to apply to some existing situations while new rules apply to future situations • Designed to allow some poor and illiterate whites to vote because their ancestors had the right to vote (even though they could not pass literacy tests or afford poll taxes)

The Ku Klux Klan and Lynching 💬

In addition to having to endure the widespread racism and discrimination prevalent in American society after the Civil War, African Americans also faced intimidation and violence at the hands of terrorist groups such as the Ku Klux Klan.

The Ku Klux Klan

- Racist terrorist group that rose to prominence in the 1860s
- Advocated white supremacy, white nationalism, and anti-immigration policies
- Attempted to overthrow Republican governments in Southern states
- Used tactics of intimidation and violence, including public lynching, against African Americans

---

The End of Reconstruction ❶

The 1876 election was a battle between Republican governor of Ohio **Rutherford B. Hayes** and New York Democrat Samuel Tilden, who had made a name for himself by aggressively going after the corrupt political boss William M. Tweed. The election results were extremely close, with some electoral votes disputed, and the result was the **Compromise of 1877,** a negotiation that enabled Hayes to become president but required the federal government to end military reconstruction and pull federal troops out of the South. This, effectively, was the end of Reconstruction which, broadly viewed, was a failure.

 Ask Yourself...

What were some of the major problems that the federal government faced in the years immediately following the Civil War? In what ways did the Reconstruction period represent opportunities for African Americans, and in what ways were African Americans still disadvantaged?

PERIOD 6 (1865–1898):
The Industrial Revolution

The Industrial Period of the United States brought the nation to great heights, as it became one of the most respected economic powers in the world. The businesses and innovations that helped improve the country also came at great cost. The working class, immigrants, and Native Americans were among some of the groups who sacrificed greatly during this period.

The Industrial Revolution 🔊

The last quarter of the 19th century is often called the **Age of Invention** because so many technological advances were made. These advances, in turn, generated greater opportunities for **mass production**, which then caused the economy to grow at a tremendous rate. Not surprisingly, the people known as the "captains of industry" to their fans (and the "robber barons" to others), who owned and controlled the new manufacturing enterprises, became extremely rich and powerful during this period.

Government Subsidized Technology 🔊

Not all breakthroughs in the Industrial Revolution were championed by entrepreneurs. Some projects were too expensive and large in scope for private business to realistically fund. Instead, the federal government took the initiative. Two such innovations were in transportation and communication.

Communication	Transportation
1843: Telegraph inventor Samuel Morse requested and received $30,000 to build a forty-mile telegraph line from Baltimore to Washington. By 1861, the transcontinental telegraph was in operation.	Pacific Railroad Acts of 1862 and 1864: Congress offered funding and land grants to the two companies (Union Pacific and Central Pacific) that lobbied for federal assistance on the project.

Factories and the Assembly Line Increase Productivity ❗

As more and faster machines became available to manufacturers, businessmen discovered that their cost per unit decreased as the number of units they produced increased. The more raw product they bought, the cheaper the suppliers' asking price.

Pros **Cons**

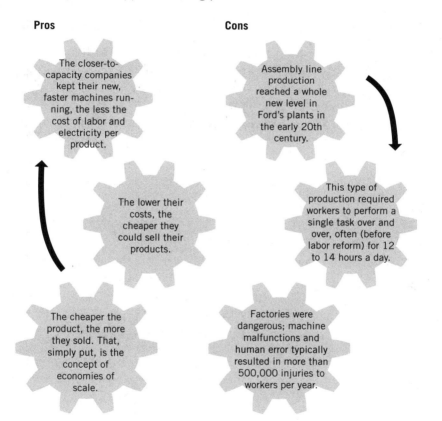

The closer-to-capacity companies kept their new, faster machines running, the less the cost of labor and electricity per product.

Assembly line production reached a whole new level in Ford's plants in the early 20th century.

The lower their costs, the cheaper they could sell their products.

This type of production required workers to perform a single task over and over, often (before labor reform) for 12 to 14 hours a day.

The cheaper the product, the more they sold. That, simply put, is the concept of economies of scale.

Factories were dangerous; machine malfunctions and human error typically resulted in more than 500,000 injuries to workers per year.

The downside of this new business practice was that it required employees to work as efficiently, and repetitively, as machines.

Electricity 💡

Thomas Edison, the "Wizard of Menlo Park," worked on two projects in New Jersey that had immeasurable impact on the ability for industrial productivity.

Try imagining a world before light bulbs. The day would end at sundown if not for inefficient, expensive, and dangerous kerosene lamps. The **light bulb** allowed factories to extend the workday by staying open late into the evening, which dramatically increased productivity.

Edison also worked on the development of the **power plant,** an electricity generator that could provide more efficient power to communities. The Edison Electric Light Station paved the way for inventors to create new uses for electricity both in industry and in the home.

Monopolies and Trusts 💡

One new form of business organization was called a **holding company.** A holding company owned enough stock in various companies to have a controlling interest in the production of raw material, the means of transporting that material to a factory, the factory itself, and the distribution network for selling the product. The logical conclusion is a **monopoly,** or complete control of an entire industry.

There were two kinds of business consolidation in the late 19th century.

Vertical integration: A company owns a means for each step of production, and therefore is self-sufficient and does not need to get resources from other companies. This is largely seen as legal. Example: Andrew Carnegie's company owned resources from iron mines to steel mills.

Horizontal integration: A holding company controls the market for a specific aspect of production. For example, a company might own all coal mines, so any consumer or company that needs coal, will have to do business with the holding company since there is no competition. This practice was found to be an illegal monopoly. Example: Rockefeller's Standard Oil.

Public pressure led to the passage of a law forbidding any "combination...or conspiracy in the restraint of trade"—the **Sherman Antitrust Act of 1890**. Unfortunately, the wording of the Sherman Antitrust Act was ambiguous enough to allow the pro-business Supreme Court at the time to interpret the law as it saw fit.

In *Northern Securities Co. vs. United States* (1904), the Supreme Court ruled that the merger of the largest railroad companies amounted to a monopoly and that the company must break up into smaller companies that would be run independently of one another. This case has been used as precedent to keep a check on monopolies ever since.

The Industrial Revolution

Captains of Industry 💬

Here is a short list of some of the more famous captains of industry:

	Captain of Industry	Company	Best known for
	John D. Rockefeller	Standard Oil	Monopolizing the oil industry
	Andrew Carnegie	Carnegie Steel (later United States Steel)	Bringing a cheap method for mass producing steel to the United States
	Cornelius Vanderbilt	New York Central and Hudson River Railroads	Being a railroad and shipping tycoon
	J.P. Morgan	J.P. Morgan and Co.	Running a banking empire; bailing out the U.S. government in the Panic of 1893; buying companies to create larger ones (AT&T, U.S. Steel, General Electric)

💬 Carnegie's secret was to use the Bessemer process—a technique for quickly converting large quantities of iron into steel. Mastered in Europe, the Bessemer process pushes air through the molten iron to rid the material of impurities through oxidation.

Increasing the Gap Between Rich and Poor 🛑

Numerous problems arose because of this consolidation of power.

Rapid Growth required lots of money.	Monopolies created an extremely powerful class.
Businessmen borrowed huge sums, and when their businesses occasionally failed, bank failures could result. - - - - - - - - - - - - - - - - - During the last quarter of the 19th century, the U.S. endured one major financial panic per decade. Although irresponsible investors caused the panics, the lower classes suffered the most, as jobs and money became scarce.	This new class's interests often clashed with those of the rest of society. - - - - - - - - - - - - - - - - - As these businessmen grew more powerful, public resentment increased, and the government responded with laws to restrict monopolies (which the courts, in turn, weakened). - - - - - - - - - - - - - - - - - Captains of industry held enormous influence over Congress.

International Trade 🛑

U.S. companies, often with the support of the federal government, looked abroad for more opportunities to maximize profits. For instance, in China:

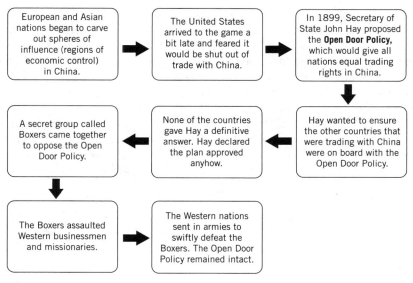

European and Asian nations began to carve out spheres of influence (regions of economic control) in China. ➡ The United States arrived to the game a bit late and feared it would be shut out of trade with China. ➡ In 1899, Secretary of State John Hay proposed the **Open Door Policy,** which would give all nations equal trading rights in China.

⬇

A secret group called Boxers came together to oppose the Open Door Policy. ⬅ None of the countries gave Hay a definitive answer. Hay declared the plan approved anyhow. ⬅ Hay wanted to ensure the other countries that were trading with China were on board with the Open Door Policy.

⬇

The Boxers assaulted Western businessmen and missionaries. ➡ The Western nations sent in armies to swiftly defeat the Boxers. The Open Door Policy remained intact.

Business and Economic Interests 🔰

During the Gilded Age, industrialists advocated an approach to governing known as **laissez-faire economics**. From the French for "allow to do," advocates of this approach reasoned that the economy works best with as little intervention as possible from the government. Similar to the idea of Social Darwinism, laissez-faire economics argued that without government interference, the natural development of the classes would take hold—anything less would be social engineering. The Supreme Court of the United States largely agreed with this idea during the Gilded Age.

Panics 🔰

The money involved in U.S. industries was unprecedented. The presence of holding companies created the first true economies of scale (large production of goods that allow for the goods to be sold at low prices) in the United States. The ability of investors and industrialists to make unfathomable fortunes in a short amount of time led to some reckless behavior in the market place. When recklessness leads to a period of declining economic activity (decreases in production, sales, wages, and employment), the nation experiences a recession, and occasionally a **financial panic**. Panics are characterized by speculation in the market that creates an artificially high value in certain goods, leading to debt, as people try to purchase more and more of the good whether they have the funds or not. A panic occurs when the bubble bursts, the goods are of little value, and people still hold debt.

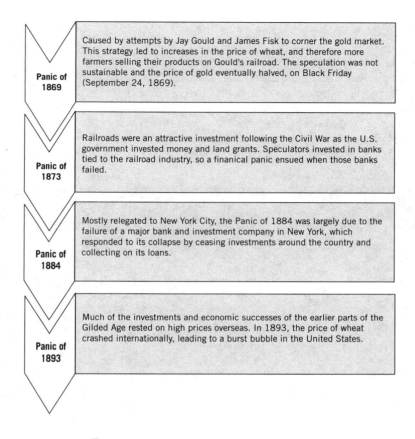

Panic of 1869	Caused by attempts by Jay Gould and James Fisk to corner the gold market. This strategy led to increases in the price of wheat, and therefore more farmers selling their products on Gould's railroad. The speculation was not sustainable and the price of gold eventually halved, on Black Friday (September 24, 1869).
Panic of 1873	Railroads were an attractive investment following the Civil War as the U.S. government invested money and land grants. Speculators invested in banks tied to the railroad industry, so a finanical panic ensued when those banks failed.
Panic of 1884	Mostly relegated to New York City, the Panic of 1884 was largely due to the failure of a major bank and investment company in New York, which responded to its collapse by ceasing investments around the country and collecting on its loans.
Panic of 1893	Much of the investments and economic successes of the earlier parts of the Gilded Age rested on high prices overseas. In 1893, the price of wheat crashed internationally, leading to a burst bubble in the United States.

Unions 🛑

Workers found their treatment by the industrialists unfair. Long hours and unsafe work conditions were only two of many factors that led to organized labor.

Child Labor 🛑

Factory jobs had also been given to children, who were hired at much lower rates. Because men did not make a high enough wage, their wives and children needed to work in order to make ends meet. According to the 1890 Census, two million children were employed. Their working conditions were dangerous and the hours were long (some experienced 18 hour days).

AFL, CIO, and the Knights of Labor 💬

Unions were considered radical organizations by many, and the government was wary of them; businesses and the courts were openly hostile
to them. Hired goons and, in some cases, federal troops often broke
strikes. Before the Civil War, the few unions that existed were small,
regional, or local and represented workers within a specific craft or industry. To enhance the power of organized labor, national labor unions
were formed. These included the following.

Knights of Labor	American Federation of Labor (AFL)	Congress of Industrial Organizations (CIO)
• Founded in 1869 • Organized skilled and unskilled workers from a variety of crafts into a single union • After a series of unsuccessful strikes under the leadership of **Terrence Powderly,** the popularity of the Knights began to decline.	• Founded in 1886 • Attempted to regain popular support of unions by focusing on such "bread and butter" issues as higher wages and shorter workdays, an approach that proved successful. • Gained more power by excluding unskilled workers	• Founded in 1935, by breaking away from the AFL • Organized industrial union workers and differed from the AFL in its early days by accept-ing African American members • Engaged in a heated rivaly with the AFL for two decades • Reunited with the AFL in 1955 to create the AFL-CIO

Strikes ❗

Although the Knights advocated arbitration over strikes, they became
increasingly violent in efforts to achieve their goals. The American public began to associate unions with violence and political radicalism.
Propagandists claimed that unions were subversive forces. One of the
reasons for this claim was the use of **strikes**, organized stoppages of
work used by unions as a bargaining tool.

Homestead and Pullman Strikes 💬

Two notable strikes occurred at the factories of notable captains of industry: Andrew Carnegie and George Pullman.

Homestead Strike, 1892	Workers at Carnegie's Homestead Steel factory went on strike, protesting a wage cut and the refusal of factory manager Henry Clay Frick to allow them to form a union.	〰 The **Pinkerton Detectives** was a private security firm founded in 1850. During the Pullman strike, Andrew Carnegie requested that Henry Clay Frick call in the Pinkerton Detective force to prevent the steel workers from protesting. The ensuing clash between the Pinkertons and the strikers led to several deaths (7 Pinkertons and 9 steelworkers) and the retreat of the Pinkertons. Eventually, the Pennsylvania state militia ended the strike, and Frick hired new workers to replace the striking workers.
Pullman Strike, 1894	Workers at the Pullman Palace Car Factory faced a wage cut and an increase in the cost of their housing. They organized a strike, and the American Railway Union joined their strike in May, leading to over 250,000 railway workers walking off the job, shutting down rail travel in 27 states.	〰 The American Railway Union president **Eugene Debs** refused to end the strike, even after President Cleveland ordered the Army to stop the strike and Debs was ordered to stop the strike because it was disrupting delivery of federal mail. Debs was convicted and jailed for refusing to follow a court order. While in jail, Debs is said to have read Karl Marx's *Communist Manifesto*. When released from jail, he became active in the socialist movement, and eventually became the leader of the American Socialist party.

 Ask Yourself...

What challenges, both private and governmental, were presented to organized labor?

Agricultural Interests 🔔

The wealth of the industrialists certainly could not be created without some help from the plains states and the southern states. The raw materials used in the northern industries came from miners and farmers who did not experience anything close to the wealth of the industrialists. In the late 19th century, these workers began to advocate for their interests and in the last decade of the century, would lead a political movement that gave northeastern industrialists a run for their money.

"New South" 🔔

After the Compromise of 1877, many southern leaders sought to emulate the industrialization of the North, coining the term "New South." Despite these aspirations, though, sharecropping and tenant farming would continue to dominate the region for many years.

Mechanization 🔔

Innovations in agricultural technology, ironically, had a detrimental effect on Gilded Age farmers. On first thought, the mechanization of agricultural tasks would seem to allow farmers to create wealth through increased production. However, consider the case of the **plow** and **reaper**:

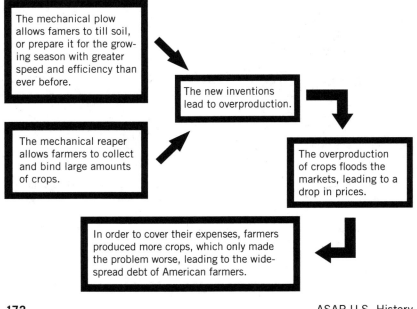

The mechanical plow allows famers to till soil, or prepare it for the growing season with greater speed and efficiency than ever before.

The new inventions lead to overproduction.

The mechanical reaper allows farmers to collect and bind large amounts of crops.

The overproduction of crops floods the markets, leading to a drop in prices.

In order to cover their expenses, farmers produced more crops, which only made the problem worse, leading to the widespread debt of American farmers.

Railroads: Benefits and Liabilities ❗

Recall that railroads were initially funded by government grants. However, they were maintained and operated by private businesses. For American workers, this dynamic provided mixed results.

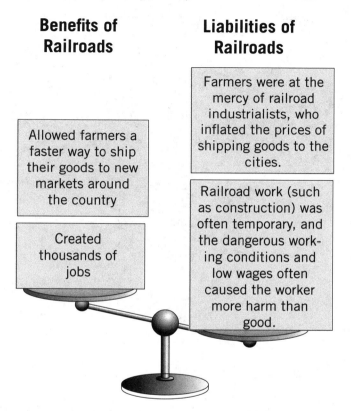

Benefits of Railroads

Allowed farmers a faster way to ship their goods to new markets around the country

Created thousands of jobs

Liabilities of Railroads

Farmers were at the mercy of railroad industrialists, who inflated the prices of shipping goods to the cities.

Railroad work (such as construction) was often temporary, and the dangerous working conditions and low wages often caused the worker more harm than good.

The Grange ❗

Looking for a solution to their increasing debt, farmers came to support a more generous money supply. An increase in available money, they correctly figured, would make payments easier. It would also cause inflation, which would make the farmers' debts (held by Northern banks) worth less. Not surprisingly, the banks opposed the plan, preferring for the country to use only gold to back its money supply. The farmers' plan called for the liberal use of silver coins. Because the debate pitted poor farmers against wealthy bankers, it had elements of class strife. Although a complicated matter, the money issue was potentially explosive. This debate led to the birth of the **Grange Movement**.

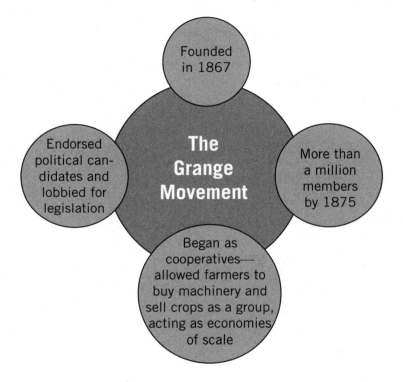

Populist Party 🛑

The Grange movement ultimately died out due to a lack of money, but the granges were replaced by **Farmers' Alliances**. The Alliances allowed women to be politically active (Mary Elizabeth Lease was a huge organizer for them) and they had branches all across the nation. The Farmers' Alliances were even more successful than the Grange movement, and they soon grew into a political party called the **People's Party**, the political arm of the **Populist** movement.

What the populists wanted:

- Increased government intervention in the business world
- Silver standard/bi-metal currency
- An end to foreclosures on farms
- Government regulation of railroads
- 40-hour work week
- Direct election of senators
- National post office
- Referendums (direct popular votes on legislation)
- Recalls (the ability to vote an elected offical out of office)
- An end to U.S. imperialism

 Ask Yourself...

In what ways was the Populist Movement a reaction to the Gilded Age?

Immigration and Urban Development ❗

Advances in **mass transportation**, such as the expansion of railroad lines, streetcars, and the construction of subways, allowed the middle class to live in nicer neighborhoods, including bedroom communities in the suburbs, and commute to work. As a result, immigrants and migrants made up the majority of city populations. Prejudice against the new arrivals was widespread, and many immigrants settled in **ethnic neighborhoods** usually in **tenements**. Worse off still were black and Latino migrants. Many employers refused them any but the worst jobs.

Asian, Italian, and Eastern European Immigration ❗

The wave of immigration that occurred during the latter part of the 19th century differed from earlier waves due to the large influx of Southern and Eastern Europeans, as well as Asian migrants. Before 1880, most immigrants arrived from northern and western Europe. The arrival of these new Americans shifted the urban demographics in terms of both population and diversity.

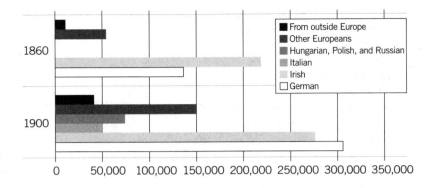

American Residents Not Born in the United States

📣 One of the great ironies that comes up when studying American history is how a nation made of immigrants can hold such prejudice against immigrants. One of the strongest backlashes against immigration came in 1882 with the passage of the **Chinese Exclusion Act**, a law that prevented immigration for Chinese workers.

Exodusters ❗

Post–Civil War racial tensions were such that it was difficult for African Americans to find gainful employment, exercise the right to vote without severe harassment and intimidation, or live free from the threat posed by white supremacists. While some freedmen saw a move to **Liberia** as the only option for true freedom, other leaders, such as **Benjamin "Pap" Singleton** advocated moving west for opportunities to work on and own land. These migrants were known as **Exodusters**.

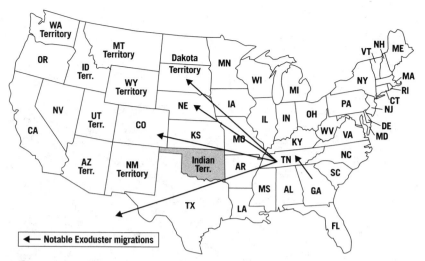

← Notable Exoduster migrations

Inspired by the biblical Exodus and the promise of free land from the 1862 Homestead Act, Pap Singleton organized former slaves in Tennessee to head toward Kansas in 1879 to seek financial and political freedom.

Without money, many former slaves were stranded in St. Louis, a situation that took its name from another biblical reference: the Red Sea.

While some African Americans did make it to Kansas and other western locations, floods of freedmen were unable to pass through St. Louis. Landowners who would find themselves competing with the new arrivals helped create roadblocks, particularly by convincing railroad companies not to let the migrants pass.

Exoduster Migration (1879–1880)

Rise of Urbanism 🔋

The late 19th-century explosion of the steel and oil industries created jobs that drew an unheard of number of migrants to America's northern cities. These technologies, combined with the expanding railroads, allowed cities to grow to new heights, literally, as steel allowed for taller and less expensive buildings (skyscrapers) that could be constructed relatively fast.

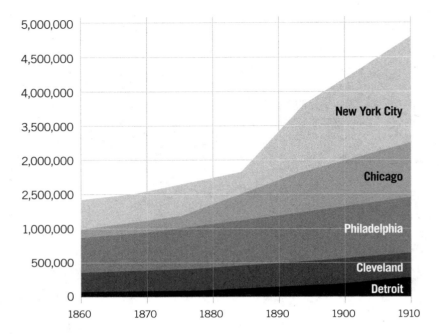

5,000,000						
4,500,000						
4,000,000						New York City
3,500,000						
2,000,000						Chicago
2,500,000						
1,000,000						Philadelphia
500,000						Cleveland
0						Detroit
	1860	1870	1880	1890	1900	1910

Urban Population Spikes (1860–1910)

Cultural Assimilation ❗

The influx of new immigrants to the United States expanded the idea of what it means to be an American. However, there were also questions raised about how much of one's original culture one could retain and still be considered "American." At **Ellis Island**, an immigration inspection station off the coast of New York City, immigrants would have their names changed to sound more consistent with the Anglo-Saxon names shared by many Americans. Some immigrants, on the other hand, chose to change their names and drop their native language in order to accelerate their **assimilation** into American society.

Ways that immigrants assimilated into American culture	Components of native culture retained despite the forces of assimilation
• Learning the history of the United States • Citizenship and civics classes • Developing literacy • Culinary education	• Elements of language of origin • Religious festivals • Skills and crafts • Foods

Political Machines 🛑

Most Americans expected churches, private charities, and ethnic communities to provide services for the poor. However, many of those services were provided instead by a group of corrupt men called **political bosses**. Political bosses gained the loyalty of new immigrants by giving back to the community. This loyalty provided the backbone for **political machines**.

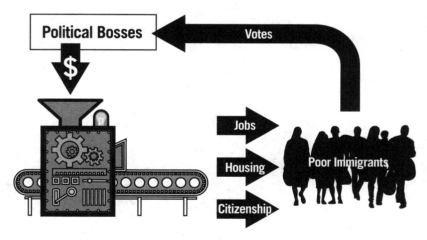

The Political Machine

~ The most notorious political boss was **William "Boss" Tweed**. As the leader of **Tammany Hall**, the political machine of New York City's Democratic Party, Tweed embezzled millions of dollars through corruption in city construction projects. By the 1870s, Tweed's power became noticeable and he was eventually found guilty of corruption and died in prison in 1878.

Growth of the Middle Class and Consumerism ❗

Trains and subways allowed wealthier people to move out from the cities to the emerging suburbs. This created a significant disparity in wealth between the majority of the city dwellers and those who could afford to live farther away. Those who were leaving the city were part of a new class of workers, more well off than factory laborers, but not really in the same ballpark of the captains of industry. This new middle class typically had management positions in factories and in retail.

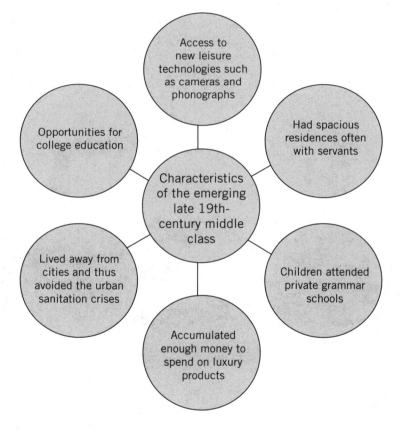

Access to new leisure technologies such as cameras and phonographs

Opportunities for college education

Had spacious residences often with servants

Characteristics of the emerging late 19th-century middle class

Lived away from cities and thus avoided the urban sanitation crises

Children attended private grammar schools

Accumulated enough money to spend on luxury products

Ask Yourself...

1. How did urbanism change the demographics of the United States?
2. What conflicts did the new urbanism create?

Westward Migration ⚡

On the western frontier, **ranching** and **mining** were growing industries, bringing many new settlers seeking employment. Ranchers drove their herds across the western plains and deserts, ignoring property rights and Native American prerogatives to the land. Individual miners lacked the resources to mine and cart big loads, so mostly they prospected; when they found a rich mine, they staked a claim and sold their rights to a mining company.

The Transcontinental Railroad ⚡

In the second year of the Civil War, Lincoln issued a challenge to America not unlike Kennedy's 1961 pledge to reach the Moon—that before the decade was out, America would have a Transcontinental Railroad connecting one side of the country to the other.

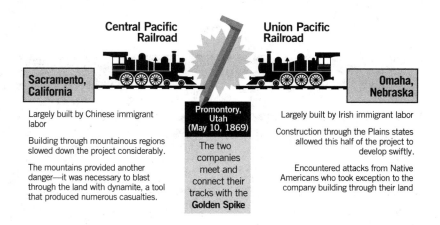

Central Pacific Railroad

Union Pacific Railroad

Sacramento, California

Omaha, Nebraska

Promontory, Utah (May 10, 1869)

The two companies meet and connect their tracks with the **Golden Spike**

Largely built by Chinese immigrant labor

Building through mountainous regions slowed down the project considerably.

The mountains provided another danger—it was necessary to blast through the land with dynamite, a tool that produced numerous casualties.

Largely built by Irish immigrant labor

Construction through the Plains states allowed this half of the project to develop swiftly.

Encountered attacks from Native Americans who took exception to the company building through their land

From 1863 to 1869, former farmers, immigrants, freed slaves, and Civil War veterans worked to make Lincoln's vision a reality. The railroad's arrival changed the West in many ways.

Beneficial Changes	Problematic Changes
• The railroad transformed depot towns into vital cities. • Western towns had more contact with ideas and technological advances from the East. • Developments in railroad technology accelerated the Industrial Revolution. • Railroad schedules gave the nation time zones.	• Industrialists who ran the railroads could charge farmers who needed the rails exorbitant rates. • The bison population was depleted. • The railroad further infringed on Native American land.

Pioneer Homesteading ❗

As the rails pushed the country westward, settlers started filling in the territory. This movement was accelerated not only by the transcontinental railroad, but also by a couple important pieces of legislation that encouraged settlement.

Homestead Act (1862)	Morrill Land Grant Act (1862)
• Offered 160 acres of land to anyone who would "homestead" it (cultivate the land, build a home, and live there) for five years • The land was often difficult to cultivate, and the winters were unexpectedly difficult for many settlers, even in their "insulated" sod homes	• Set aside land and provided money for agricultural colleges • Many colleges that still exist owe their founding to the Morrill Act, from the more obviously agriculturally based schools such as Texas A&M to traditional state schools such as Penn State.

During construction and following the completion of the transcontinental railroad, new states could join the United States due to the rapid population growth:

1864: Nevada
1867: Nebraska
1876: Colorado
1889: North Dakota, South Dakota, Montana, Washington
1890: Idaho, Wyoming
1896: Utah

Near-Extinction of the Bison ❗

As railroad construction crawled across the nation, rail companies organized massive hunts for bison (considered a nuisance). Railroad bounty hunters hunted the herds to near extinction, destroying a resource upon which local Native Americans had depended.

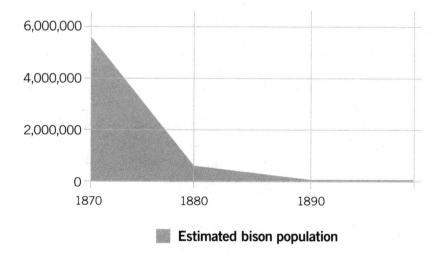

Estimated bison population

Conflict Between White Settlers, Indians, and Mexican Americans ❗

Some tribes, such as the Sioux, fought back, giving the government an excuse to send troops into the region.

- **Sand Creek Massacre,** Colorado (1864)
  More than 200 Indian men, women, and children were killed by the U.S. Army under Col. Chivington, breaking a peace agreement between the army and the Cheyennes.
- **Battle of Little Bighorn,** Montana (1876)
  Cheyenne and Lakota Sioux refused an army order to leave their land after gold was discovered. Lt. Col. Custer attacked the tribes but were outnumbered. This is the most well-known Indian victory, better known as "Custer's Last Stand."
- **Wounded Knee,** South Dakota (1890)
  The Sioux had been performing a sacred ritual known as the Ghost Dance on their reservation when the U.S. Army fired upon them mistaking the dance for a preparation for war. The Sioux fought back, but in the end 300 Indians were killed as well as 25 infantry men.

The American expansion westward also marginalized the former Mexicans who now found themselves living in the United States following the Treaty of Guadalupe Hidalgo. Mariano Vallejo was a military commander who envied American democracy and welcomed his new government. However, Vallejo lost much of his land to new settlers, and by the time of the Gold Rush, he and his people could find little political recourse, outnumbered by thousands of new settlers.

Indian Reservations ❗

Those who suffered the greatest losses in this expansionist era were, of course, the Native Americans. At first, pioneers approached the tribes as sovereign nations. They made treaties with them, which the settlers or their immediate successors broke. The result was warfare, leading the government to try another approach—to force Native Americans onto reservations, which typically were made up of the least desirable land in a tribe's traditional home region. The reservation system failed for a number of reasons.

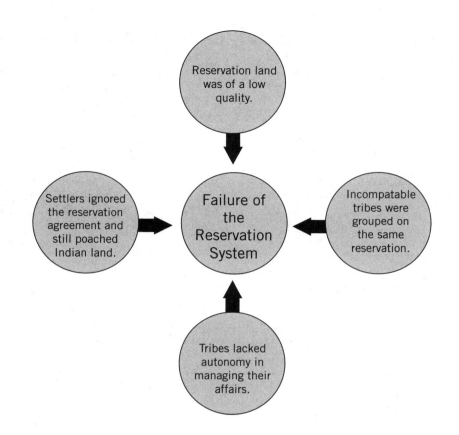

Assimilation vs. Cultural Preservation ❗

A central tension of American expansion dealt with Indian identity. Native Americans wanted to maintain their culture and customs, yet found themselves increasingly pressured to conform to settler cultural standards. The pressure put on the tribes by the United States is known as **Americanization.** This occurred in a number of ways.

Carlisle Indian Industrial School	Dawes Act
• Pennsylvania school to which Indian children were sent to learn American culture and skills • The intention of the school was to benefit the Indians by dismantling their culture through assimilation. For instance, students were forced to change their names and cut their hair (hair was sacred in many tribes).	• An 1887 act that broke up the reservations and distributed some of the land to the head of each Native American family, offering citizenship as an ultimate goal • A hidden effect of the Dawes Act was that it forced land ownership onto Indian tribes, a concept that ran counter to the core beliefs of many tribes.

The **Nez Perce** were an Indian tribe in northeast Oregon. As it did with many tribes, the U.S. government forced them to migrate to a small reservation in Idaho. **Chief Joseph** led his people in resistance to this removal, but eventually surrendered to federal power. Along with Sitting Bull, Chief Joseph became one of the most well-known Indians of his time.

 Ask Yourself...

To what extent was the American westward expansion consistent with the American values as expressed in the Declaration of Independence and the Constitution?

The Gilded Age

Mark Twain dubbed the era between Reconstruction and 1900 the **Gilded Age** of politics. Gilded metals have a shiny, gold-like surface, but beneath lies a cheap base. America looked to have entered a period of prosperity, with a handful of families having amassed unprecedented wealth, but the affluence of a few was built on the poverty of many. Similarly, American politics looked like a shining example of representative democracy, but just beneath the surface lay crass corruption and patronage.

Corruption and the Captains of Industry 😬

Politics and money can be a dangerous combination and the captains of industry (alternatively known as **robber barons**) were able to use their money to influence politicians in ways that would undermine democracy. **Jay Gould**, a railroad magnate, is a great example of the toxicity of money in politics.

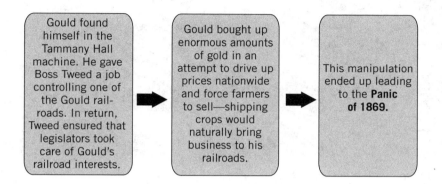

Gould found himself in the Tammany Hall machine. He gave Boss Tweed a job controlling one of the Gould railroads. In return, Tweed ensured that legislators took care of Gould's railroad interests.

➡

Gould bought up enormous amounts of gold in an attempt to drive up prices nationwide and force farmers to sell—shipping crops would naturally bring business to his railroads.

➡

This manipulation ended up leading to the **Panic of 1869.**

Andrew Carnegie's Inconsistent Philosophy 😮

In response to public pressure for reform, steel mogul Andrew Carnegie promoted a philosophy based on the work of Charles Darwin. While he held a cynical view that some people were more worthy of wealth than others, he also felt a strong compulsion to give back.

 Gould even caused an international incident between the United States and Canada for kidnapping a British conman. Who *does* that?

Gospel of Wealth: Carnegie asserted that with great wealth comes great responsibility. He advocated philanthropy, as by building libraries and museums or funding medical research, but not charity.

Social Darwinism: Using Darwin's theory of evolution as an analogy, Carnegie argued that in business, as in nature, unrestricted competition allowed only the "fittest" to survive. He was against government regulation yet supported government assistance to business (e.g., tax abatements, grants, tariffs, etc.). Carnegie claimed that the concentration of wealth among a few was the natural and most efficient result of capitalism.

Rise of Socialism ❗

A phenomenon that coincided with the Gilded Age was the rise of **socialism** in the United States. Derived from the Marxist ideals brought by German immigrants in the mid to late 19th century, critics saw socialism as incompatible with the capitalistic roots of American entrepreneurialism. A xenophobic distrust of immigrants further hampered socialism's chances at widespread American acceptance.

Characteristics of Socialism:

- Derived from the ideas of Karl Marx
- Advocates public ownership of necessary industries
- Uses a planned economy
- State is responsible for basic needs of all individuals
- Limits or eliminates competition

Since the terms often get conflated, it is probably good to take a minute to distinguish socialism from communism and Marxism.

Marxism	Communism	Socialism
• A historical theory put forth by Karl Marx (1818–1883) explaining the origins of conflict in societies • Conflict exists because of class struggles; social class are pitted against one another • Logical conclusion of this struggle: the working class takes control of the means of production and shares ownership of goods	• An outgrowth of Marxism that describes the society that exists at the end of Marxist struggle • In this society, there is no ownership or class distinction • In a true Marxist sense, there have been no large-scale attempts at Communism since there has been no lasting post–Industrial Revolution, working-class seizure of the means of production	• Refers to govt. policies that provide public ownership of certain industries and services • Socialist programs have existed around the world for years, even in the U.S. (taxes, funding for public schools, fire departments, etc.) • Some govts. employ large-scale socialist programs; others have limited applications of such programs

It is important to note that socialism, and the organized political party the Socialist Party of America, were often associated with unions due to the fact that (1) the German immigrants who brought the ideals to the United States were working class and joined labor unions and (2) the beliefs of Marxism focus on the ability of laborers to seize of the means of production.

Ask Yourself...

How did the challenges of the Gilded Age illustrate contradictions between American life and the ideals of the America's founding documents?

Social Change 🔔

The corruption and social ills evident in the Gilded Age made the period ripe for social change. While small changes were created, they were often at the local and private level. In many ways, the Gilded Age continued to create a less equal society for all but the wealthy and privileged. It would not be until the first decade of the 20th century that the government began to take action, thanks to the Progressive Movement. But more on that later.

Government Corruption 🔔

The "**spoils system**" pioneered by Andrew Jackson meant that every time a new president took office, thousands of government jobs opened up, and it was the president's responsibility to fill them. The debate between stalwarts and half-breeds was the source of a serious debate within the late 19th century Republican Party:

- **Stalwarts**—believed that all government jobs should go to loyal Republicans
- **Half-Breeds**—thought that qualified Democrats should be able to keep their jobs after a Republican was elected

Congress finally had to do something about the spoils system in 1881:

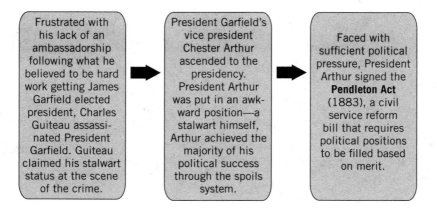

Frustrated with his lack of an ambassadorship following what he believed to be hard work getting James Garfield elected president, Charles Guiteau assassinated President Garfield. Guiteau claimed his stalwart status at the scene of the crime. ➡ President Garfield's vice president Chester Arthur ascended to the presidency. President Arthur was put in an awkward position—a stalwart himself, Arthur achieved the majority of his political success through the spoils system. ➡ Faced with sufficient political pressure, President Arthur signed the **Pendleton Act** (1883), a civil service reform bill that requires political positions to be filled based on merit.

Tariffs ❗

The end of the Civil War saw the United States change from an agriculture-based economy to an industrial one. In fact, by 1900, the United States was the world's leading industrial power. With no federal income tax (this does not come until the 16th Amendment), tariffs were seen as a source of revenue for the government as well as a way to protect American industries from foreign competition. It is important to remember that tariffs can backfire with foreign countries responding to an American tariff with one of their own.

The tariff issue was the most controversial debate of the 1890s with two significant tariffs getting passed.

- **McKinley Tariff, 1890**: A 50 percent tariff was placed on foreign imports (with the exception of raw sugar, the result of a clever lobbying effort by the American sugar trust).
- **Wilson-Gorman Tariff, 1894**: A Democratic plan to reform tariffs, it decreased the McKinley Tariff slightly and created a 2 percent income tax.

Supporters of Tariffs	Opponents of Tariffs
• Republicans • Urban industrialists • Saw tariffs as a way to prevent cheaper goods from overseas harming American jobs	• Democrats • Rural agriculturalists • Saw an income tax (which would collect more from the wealthy) as a more fair way to bring revenue into the government

Women in the Gilded Age ❗

Unlike those living in the early 19th century, women of the Gilded Age tended to be more educated and wished to work within the women's sphere to help reform society.

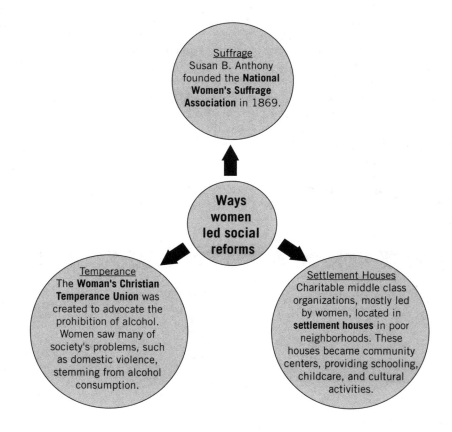

Suffrage
Susan B. Anthony founded the **National Women's Suffrage Association** in 1869.

Ways women led social reforms

Temperance
The **Woman's Christian Temperance Union** was created to advocate the prohibition of alcohol. Women saw many of society's problems, such as domestic violence, stemming from alcohol consumption.

Settlement Houses
Charitable middle class organizations, mostly led by women, located in **settlement houses** in poor neighborhoods. These houses became community centers, providing schooling, childcare, and cultural activities.

Jane Addams 😎

In Chicago, **Jane Addams** lobbied local governments for building-safety codes, better sanitation, and public schools. Frustrated by government's slow pace, Addams founded Hull House to provide such services as English lessons for immigrants, day care for children of working mothers, childcare classes for parents, and playgrounds for children. Addams also campaigned for increased government services in the slums. She was awarded the Nobel Peace Prize for her life's work in 1931.

💬 Similar to the Hull House, the **Henry Street Settlement** was founded in 1893 as a community center for nurses to offer home health care education to the immigrant poor of New York City.

Plessey v. Ferguson 🔔

Following the marginal gains to ensure civil rights in the years immediately following the Civil War, the courts began to chip away at laws aimed at protecting African Americans. The most infamous Supreme Court case was *Plessey v. Ferguson* (1896). It created a 60-year precedent ensuring that African Americans would not receive equal treatment.

The background—Homer Plessey, who identified as one-eighth African American, acted on behalf of a civil rights advocacy group in Louisiana by purposefully violating the Separate Car Act.

The case—Plessey argued that separating people in different train cars based on race violates the Equal Protection Clause of the 14th Amendment, since it enshrines unequal treatment into law.

The outcome—The Supreme Court ruled that the Equal Protection Clause had not been violated and introduced an interpretation of the clause known as **separate but equal.** States around the country, particularly in the South, introduce discriminatory Jim Crow laws consistent with the "separate but equal" decision.

 Ask Yourself...

What challenges existed during the Gilded Age that made social change a difficult process?

PERIOD 7 (1890–1945):

The Early 20th Century

The period spanning the 1890s through World War II was one of sweeping modernization. This section examines the profound economic, technological, social, and cultural changes that took place during this era. It also discusses the impact of unprecedented crises in America—the Great Depression and two world wars.

The Industrial Economy ❗

The economic progress and technological advances of the early 20th century began to shape American culture into the modern industrialized nation of today. Science and innovation progressed at a tremendous rate and the inventions that resulted, and which were made readily available to the masses, made life easier. The economic boom of the 1920s and the increased standard of living for many Americans allowed the middle (and even working) classes to enjoy benefits and conveniences that were once reserved for the wealthy. Moreover, advances in communications created a unity of popular culture in America and a heightened sense of national pride.

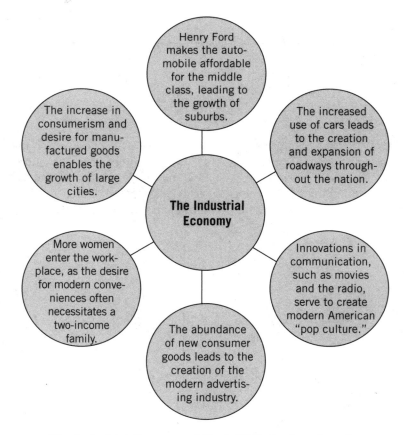

The Industrial Economy of Early 20th-Century America

The American industrial economy got a major boost from some extraordinary feats of engineering that were accomplished during the first half of the century! The **Hoover Dam**, built on the border of Nevada and Arizona, allowed the power of the Colorado River to be harnessed for the first time in history and remains a world-renowned structure to this day. The dam provided a major source of hydroelectric power, allowed for the irrigation of millions of acres of farmland, and met the water needs of millions of homes and businesses. The **Panama Canal**, which created a much faster sea route between the west and east coasts, was also a monumental achievement that greatly facilitated maritime trade and advanced American economic interests.

Ask Yourself...

Some modern Americans romanticize the 1890s as the time before life became—at least in their view—hectic, impersonal, unhealthy, materialistic, and jaded. This has led to a "back to basics" mentality, whereby some people strive to live a simpler and supposedly better life by embracing elements of 19th-century living (such as growing their own food). While 20th-century conveniences like the car, radio, and telephone have obviously advanced American society, in what ways, if any, might they have worsened our quality of life?

 One of the first films ever shown to a theater audience was a 50-second shot of an approaching train in 1896. Legend has it that the people panicked and ran to get out of the way!

The Progressive Era (1890–1920) ❶

The **Progressive Movement**, unlike the working-class **populism** of the 19th century, was a reform movement involving mostly middle- and upper-class men (although some women were highly influential as well). These reformers wanted to greatly increase the role of the federal government in achieving their vision of social justice on a wide variety of issues. They were somewhat successful in this regard, as the reach of federal power expanded exponentially during this period. Eliminating corruption among the rich and powerful was a major goal, as was equality and alleviating the plight of the poor and downtrodden.

Corruption in Politics and Business ❶

The following are some important instruments and methods of the Progressive Era fight against corruption.

The Sherman Antitrust Act	• A federal legislative act that prohibited businesses from conspiring to unreasonably restrict trade or supply in a given area of the market (and therefore raise prices artificially by limiting competition) • Was enacted in 1890 under President Benjamin Harrison, but was later used more effectively by President Roosevelt
The Clayton Antitrust Act	• A federal legislative act that expanded upon the Sherman Antitrust Act by prohibiting additional practices that reduce market competition (e.g., the merger of two large businesses that would effectively create a monopoly) • Was enacted in 1914 by President Woodrow Wilson
The Federal Trade Commission (FTC)	• An agency of the federal government charged with enforcing the Clayton Antitrust Act and with otherwise eliminating unfair business practices and protecting the American consumer • Was established in 1914 by President Woodrow Wilson

ASAP U.S. History

The Interstate Commerce Commission (ICC)	• An agency of the federal government charged with regulating monopolistic or otherwise unfair practices in the railroad industry; was later given authority to regulate other modes of commerce • Was created in 1887 by President Grover Cleveland by means of the **Interstate Commerce Act;** the first instance of federal regulation of a private industry
The Referendum	• A system whereby an issue of public importance (e.g., proposed legislation) is put to a direct vote by the people, bypassing their elected representatives and avoiding any corrupt or self-serving influence that politicians might otherwise exert • Was first used during the colonial period, but was widely adopted and developed during the Progressive era as a way of bringing about social reform
The Recall Election	• A procedure whereby citizens can vote directly to remove an elected official (state or local only) from office before his or her term expires • Was adopted during the Progressive era as a means of eliminating corrupt officials at the will of the people (unlike impeachment, which requires action by legislators)
Municipal Reform	• A movement designed to promote honest and efficient regulation at the local level; "council-manager government" involved the appointment (by an elected city council) of an independent and presumably ethical **city manager** to oversee local affairs • Was adopted during the Progressive era as a means of reducing the influence of corrupt politicians who were controlled by "big business"
Muckraking	• A common journalistic practice whereby one seeks to uncover and expose corruption, particularly in the realm of politics; muckrakers were the forerunners of modern "investigative journalists" • Was largely developed by journalists of the Progressive era, although instances were seen in the previous century

Instruments and Methods of the Progressive Era Fight Against Corruption in Politics and Business

Theodore Roosevelt was one of the most dedicated and effectual champions of the Progressive movement. During his tenure as president (1901–1909), he fought successfully to expand the federal government's role in regulating business and promoting social and environmental causes. He promised the American public a **"square deal"** through which he would destroy the monopolies that thwarted business competition and thus burdened the consumer. For his efforts he was aptly nicknamed **"the trustbuster."**

❗ As part of a banking and currency reform plan **Woodrow Wilson,** Roosevelt's similarly progressive successor, signed the **Federal Reserve Act** into law in 1913. The Act created the **Federal Reserve System,** which is essentially the central bank of the United States, in order to ensure a safer, stabler, and more flexible monetary system. In the spirit of Hamilton and the Federalists (who had tried unsuccessfully to create a permanent national bank in the 18th century), the federal government now had substantially more control over the nation's finances.

Labor Reform ❗

As in other periods of reform, Progressive era activists turned their attention to the impoverished and vulnerable members of society and sought equality and justice. Industrialization had created a strong need for labor and, with virtually no legal protections in place, workers were terribly exploited. **Child labor** was particularly attractive and efficient for employers because children (often as young as 5 or 6) were easily trained and manipulated and would work for the lowest of wages. Presidents Roosevelt and Wilson tried to restrict child labor through federal legislation but such laws were deemed unconstitutional. By the 1920s, however, public sensibilities were increasingly offended by child labor practices and the number of working children had substantially decreased.

Upton Sinclair, a dedicated muckraker of the day, published a fact-based novel in 1906 entitled *The Jungle*. The book vividly depicted the appallingly harsh conditions in the meatpacking plants. Sinclair illustrated the deep-seated corruption of the rich and powerful, as well as the abject poverty and utter hopelessness of immigrant factory workers. While the novel did spark some outrage over the plight of the poor, the main outcry (much to Sinclair's dismay) concerned the unsanitary conditions within the food industry and the health implications for the public. Sinclair said of his most famous work: "I aimed for the public's heart, and by accident I hit it in the stomach."

Women's Suffrage

The longstanding fight for women's suffrage continued into the 20th century as activists lobbied both Congress and state legislatures for female voting rights. While the abolitionist and women's suffrage movements were often linked during the 19th century, and women were instrumental in the fight to end slavery, women were not afforded the right to vote until 50 years after universal male suffrage had been granted! In 1920, over 70 years after the first women's rights convention in Seneca Falls, the **19th Amendment** to the Constitution finally extended suffrage to women.

NOTABLE FIGURE:

Susan B. Anthony (1820–1906) was a gifted writer and orator whose feminist activism was critical to the women's suffrage movement. In 1869, she cofounded the National Woman Suffrage Association and won the support of many through her eloquent speeches. In 1872, she was famously arrested for illegally voting in a national election and then tried and convicted in federal court. She refused to pay the resulting fine. She would not live to see the ratification of the 19th Amendment.

Prohibition ❗

The 19th century **temperance movement**, which had been largely spear-headed by women, finally came to fruition in 1920 (on the eve of women's suffrage) when the **18th Amendment** to the Constitution took effect. The Amendment prohibited the manufacture, sale, and transport of intoxicating liquors, although many state and local laws criminalized possession and consumption as well. The success of **Prohibition** is often understated, as alcohol use and related crimes were substantially reduced. However, crimes related to the illegal manufacture and sale of alcohol were highly problematic, and organized crime soared. Prohibition laws met with widespread disobedience, especially in large cities, with underground drinking establishments known as "speakeasies" routinely flouting the law. Opposition to Prohibition continued to grow until 1933 when it was repealed by the **21st Amendment**.

Prohibition was repealed because it was basically unenforceable, caused routine and widespread disregard for the law, empowered organized crime, and regulated behavior that many considered a matter of personal choice. Can this same reasoning be properly applied to our modern "war on drugs"? Does the fact that street drugs like heroin and methamphetamine are much more dangerous than alcohol simply negate the comparison? What do you think?

Environmentalism ❗

At the turn of the 20th century, the nation was feeling the negative effects of industrialization not only in the form of pollution and excess waste, but also in terms of the depletion of natural resources and the destruction of wildlife and natural beauty. Accordingly, Progressive-era activists adopted environmental conservation as one of their many social causes. President Roosevelt once again spearheaded the campaign, establishing the United States Forest Service during his tenure. Roosevelt was ultimately responsible for creating millions of acres of national forests, parks, and wildlife reserves. He is often referred to as America's "conservation president."

The End of the Progressive Era ❗

The various reformers of this period managed to transform American society in such a way that the nation could never fully go back to its pre-Progressive era policies. While the activists were not all of like mind and often disagreed on important issues (such as immigration and segregation), they all believed that government should take an active role in achieving social justice. The progressives may not have won every individual battle they fought, but they forever changed the way that Americans would view the federal government and the level of power that it exerts. The movement would be curtailed in the 1920s during the conservative presidencies of Harding, Coolidge, and Hoover, who attempted to reverse progressive reforms and reduce the extent of governmental regulation.

 Ask Yourself...

The "trustbusting" legislation that was enacted during the Progressive era sparked its share of criticism and controversy and is even condemned by some economists and businesspeople today. Proponents of antitrust laws believe that it is inherently unfair for a single business (or perhaps a small group of businesses) to dominate a given market to the point at which it can control prices. Opponents argue that trustbusting simply penalizes successful enterprises in favor of less able and efficient ones, sacrificing ambition and excellence in favor of mediocrity. What do you think? If a business is good enough to acquire the lion's share of the market, should it be legally prevented from doing so?

The Great Depression 🛑

The **Great Depression** of the 1930s was the worst economic crisis in American history. Hoover's "hands off" policy did virtually nothing to help this desperate situation, which paved the way for Franklin D. Roosevelt's tenure as one of the most politically active presidents. Despite the innumerable federal agencies that Roosevelt created for poverty relief, which did help many Americans, it was ultimately the economic boom caused by World War II that finally ended the Depression.

The Stock Market Crash 🛑

Prior to the **stock market crash of 1929,** stock traders had been allowed to buy on **margin**, a destabilizing practice that enables one to borrow against future profits that might or might not materialize. Eventually the bottom fell out of the market: Prices dropped, but no matter how far they dropped nobody wanted to buy. The crash, along with other national and global economic factors, ultimately led to deflation, high unemployment, and widespread business failure. Many Americans lost their homes and life savings and were driven to abject poverty.

The Presidential Response 🛑

NOTABLE FIGURES: 🛑

Herbert Hoover (1929–1933) was a highly conservative president who did not believe the federal government should intervene in economic affairs. He underestimated the gravity of the stock market crash and did little to alleviate the crisis. Many Americans consequently blamed Hoover for the Depression, and the ramshackle shacks of the poor came to be known as **"Hoovervilles."** Eventually Hoover did intervene by creating a few farm assistance programs and federal work projects. However, he was still easily defeated by Roosevelt in the 1932 election.

Franklin Delano Roosevelt (1933–1945) was a highly liberal president who created a vast number of federal agencies in his attempt to help the poor and end the Depression. (So many of these organizations were known by their acronyms that they were referred to as the **"alphabet agencies"**). His economic policy consisted of **"relief, recovery, and reform"** (the "3 R's")—collectively known as the **"New Deal."** In reference to the unprecedented economic devastation of the Depression, he uttered his most famous quote: "The only thing we have to fear is fear itself." While Roosevelt did face considerable opposition to his policies from the Supreme Court, many of his federal agencies and programs survive to this day.

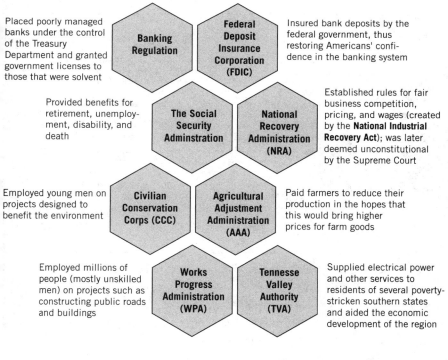

Placed poorly managed banks under the control of the Treasury Department and granted government licenses to those that were solvent — **Banking Regulation**

Federal Deposit Insurance Corporation (FDIC) — Insured bank deposits by the federal government, thus restoring Americans' confidence in the banking system

Provided benefits for retirement, unemployment, disability, and death — **The Social Security Adminstration**

National Recovery Administration (NRA) — Established rules for fair business competition, pricing, and wages (created by the **National Industrial Recovery Act**); was later deemed unconstitutional by the Supreme Court

Employed young men on projects designed to benefit the environment — **Civilian Conservation Corps (CCC)**

Agricultural Adjustment Administration (AAA) — Paid farmers to reduce their production in the hopes that this would bring higher prices for farm goods

Employed millions of people (mostly unskilled men) on projects such as constructing public roads and buildings — **Works Progress Administration (WPA)**

Tennesse Valley Authority (TVA) — Supplied electrical power and other services to residents of several poverty-stricken southern states and aided the economic development of the region

Some Agencies and Tools of the New Deal 😀

💬 Roosevelt frequently clashed with the Supreme Court, frustrated by its decisions that declared much of the New Deal legislation unconstitutional. In response he attempted to **"pack the court"** with new justices who would be more likely to support his policies. In 1937, Roosevelt proposed the **Judicial Reorganization Bill,** which would allow him to name a new additional justice for every sitting justice over the age of seventy years and six months. Had the bill passed it would have allowed Roosevelt to appoint a maximum of six new Supreme Court justices. This blatant attempt at **court-packing** was met with disdain by republicans and democrats alike, and the bill was eventually defeated by Congress.

NOTABLE FIGURE: 💬

Roosevelt's response to the Great Depression was guided by the work of the British economist **John Maynard Keynes** (1883–1946). Keynes contended that depressions are the result of a vicious cycle in which people see that the economy is bad, so they fear that money will be hard to come by, so they don't spend the money they have, so businesses fail, so the economy worsens, so people fear that money will be hard to come by, and so on. The solution, Keynes argued, was for the government to step in and embark on a program of deliberate deficit spending: The "multiplier effect" would ensure that every dollar spent would do several dollars' worth of good in reviving the economy.

As if Americans didn't have enough problems in the midst of the Depression era, during the 1930s the Great Plains states suffered one of the worst environmental disasters in American history. A deadly combination of low rainfall, high winds, and loose soil caused "black blizzards" of dirt that rose thousands of feet in the air and sometimes traveled as far as the East Coast! Residents were devastated by the crisis, which exacerbated the extreme poverty seen in much of the area, and the region became known as the **"Dust Bowl."**

Ask Yourself...

Many people criticized Roosevelt for interfering too much in the nation's economics and in the daily lives of Americans. Other people criticized him for not interfering enough. What do you think? How much responsibility should the federal government have to take care of Americans who have fallen on hard times? Should different rules apply during an economic crisis like the Great Depression than in times of general prosperity?

Popular Culture ❗

The first half of the 20th century saw the beginnings of modern American popular culture, and this unifying force contributed to a stronger national identity. The popularity of radio and film, and especially the influence of Hollywood, gave the country a stronger sense of what it meant to be American. New ideas traveled faster and more easily, and traditional beliefs, attitudes, and practices were supplanted by modern ones. Victorian-era ideas about gender, race, science, religion, art—and just about everything else—gave way to more progressive ways of thinking.

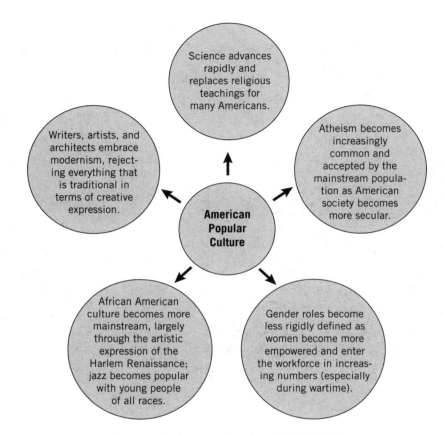

Science advances rapidly and replaces religious teachings for many Americans.

Writers, artists, and architects embrace modernism, rejecting everything that is traditional in terms of creative expression.

American Popular Culture

Atheism becomes increasingly common and accepted by the mainstream population as American society becomes more secular.

African American culture becomes more mainstream, largely through the artistic expression of the Harlem Renaissance; jazz becomes popular with young people of all races.

Gender roles become less rigidly defined as women become more empowered and enter the workforce in increasing numbers (especially during wartime).

Cultural Changes in America (1890–1945)

The Scopes Monkey Trial 😎

The clash between traditional Christian values and modern science came to a head in the "**Scopes Monkey Trial**" of 1925. John Scopes, a Tennessee school teacher, was arrested for violating a controversial state law known as the Butler Act. The law made it a crime to teach Darwin's theory of evolution (as it pertains to human beings) in a public school. The trial became a media circus as two of the most renowned lawyers of the day, Clarence Darrow and William Jennings Bryan, argued legally irrelevant issues in court. Ultimately Scopes was convicted and the constitutionality of the Butler Act was upheld on appeal, although Scopes's conviction was overturned on a technicality.

The Reproductive Rights Movement 💬

Margaret Sanger (1879–1966) was the founder of the American reproductive rights movement. Since women could not break out of traditional gender roles or gain independence if forced to bear a child every year, Sanger's battle for legalized contraception was critical. She opened the first birth control clinic in 1916 (for which she was arrested for disseminating "obscene material") and founded the organizations that developed into the prominent **Planned Parenthood** of today. Sanger's revolutionary life's work was influenced by her mother who, after eighteen pregnancies and twelve children, died at the age of forty.

The Harlem Renaissance ❗

In the 1920s, in the largest black neighborhood of New York City, theaters, cultural clubs, and newspapers sprang up—a development called the **Harlem Renaissance**. Among the great figures of the Harlem Renaissance were the poets **Langston Hughes**, **Countee Cullen**, and **Zora Neale Hurston**. Another major black cultural development was the popularization of **jazz**. Because jazz featured improvisation and free-spiritedness, it came to be seen as emblematic of the era (which is how the decade came to be known as the Jazz Age). Probably the most popular and most gifted of the era's jazz musicians was trumpeter **Louis Armstrong**.

Cultural Changes and African Americans ❗

While the revolutionary impact of the 1960s civil rights movement was still decades away, African Americans did make considerable strides during the early 20th century. More blacks began to reject the inferior self-image and subservient attitudes that had been instilled in their 19th-century counterparts. In 1909, the **National Association for the Advancement of Colored People (NAACP)** was formed as a biracial organization aimed at achieving equal rights. Gradually attitudes began to change, among both blacks and whites, largely through the efforts of activists and social reformers.

NOTABLE FIGURES: 💬

Booker T. Washington
Born into slavery in the South, Washington promoted economic independence as the means by which African Americans could improve their lot. To pursue that goal he founded the Tuskegee Institute, a vocational and industrial training school for blacks. Some accused Washington of being an accommodationist because he refused to press for immediate equal rights. Others believed that Washington simply accepted the reality of his time when he set his goals.

W.E.B. Du Bois
Du Bois believed that a "Talented Tenth" of the African American population should assume roles of academic and community leadership, advancing the race through intellect and skill. He headed the NAACP in the quest for racial justice, a task he found so strenuous that, after a lifelong struggle, Du Bois abandoned the United States and moved to Africa.

Marcus Garvey
A Jamaican immigrant and founder of the Universal Negro Improvement Association (UNIA), Garvey believed that blacks should separate from white society, which he saw as corrupt. Garvey promoted black-owned businesses and founded the Black Star Line to help blacks emigrate through his "back to Africa" movement. Although he was viewed as extreme, he still attracted many African American followers.

💬 Not everyone supported the egalitarian way of thinking that was developing in the early 20th century. The **Ku Klux Klan ("KKK")**, a reactionary white supremacist group that often used intimidation and violence, had been prominent during the **Reconstruction Era** but was eventually suppressed by the federal government. The group reemerged during the early 20th century and became prominent in the 1920s, this time targeting not only blacks but Jews, Catholics, and immigrants as well. Beliefs in the superiority of one race or ethnicity over another found support in the **eugenics** movement, which proposed that the human race could be vastly improved by encouraging only those who are "fit" to reproduce to have children.

Ask Yourself...

The battle between science and creationism that culminated in the *Scopes'* trial of 1925 is still going on today, the crux of which is the ongoing question of federal power versus states' rights. From a constitutional perspective, the issue in *Scopes* was not whether evolution or creationism is true, but whether the people of Tennessee had the right to have their children taught in accordance with their own beliefs. Some 21st-century Americans believe that our society now has an unfair bias toward science, as federal courts and legislatures have no qualms about forcing children to learn evolutionary theory. What do you think?

Migration and Immigration ❗

The America of the 1940s was a very different place from the America of the 1890s, due in part to the changing makeup of the nation. New patterns of immigration, as well as patterns of internal migration throughout the country, had a profound effect on the culture. These changes also increased tensions, however, as clashes of ideologies and an ever-present fear of "foreigners" led to anti-immigration sentiments and ethnic conflict.

The Immigration Acts of the 1920s ❗

The period preceding World War I saw an influx of immigrants from various countries, particularly from Southern European countries (such as Italy) and Eastern European countries (such as Russia). This situation caused many Americans concern, as the United States had traditionally been a people of Northwestern European descent. These new immigrants were often disliked and viewed as undesirable and even dangerous. Consequently, the **Emergency Quota Act of 1921** and the **Immigration Act of 1924** (the "Immigration Acts") limited the number of immigrants annually from a given country (with certain exceptions) to a percentage of the number of residents from that country already living in the United States (based on an older census).

Northern and Western Europeans	• Immigration rates were high in the 19th century but then tapered off; the Immigration Acts did not *increase* Northern/Western immigration per se, but did achieve the goal of increasing the *percentage* of immigrants from this region.
Southern and Eastern Europeans	• Immigration rates were high in the early part of the 20th century, but greatly decreased as the result of the Immigration Acts, which effectively (and deliberately) restricted their numbers to a disproportionate degree.
Asians	• Immigration rates were high in the 19th century, although the Chinese had been explicitly barred as early as 1882; most other Asians were explicitly barred by the Immigration Acts, as well as by earlier 20th-century immigration legislation.
Mexicans	• Immigration rates were high in the 19th and 20th centuries, particularly during the Gold Rush and the Mexican Revolution; the Immigration Acts originally exempted residents of the Americas from the quotas, but measures were eventually taken to restrict Mexican laborers.
Other Countries	• The Immigration Acts were designed to specifically restrict immigration from Southern/Eastern Europe and Asia, but countries with already low immigration rates were effectively limited accordingly (e.g., a country with only 1,000 immigrants residing in the U.S. might be limited to only 20 or 30 new entrants per year).

Effects of the Immigration Acts of the 1920s

ASAP U.S. History

The First Red Scare 🔔

The rise of communism following the **Russian Revolution** served to intensify the fear of Eastern and Southern European immigrants, particularly those who embraced communist, socialist, or anarchist ideologies. As some on the radical left did resort to bombing campaigns and other means of violent protest, a "siege mentality" developed. Civil liberties were often suspended as law enforcement and government officials sought to eliminate what they perceived as a major threat to law and order.

Palmer Raids, 1919 💬	Sacco and Vanzetti, 1920 💬
• A series of anarchist bombings targeted prominent public officials, newspaper editors, and businessmen. Attorney General A. Mitchell Palmer was one of the victims. • In response, govt. agents raided union halls, pool halls, social clubs, and residences. About 500 immigrants were deported. • Over 10,000 people were arrested, but few weapons or bombs were discovered.	• Nicola Sacco and Bartolomeo Vanzetti were Italian immigrants arrested for murder. • They were members of an anarchist movement that advocated warfare against the govt. • The trial attracted nationwide attention; protests were often violent. Many leftists believed the men were innocent and being persecuted for their beliefs. • Though the two men were convicted and ultimately executed, whether they were, in fact, guilty remains a subject of intense debate.

Migration 🔔

The nation also changed during the first half of the 20th century in terms of how the population was geographically dispersed. During WWI, southern blacks undertook a **Great Migration** to the major cities of the North in search of the jobs that the war effort had created. Then during the economic desperation of the Great Depression, even white Americans were forced to seek work anywhere they could get it, which often meant leaving their homes in rural areas and moving to large cities as well. However, even though migration patterns caused blacks and whites to reside in the same cities, neighborhoods remained racially segregated due to discrimination in housing and education.

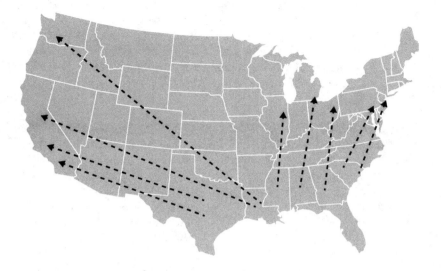

20th-Century African American Migration Patterns

 Ask Yourself...

One recurring pattern in American history is that, during times when the nation is under a significant threat, individual civil liberties are violated. When faced with widespread lawlessness, terrorism, or foreign aggression, government officials and law enforcement officers often take action that they would never condone under ordinary circumstances. Some would argue that this makes perfect sense, as self-preservation is our first priority, while others believe that disregarding constitutional rights involves crossing a line that should simply never be crossed. What do you think?

Foreign Diplomacy ❗

By the 1890s, the United States had become an important player on the international scene. At a time when the nations of Europe, such as Great Britain, were establishing vast colonial empires, American leaders feared that the nation would be overpowered if it did not soon acquire territories of its own. Despite the longstanding foreign policy of non-entanglement in international affairs, victory in the Spanish-American War turned the United States into a major imperial power.

Imperialism vs. Isolationism ❗

When the United States was in its infancy following the Revolution and lacked the military might to challenge stronger nations, it was undoubtedly wise to stay out of European affairs. As the country grew in size and strength, however, the question of which foreign policy to adopt became debatable.

Imperialism { A foreign policy of forcefully extending authority over other nations, either through territorial gain or through economic or political dominance

Isolationism { A foreign policy of non-interaction with other nations, as by abstention from alliances and other economic and political relations

---

The United States did not necessarily need to acquire colonies or territories to become an imperialistic world leader. "**Dollar diplomacy**," a practice closely associated with **President Taft**, involves securing advantageous relationships with poorer countries through financial means (such as the granting of monetary loans).

The Spanish-American War 🔔

Whatever isolationist ideals the nation may have had were abandoned in 1898 when America became embroiled in Spanish-Cuban relations and ultimately went to war with Spain.

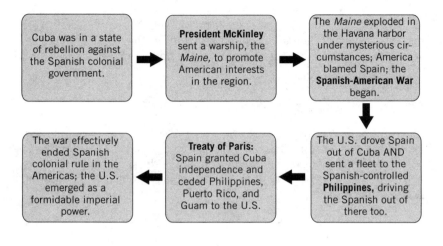

Cuba was in a state of rebellion against the Spanish colonial government. ➡️ President McKinley sent a warship, the *Maine*, to promote American interests in the region. ➡️ The *Maine* exploded in the Havana harbor under mysterious circumstances; America blamed Spain; the **Spanish-American War** began.

⬇️

The war effectively ended Spanish colonial rule in the Americas; the U.S. emerged as a formidable imperial power. ⬅️ **Treaty of Paris:** Spain granted Cuba independence and ceded Philippines, Puerto Rico, and Guam to the U.S. ⬅️ The U.S. drove Spain out of Cuba AND sent a fleet to the Spanish-controlled **Philippines,** driving the Spanish out of there too.

💬 Many believe that American pro-war sentiment was due in part to the horrific details of Spanish mistreatment of the Cubans that were reported in the press. Stories were often lurid, highly sensationalized, and grossly exaggerated (much like the tabloid press of today!), with the desire for newspaper sales outweighing the need for accurate reporting. Newspaper mogul **William Randolph Hearst**, a reputed **war hawk**, was often accused of publishing such articles. The term "**yellow journalism**" was coined to describe this type of shoddy and disreputable journalistic practice.

Teddy Roosevelt, the Rough Riders, and a "Big Stick" 💬

Back in 1886, future president Theodore Roosevelt was President McKinley's Assistant Secretary of the Navy. An intrepid man with aggressive ideas about foreign policy, Roosevelt pushed hard for America's entry into the war. He went as far as to resign his post when the hostilities began so that he could serve with the First Volunteer Cavalry Regiment (better known as the **"Rough Riders"**)! When he became president a few years later, Roosevelt would expand upon the **Monroe doctrine** to accommodate his imperialist views:

> **Roosevelt Corollary:** Not only should Europe stay out of the Americas but the United States would intervene on behalf of any European nation with a legitimate claim in Latin America. This proclamation essentially reserved the right to use military force in the Americas.

Ask Yourself...

The issue of whether the United States should intervene in international conflicts remains as controversial today as it was during the Spanish-American War. Many believe that the United States, as the world superpower, has a moral obligation to defend oppressed or subjugated weaker nations that cannot defend themselves. Others condemn U.S. interference, accuse America of presumptuously "policing the world," and emphatically suggest that it mind its own business. What do you think?

 Roosevelt was famously fond of the motto "speak softly and carry a big stick."

World War I 😮

The First World War was the most devastating war humankind had ever known. A highly complicated web of European alliances created a precarious situation: Any armed conflict between nations on opposing sides now had the potential to become a global catastrophe! At first, the United States wisely chose to stay out of the scourge, but maintaining a neutral stance amidst a world war was not so easy. Eventually America joined the Allied forces and its entry was a major turning point for victory.

From Neutrality to War 😮

When the Austrian **Archduke Franz Ferdinand** was assassinated by a Serb in 1914, Europe went to war. Woodrow Wilson immediately declared the United States neutral, but in truth America favored Great Britain and its allies. When the Germans torpedoed the passenger ship *Lusitania* on its voyage from New York to Liverpool and killed over 1,100 people (128 of whom were Americans), the public outcry was enormous. It was later revealed that the ship had actually been carrying munitions to aid Britain's war effort. The continued German use of **unrestricted submarine warfare** near the British Isles, along with other acts of aggression by Germany, ultimately led to a declaration of war by the United States.

💬 In February of 1917, the German foreign secretary, Arthur Zimmerman, sent a telegram to the German ambassador to Mexico. Its contents revealed Germany's plan to use "ruthless" submarine warfare and proposed a German-Mexican alliance in the event that the United States joined the Allied war effort. Should Germany win, it would give Texas, New Mexico, and Arizona back to Mexico! British intelligence operatives intercepted the now infamous **Zimmerman telegram** and alerted the Americans. President Wilson was none too pleased, nor was the American public, and the United States declared war on Germany in a matter of weeks.

Causes of U.S. Entry Into WWI

- **Strong Pro-British Sentiment** (close economic ties)
- **Strong Anti-German Sentiment** (stories of wartime atrocities)
- **The Sinking of the *Lusitania*** (American casualties)
- **Unrestricted Submarine Warfare** (neutral countries would be attacked)
- **Instigation of War between the U.S. and Mexico** (the Zimmerman telegram)

The Treaty of Versailles and the League of Nations ❗

When the Allied forces won the war, France and Great Britain wanted a peace treaty that would punish Germany severely for the devastation. President Wilson, however, was at odds with this hard-line approach. Instead he opted for a more conciliatory agreement and pressed for the adoption of his brainchild—the **League of Nations**—which would function as a peacekeeping organization much like the United Nations of today. In the end, the terms were harsh and punitive, and a humiliated Germany signed the **Treaty of Versailles** under protest. The Treaty did in fact establish the League of Nations, but, in an ironic twist, the U.S. Senate took issue with some of the provisions concerning the League and refused to approve the Treaty. Consequently, the United States never signed the Treaty of Versailles, nor did it ever join the League of Nations.

Under the Treaty of Versailles Germany must

Admit total fault for the war	Cede colonies and other territories to the Allies	Pay Reparations	Disarm

1914	Austrian Archduke Ferdinand is assassinated in Sarajevo.
1914	The nations align themselves for war (the Central Powers vs. the Allies) and WWI begins in Europe.
1914	Wilson declares U.S. neutrality.
1915	Germany declares the waters around the British Isles a war zone.
1915	The Germans sink the *Lusitania.*
1917	The contents of the Zimmerman Telegram are published in the U.S.
1917	The **Russian Revolution** further destabilizes Europe and causes concern for the Allied war effort.
1917	The U.S. enters WWI by declaring war on Germany and its allies.
1918	The **American Expeditiary Forces** (the U.S. troops sent abroad) win their first major offensive, a turning point for the Allies.
1918	Germany is defeated and an **Armistice** is signed, ending WWI.
1919	Germany accepts the **Treaty of Versailles.**
1919	The U.S. adopts a policy of **isolationism.**

Timeline of U.S. Involvement in WWI

 Kaiser Wilhelm II of Germany, King George V of England, and Czar Nicholas II of Russia were all cousins. So much for family ties!

Post–WWI Isolationism 🛑

The carnage and large-scale suffering of World War I had been unprecedented and had a profound impact on the collective psyche of the American people. The United States understandably wanted nothing more to do with European conflicts and adopted a strict isolationist foreign policy. To prevent once again becoming entangled in Europe's wars, Congress passed a series of **neutrality acts** in the 1930s. These laws prohibited practices such as selling arms or granting loans to nations at war—a clear attempt to avoid the pattern that had led to WWI involvement. This stab at neutrality was sorely undermined in 1941 when the Japanese attacked Pearl Harbor, forcing America into World War II.

Ask Yourself...

The Treaty of Versailles was designed to leave Germany in such a weakened and dejected state that it could never wreak havoc upon Europe again. In what might be the most epic instance of backfiring in history, however, that is precisely what happened. Some argue that it was a mistake to humiliate Germany at Versailles, and that a compassionate treaty would have prevented any need for revenge and fanatical nationalism. Others believe the Allies simply weren't harsh enough and that it was laxity in *enforcing* the Treaty that allowed Germany to once again dominate Europe. If you were at Versailles, what would you have done?

World War II 🛑

The Second World War was the defining conflict of the 20th century. During the 1930s, Nazi Germany and the Japanese Empire embarked upon their respective campaigns for world dominion, while the **Allies** attempted to appease them in order to avoid another drawn-out bloody war. Ultimately war in Europe began with the 1939 German invasion of Poland, and the United States was forced to join in with the 1941 **Japanese attack on Pearl Harbor**. After the **Axis** powers were defeated in Europe, the United States ended the war in Asia by dropping atomic bombs on Japan, ushering in the Cold War **nuclear age**.

Democracy vs. Totalitarianism ❗

World War II was, in many ways, a conflict of ideology. The govern-ments of the German Nazi state, **Fascist** Italy, and Imperial Japan were highly militant totalitarian regimes that oppressed their own people and sought to conquer foreign lands. The cause of freedom thus became a rallying cry for America and its allies.

The Major Players:

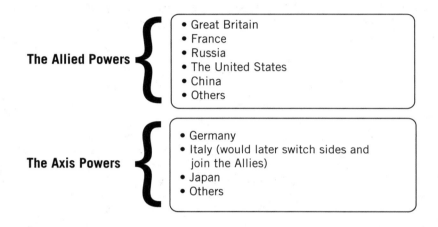

The Allied Powers {
- Great Britain
- France
- Russia
- The United States
- China
- Others

The Axis Powers {
- Germany
- Italy (would later switch sides and join the Allies)
- Japan
- Others

💬 The WWII "alliance" between Russia and the United States was tenuous and strained at best. The Soviet Union, led by ruthless communist dictator **Josef Stalin,** was totalitarian and brutally oppressive. Stalin had originally aligned himself with Hitler and the Nazis (even though they were ideological enemies) and joined the Allies (who reluctantly joined forces with the Soviets) only when Hitler double crossed him and invaded Russia. When Stalin's forces ultimately invaded Germany, they perpetrated heinous crimes against the German civilian population. As soon as the war was over, **Cold War** tensions between the Soviets and the free world began in full force.

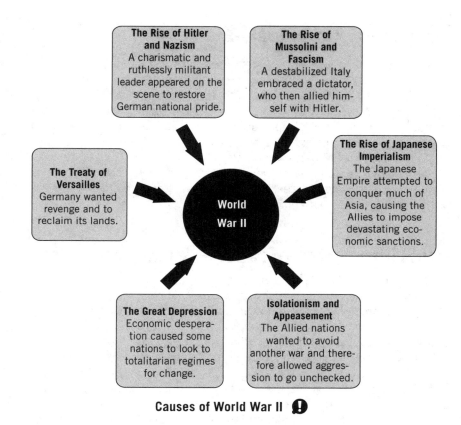

The Rise of Hitler and Nazism A charismatic and ruthlessly militant leader appeared on the scene to restore German national pride.	**The Rise of Mussolini and Fascism** A destabilized Italy embraced a dictator, who then allied himself with Hitler.

The Treaty of Versailles Germany wanted revenge and to reclaim its lands.

The Rise of Japanese Imperialism The Japanese Empire attempted to conquer much of Asia, causing the Allies to impose devastating economic sanctions.

The Great Depression Economic desperation caused some nations to look to totalitarian regimes for change.

Isolationism and Appeasement The Allied nations wanted to avoid another war and therefore allowed aggression to go unchecked.

Causes of World War II 🔔

Nazi Germany and the Holocaust 🔔

NOTABLE FIGURE:

Adolf Hitler (1889–1945) rose to power in the destabilized Germany of the 1930s and quickly and ruthlessly eliminated any opposition. He had an almost hypnotic hold on his followers and indoctrinated (some would argue "brainwashed") the nation in his racist and hateful ideologies. German **"Aryans"** were the superior "master race" and all those deemed racially inferior or otherwise undesirable (most notably the Jews) were viciously persecuted and eventually murdered. Hitler's **"Final Solution"** entailed the systematic gassing of Jews to death in the extermination camps of Poland, with an estimated six million Jews murdered. Other victims included homosexuals, Sinti and Roma ("Gypsies"), people who were physically disabled or mentally ill, Communists and other political dissidents, and basically anyone unfortunate enough to offend his established power structure in any way.

Japanese Atrocities ❗

While many think primarily of Nazi misdeeds when considering atrocities of the WWII era, some of the most brutal war crimes were actually committed by Japanese soldiers. The 1937 **Nanjing Massacre** left over 200,000 Chinese civilians dead. Later during the war, Japanese forces cruelly murdered millions of additional civilians in occupied areas in what has become known as the "**Asian Holocaust**." Tens of thousands of Allied POWs and noncombatants were tortured and killed as well. Particularly disturbing were the vicious attacks upon women (including nuns and Red Cross nurses), infants and children, the elderly, and the sick and wounded.

U.S. Internment of Japanese Americans ❗

The surprise attack on Pearl Harbor by the Japanese stunned the United States. The thousands of Japanese Americans living in the United States, many of whom were native born, were suddenly perceived as a potential threat to national security. In stark disregard of civil liberties, over 100,000 people, most of whom had committed no crime or disloyal act, were forcibly relocated to internment camps for the duration of the war. No comparable act was passed for Americans of German or Italian descent. While the Japanese Americans were generally not abused or mistreated (apart from the internment itself), many lost their homes and property as well as their freedom. The Supreme Court upheld the constitutionality of the internment as a necessary evil during time of war. It took more than forty years for the U.S. government to issue an apology and attempt to compensate the victims.

The End of the War ❗

On June 6, 1944, the Allies turned the tide of the war in Europe with the risky **D-Day invasion**, in which over 130,000 troops stormed the beaches at Normandy. Within weeks, over a million men had landed and the Allies soon took back the continent. Hitler committed suicide in April of 1945 and Germany surrendered unconditionally eight days later.

While the Japanese were undoubtedly losing the war in Asia, the tenacity of their fighting forces was a cause for concern for the Allies. The Japanese did not believe that surrender was honorable, and the United States feared that the war would continue (perhaps for years) with a tremendous loss of life. President Truman consequently decided to drop an atomic bomb on **Hiroshima**, which annihilated the city and killed well over a hundred thousand innocent civilians. When the Japanese still did not surrender, a second bomb was dropped on **Nagasaki**, after which the Japanese had little choice but to surrender unconditionally to the Allies. The suffering and devastation caused by the use of nuclear weapons would impact Japan for generations.

⦿ The **Manhattan Project** was the top-secret U.S. government research project designed to create the first atomic bomb. It was devised after the scientific community learned that Nazi physicists had discovered the secrets of splitting a uranium atom. Understandably alarmed at the prospect of nuclear weapons at Hitler's disposal, the United States was determined to beat the Germans to the punch! The government engaged a team of more than 100,000 scientists and technicians who ultimately produced the first atomic weapon, thereby ushering in the **nuclear age**.

The Germans anticipated an invasion of the continent but didn't know exactly where it would occur, so the Allies thought of a clever ruse. To throw the Germans off track, they created a massive fake army out of rubber inflatable tanks and aircraft, as well as dummy soldiers, and put it near Pas de Calais, a hundred miles away from Normandy! The deception was enhanced by fake radio transmissions and other false intelligence. To the German aerial reconnaissance, it looked as though a mighty army was about to invade at Pas de Calais, and the Germans sent the bulk of their forces there. The rest is D-day history.

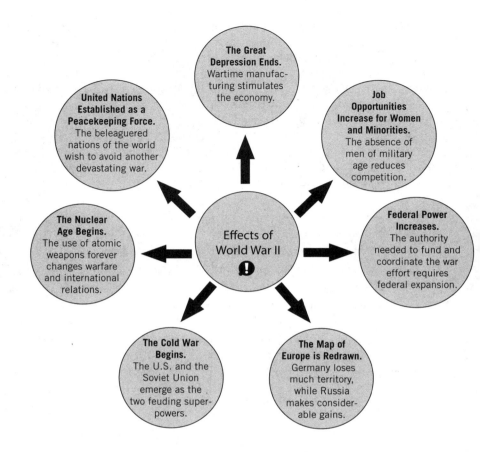

The Great
Depression Ends.
Wartime manufac-
turing stimulates
the economy.

United Nations
Established as a
Peacekeeping Force.
The beleaguered
nations of the world
wish to avoid another
devastating war.

Job
Opportunities
Increase for Women
and Minorities.
The absence of
men of military
age reduces
competition.

The Nuclear
Age Begins.
The use of atomic
weapons forever
changes warfare
and international
relations.

Effects of
World War II

Federal Power
Increases.
The authority
needed to fund and
coordinate the war
effort requires
federal expansion.

The Cold War
Begins.
The U.S. and the
Soviet Union
emerge as the
two feuding super-
powers.

The Map of
Europe is Redrawn.
Germany loses
much territory,
while Russia
makes consider-
able gains.

Ask Yourself...

Were the world leaders of the 1930s right or wrong in trying to appease
Hitler and avoid the ravages of WWII? In the generations that followed,
many Americans developed strong anti-war sentiments (particularly those of the 1960s and 1970s counterculture movement) and
condemned any military action whatsoever as immoral. Moreover,
many today believe that the billions of dollars spent annually on weaponry would be better spent alleviating poverty and improving the daily
lives of American citizens. Should America always seek to avoid war at
all costs? What might have happened if the United States had been too
weak militarily to fight the Japanese and the Nazis?

ASAP U.S. History

PERIOD 8 (1945–1980):
The Postwar Period and Cold War

The postwar period was a time of international tensions and domestic turbulence. This section examines how the Cold War between the United States and the Soviet Union dominated American foreign policy. It also explores how radical social and political movements at home (mostly in the 1960s and 1970s) changed the nation.

The Cold War ❗

The period immediately following the Second World War through the 1980s was dominated by the epic power struggle between the United States and the Soviet Union and their respective allies. Fueled largely by fundamental ideological differences, the capitalistic United States and the communist U.S.S.R. each feared that the other was intent upon taking over the world and acted accordingly. While the two superpowers never actually engaged each other in combat, "hot" **proxy wars** were fought in Korea and Vietnam as the hostilities reshaped the map and governed international politics in every corner of the world.

Containment ❗

After World War II, the United States adopted a policy of **containment**, which aimed to halt the spread of communism around the globe while avoiding war with the Soviet Union. The nation's policies and interactions with other countries were invariably grounded in this concept and based upon this overarching goal. In response, the Soviets made every attempt to thwart the United States in these efforts and to build a powerful communist alliance. Here are some important Cold War polices and alliances:

The Truman Doctrine	The Marshall Plan
• Involved U.S. economic and military support for countries that resisted Communist subjugation	• Involved large amounts of U.S. financial aid for war-torn European nations in exchange for their allegiance
• Initiated by the U.S. (at the behest of President Truman) in 1947 in response to Communist threats to take over Greece and Turkey 〰	• Initiated by the U.S. (and named after Secretay of State George Marshall) in 1948 in response to the destabilization of Europe due to WWII
• Resulted in a reduction in worldwide Communism and an increase in Cold War hostilities	• Resulted in reduced support for Communism in Europe, increased U.S. power, and greater economic stability on the European continent

The North Atlantic Treaty Organization (NATO)	The Warsaw Pact
• Involved a mutual defense alliance among the U.S., Canada, and several western European nations • Initiated by the U.S. in 1949 in response to the Soviet blockade of Berlin • Resulted in increased U.S. global influence and the ultimate creation of the Warsaw Pact in response	• Involved a mutual defense alliance among the Soviet Union and several Central and Eastern European countries • Initiated by the Soviet Union in 1955 in response to the integration of West Germany into NATO • Resulted in increased Soviet influence over member nations, a counterbalancing of NATO power, and a formalized political division of Europe

Cold War Policies and Alliances

The Korean War ⚠

The United States intervened in Northeast Asia in 1950 to prevent communist expansion into the southern region of Korea, a destabilized former Japanese colony. Victory against the Soviet-backed communist forces of North Korea seemed assured until China unexpectedly entered the war and attacked American troops. Fearing the outbreak of World War III, the United States wisely refrained from the use of atomic weaponry and avoided further escalation of the war, ultimately achieving peace between North and South through a negotiated truce.

1910 Japan formally makes Korea its colony and controls the region for several decades.

1945 Japan is defeated in WWII and victorious Russian troops enter Korea in an attempt to claim the territory.

1945 The U.S., fearing Communist expansion, demands that the Soviets advance no farther into Korea than the 38th parallel.

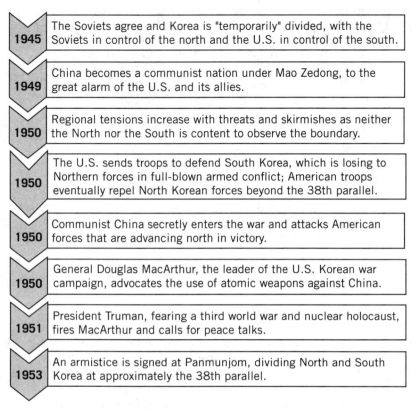

1945	The Soviets agree and Korea is "temporarily" divided, with the Soviets in control of the north and the U.S. in control of the south.
1949	China becomes a communist nation under Mao Zedong, to the great alarm of the U.S. and its allies.
1950	Regional tensions increase with threats and skirmishes as neither the North nor the South is content to observe the boundary.
1950	The U.S. sends troops to defend South Korea, which is losing to Northern forces in full-blown armed conflict; American troops eventually repel North Korean forces beyond the 38th parallel.
1950	Communist China secretly enters the war and attacks American forces that are advancing north in victory.
1950	General Douglas MacArthur, the leader of the U.S. Korean war campaign, advocates the use of atomic weapons against China.
1951	President Truman, fearing a third world war and nuclear holocaust, fires MacArthur and calls for peace talks.
1953	An armistice is signed at Panmunjom, dividing North and South Korea at approximately the 38th parallel.

The Korean War

The Vietnam War ❗

The United States similarly intervened in Southeast Asia during the Cold War to prevent Vietnam, a destabilized former French colony, from becoming communist. American involvement in this conflict was protracted, divisive, and traumatic for the nation as U.S. service-men were forced to fight a long grisly war for reasons that, to many, remained elusive. Despite the fact that enemy casualties far exceeded U.S. casualties, increasingly vitriolic public opposition to the war even-tually forced a complete withdrawal of American troops and Vietnam ultimately fell to communism. The following chart summarizes the events of the Vietnam War.

1800s –1940	Vietnam is a French colony and remains under French control.
1940– 1945	Japan invades Vietnam during WWII but is ultimately defeated.
1945	Ho Chi Minh, a communist, declares Vietnam independent.
1946	France attempts to regain control and the Franco-Vietnamese War begins.
1948– 1950	The U.S. supports the French war effort, while the Soviet Union and China recognize Vietnam.
1954	France is defeated and the Geneva Accords "temporarily" divide Vietnam in two, with the communists in control of the north.
1955– 1963	The region remains destabilized as the U.S. struggles for political control of the South; Southern insurgents are called "Viet Cong."
1964	U.S. ships are reportedly attacked by the North Vietnamese; the Gulf of Tonkin Resolution gives Johnson the power to use military force in Southeast Asia.
1965	The U.S. aerial bombing campaign begins, followed by the ground war; increasing numbers of U.S. troops are deployed.
1966– 1969	News footage of the conflict and reports of U.S. casualties shock Americans; public opposition to the war increases.
1969	Nixon speaks of "Vietnamization" and begins to withdraw troops.
1973	The U.S. ends its involvement in the conflict with the Paris Peace Accords.
1975	The North is victorious and Vietnam becomes a communist nation.

The Vietnam War

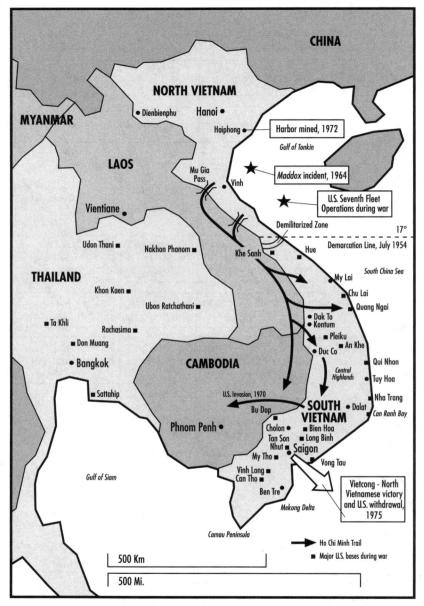

Southeast Asia During the Vietnam War

**The Gulf of Tonkin Resolu-
tion** was passed by Congress
in August of 1964 in response to
reported attacks upon the *USS Mad-
dox* by the North Vietnamese. It gave the
president authorization to use conventional
military force in Southeast Asia, without a
congressional declaration of war, in order to
protect American interests. Many believe this
was an appropriate emergency measure
in the face of foreign aggression, while
others consider it a reckless violation
of our constitutional doctrine of
separation of powers. What
do you think?

Cold War Politics in the Third World ❗

The end of World War II brought about the decline of the European
empires that had colonized Africa and South America and the creation of many newly independent nation-states. While the nationalist
pride of these countries, and their respective histories with imperialism, led them to avoid entanglements with the American and Soviet
superpowers, most became pawns to some extent in the ongoing Cold
War struggle. The term "third world" was coined during this period,
referring to a state that was neither part of the "first world" U.S. alliance nor part of the "second world" alliance with the Soviet Union.

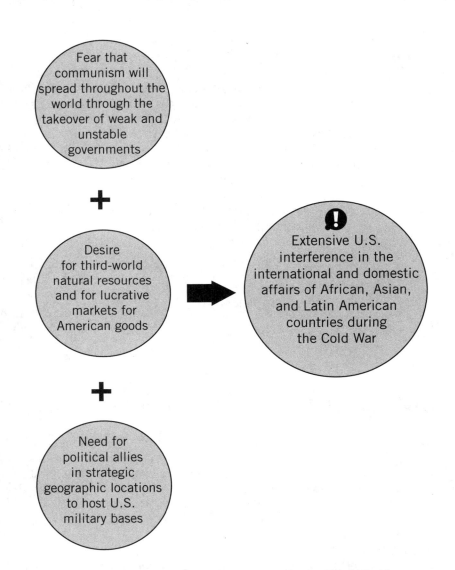

Causes of U.S. Cold War Interference in the Third World

The phrase **"mutually assured destruction"** ("MAD") was often used during the Cold War to justify the proliferation of nuclear weapons among the superpowers. Ironically, the fact that each side had accumulated enough nuclear weapons to obliterate the other (many times over) was thought to serve as a perfect deterrent to the use of any nonconventional weapons whatsoever. What do you think?

The Space Race 💬

The intense rivalry and territorial ambitions of the Cold War were not restricted to planet Earth! When the Soviets managed to launch *Sputnik* in 1957, the first satellite in space, the United States took it as a "wake-up call." Shortly thereafter the government created the National Aeronautics and Space Association ("NASA") and the **space race** began. Both nations scrambled to beat the other in developing the technological advancements needed for space exploration. The United States made great strides and, twelve years after *Sputnik*, launched the *Apollo* 11 spacecraft with the first men to walk on the moon.

Nixon and Détente ❗

After several decades of bitter hostilities and proxy war with the Soviet Union, President Nixon tried to usher in a new period of relative tolerance and conciliation. This policy, known as **détente** (or "openness"), entailed respecting one another's ideological differences and attempting to cooperate more successfully. This liberal approach was short-lived, however, as the 1979 Soviet invasion of Afghanistan alarmed the free world and revitalized Cold War tensions in the 1980s.

💬 Perhaps the most enduring and infamous symbol of the deep divisions between East and West during the Cold War is the **Berlin wall**, which separated communist East Berlin from democratic West Berlin. Constructed of concrete and barbed wire and patrolled by armed guards, the wall was erected in 1961 by the communist government in order to prevent ever-increasing defections to the West. Any East German attempting to scale the wall or otherwise escape was shot on sight, and many died as they tried desperately to reach the freedom that lay just yards away. However, thousands did succeed by digging tunnels, crawling through sewers, and even floating in a hot-air balloon! The wall, which had become the embodiment of communist oppression, was joyfully torn down nearly thirty years later when the Cold War finally ended.

Ask Yourself...

Was the United States justified in fighting communism so aggressively in the postwar 20th century, at the cost of untold resources and countless American lives? What might have happened if it hadn't? Would communism have eventually fallen from the weight of its own inherent flaws, or might there be a very different world today—a world in which even the United States languishes under Soviet rule?

Federal Power vs. Individual Civil Liberties ❗

How to strike an appropriate balance between the power of the state and the rights of the individual is a question that has perpetually confronted Americans since colonial times. The second half of the 20th century, however, brought radical changes in popular ideas about personal liberty and individualism that caused Americans to reject conventional beliefs and challenge authority as they never had before. This newfound emphasis on self-determination inevitably led to some bitter clashes between the United States government and its citizens.

McCarthyism	• Involved the aggressive (and often slanderous) outing of actual or suspected communists by Senator Joseph McCarthy during the **"Second Red Scare"** • Occurred in the 1950s • Resulted in **blacklisting,** persecutions, and the ruination of many reputations, along with a paranoid national mentality • Pitted the government's need to maintain national security and identify potential spies against the individual's right to privacy and freedom of belief
The Development of the Military-Industrial Complex	• Involved the creation of a mutually profitable alliance between the U.S. military and the arms industries, making war a desirable enterprise for a powerful few at the expense of the general welfare • Occurred in the late 1940s and the 1950s; the term was popularized by President Eisenhower in his farewell address • Resulted in the massive build-up of military weapons and, many argue, caused the nation's protracted involvement in the Vietnam War • Pitted the government's need to defend the nation militarily and maintain superpower status against the individual's right to live peacefully and to reap the benefits of federal funds otherwise spent on the military

The Vietnam War Protests	• Involved large-scale disruptive and often violent protests against the war in Vietnam • Occurred in the late 1960s and early 1970s • Resulted in national turmoil that ultimately caused the U.S to end its involvement in Vietnam without achieving its military or political objectives • Pitted the government's need to maintain domestic order and make foreign policy decisions against the individual's right to protest
The Pentagon Papers 〜	• Involved President Nixon's attempt to suppress highly classified damaging information (leaked to the press) about U.S. government action during the Vietnam War • Occurred during the early 1970s • Resulted in a Supreme Court decision favoring the press and a reduction in the power and prestige of the U.S. government • Pitted the government's need to maintain national security and preserve American international credibility against the individual's right to be informed
Energy Policy and the Oil Crisis	• Involved exorbitant prices for petroleum as the result of an oil embargo by Arab countries in response to U.S. support for Israel • Occurred during the 1970s • Resulted in hardship and disruption of daily life for the American public due to gas and energy shortages • Pitted the government's need to form political alliances and offer support to friendly nations against the individual's right to live comfortably in a prosperous nation

**Postwar Clashes Between Governmental Power
and the Individual Liberties of Americans**

The Power of OPEC 💬

The ability of Middle Eastern nations to effectively manipulate the United States and its allies during the 1970s energy crisis was largely due to the **Organization of Petroleum Exporting Countries ("OPEC")**. The member nations, which controlled the better part of the world's oil supply, endeavored to use their unified strength to exploit the western need for oil and control the United States politically. Since the crisis of the seventies, however, technological advancements have allowed for greater domestic oil production and more efficient energy use. Consequently, the United States no longer maintains a crippling dependency on foreign oil, and OPEC has lost much of its coercive international power.

 Ask Yourself...

How successful was American society in achieving the proper balance between governmental power and civil liberties in the postwar 20th century? During which of the conflicts and crises, if any, were the rights and freedoms of U.S. citizens wrongly denied so that federal power could thrive? Conversely, were there times when the good of the country, and of the American people in general, was recklessly sacrificed to the spirit of modern individualism?

The Civil Rights Movement ❗

One of the most prominent and pervasive social issues at the heart of the postwar turmoil was that of civil rights for African Americans. While legal discriminatory practices based on race, such as segregated public facilities, were typically confined to the Southern states, blacks all throughout America began to challenge societal norms and fight for equal status with whites. The methods through which civil rights activists sought change varied greatly, ranging from use of the judicial system to orchestrated acts of peaceful defiance, and even to acts of extreme violence designed to unhinge American society at large.

The following are some important tools and methods of the Civil Rights Movement.

Nonviolent Protest and Peaceful Activism	• Entailed organized efforts to end racial discrimination while either acting within the law or with a determination to avoid violence and bloodshed • Is closely associated with the leadership of **Martin Luther King, Jr.** • Resulted in great gains for the black community in the 1960s and 1970s and in changing racial attitudes, largely because the methods used, while still greatly divisive, gained the respect of blacks and whites alike
Violent Protest and Militant Activism 💬	• Entailed organized efforts to end racial discrimination through violence, intimidation, and a fundamental disruption of American society • Is closely associated with the leadership of **Malcolm X** (who advocated change "by any means necessary"), with the **Black Panther Party,** and (some argue unfairly) with the "Black Power" movement • Resulted in some gains for the black community through increased attention to racial issues in the 1960s and early 1970s, yet alienated most whites, as well as many blacks, and greatly exacerbated racial tensions
Civil Disobedience 💬	• Entailed organized efforts to end racial discrimination by publicly disobeying racial laws that were deemed unfair or immoral (e.g., an African American deliberately sitting in the "whites only" section of a restaurant) • Is closely associated with the teachings of Thoreau and Ghandi, which were then adopted by Martin Luther King, Jr and his followers • Resulted in the eventual overturning of laws that overtly discriminated against blacks in America, and also in an enhanced spirit of nonconformity and widespread anti-authoritarian sentiments in the 1960s and 1970s

Desegregation	• Entailed a combination of protest activities and decisive court decisions aimed at ending racial segregation, which existed predominantly in the South • Is closely associated with **Brown v. Board of Education of Topeka (1954),** in which the Supreme Court held that the existing "separate but equal" legal doctrine of racial segregation was unconstitutional • Resulted in an eventual end to legal segregation practices in the U.S., the forced integration of public schools, and a period of heightened racial tensions in the late 1950s, 1960s, and early 1970s
The Civil Rights Acts	• Entailed the use of federal legislation, including the Civil Rights Act of 1965, the Voting Rights Act of 1965, and the Fair Housing Act of 1968, to achieve racial equality • Closely associated with the liberal expansion of federal power in the 1960s; the Acts were successfully used to fight racial discrimination in myriad contexts • Resulted in substantial gains for the black community in many different areas, along with an expansion of federal involvement in racial issues
Affirmative Action	• Entailed the widespread systematic practice of giving preferential treatment to African Americans over whites in terms of college admissions, hiring practices, etc. • ◯ Is closely associated with **Regents of University of California v. Bakke (1978),** in which the Court held that, while quotas are unconstitutional, race could be considered as a factor in university admissions • Resulted in very substantial gains for the black community in terms of education and employment, but also in allegations of reverse discrimination by the white community

Tools and Methods of the Civil Rights Movement

The attorney who eloquently argued the case for desegregation in **Brown v. Board of Education** was none other than **Thurgood Marshall,** who would later become the first black justice on the United States Supreme Court! Marshall, who was an NAACP lawyer when he litigated the case, was appointed to the Court in 1967 in a bold move by President Johnson. Justice Marshall's unwavering commitment to civil rights issues throughout his twenty-four year tenure became a critical aspect of the movement, as his name became synonymous with Court decisions favoring racial equality for the African American community.

Resistance to Desegregation ❗

While some southern whites favored the racial integration that was taking place in postwar America, and even fought alongside their black compatriots in the civil rights movement, others greatly resented the changes to the status quo. Many were outraged by what they saw as a violation of their fundamental right to choose to associate with whomever they wished. The federal government, which had arguably stretched its constitutional powers to an impermissible degree in taking such an active role in the lives of its citizens, was often vilified. Some southern officials simply refused to obey desegregation edicts, while others found ways to circumvent the law, such as paying tuition for white children to attend private schools. Violence was not uncommon. While forced desegregation of schools continued to be an issue in some areas during the early 1970s (even in the North), by the latter part of the decade, integration had itself become the status quo and tensions had largely dissipated.

Just Another Form of Civil Disobedience?

Rather than comply with federal orders to desegregate their schools, some southern officials simply shut down their entire school systems (sometimes for years)! While this behavior might seem odd and indefensible to the modern American mind, many were in fact acting in accordance with their consciences. Were the officials who publicly disobeyed what they viewed as immoral desegregation laws engaging in civil disobedience in the traditions of Thoreau and Ghandi? Alternatively, does the term *civil disobedience* properly apply only to acts of defiance of which 21st-century Americans are inclined to approve?

Ask Yourself...

Is affirmative action for African Americans an ethically or constitutionally acceptable way to remedy past racial discrimination? Some would assert the adage that "two wrongs don't make a right": If preferential treatment based on race is abhorrent when it disadvantages one group, is it not hypocritical to condone the practice when it disadvantages another group? Others would argue that societal context must be considered, and that affirmative action is necessary to counteract past and ongoing discrimination in favor of whites and against African Americans. What do you think?

Other Social Movements ❗

As Americans became more socially conscious and inclined toward political activism, many different movements took shape. Some of these sought equality for groups such as women, gays, and Native Americans, while others fought for causes such as environmental protection and awareness. While the agendas may have differed in the postwar era from those of 21st-century activists (e.g., national legalization of same-sex marriage was not viewed as feasible in the 1970s, much less in the 1940s), the strides that were made during this early period were critical in the development of these various modern-day movements. The following chart summarizes some of these social movements in America.

Women's Rights	• Centered primarily on equality of opportunity in education and employment, fair and comparable pay in the work force, reproductive rights to birth control and abortion, and domestic emancipation • Obstacles included deeply ingrained cultural beliefs about traditional gender roles and the social stigma typically applied to women who flouted these conventions. • 💬 Milestones include the **Equal Pay Act of 1963,** which requires that males and females receive equal pay for equal work; the formation of the **National Organization for Women (NOW)** in 1966, which remains the most prominent feminist organization in the U.S.; and *Roe v. Wade* **(1973),** which legalized first-trimester abortion (although the decision remains highly controversial).
Gay Rights	• Centered primarily on the fight against the criminalization and pathologization of homosexuality and on efforts to organize the gay community • Obstacles included the widespread belief that homosexuality is immoral and deviant, as well as the strong reluctance of many gays to publicly reveal their orientation. • Milestones include the **Stonewall** protest of 1969, during which gay men, lesbians, and transgender people rioted for several days in response to a police raid on a gay bar.

Latino Rights	• Centered primarily on the issues of fairness in immigration, bilingual education, and farm workers' rights • Obstacles included the opposition of the native-born community, many of whom viewed Latinos as foreign intruders and resented the use of Spanish in a traditionally English-speaking country. • Milestones include the Equal Education Opportunity Act of 1974, which made bilingual education more readily available.
Native American Rights	• Centered primarily on safeguarding tribal sovereignty and treaty rights, as well as on preserving Native American culture • Obstacles included the unique legal relationship between the Native American community and the federal government, in which individuals are considered both U.S. citizens and citizens of their respective tribal nations. • Milestones include the **Indian Civil Rights Act of 1968,** which prevented civil rights abuses of Native Americans by their tribal governments by applying most Bill of Rights restrictions to these entities.
The "War on Poverty"	• Centered primarily on providing low-income individuals with myriad government-funded assistance, such as job training, subsidized housing, free legal services, and novel educational opportunities • Obstacles included the traditional belief that poverty, absent illness or disability, is the result of laziness and vice and that the government should not reward the indolent by supporting them with tax dollars. • Milestones include the **Economic Opportunity Act,** initiated by President Johnson, which appropriated nearly a billion dollars for poverty relief.

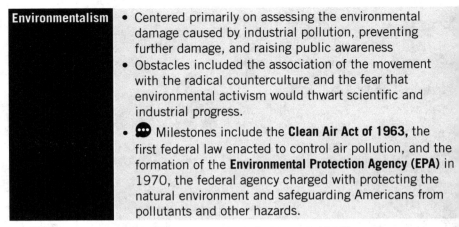

Environmentalism	• Centered primarily on assessing the environmental damage caused by industrial pollution, preventing further damage, and raising public awareness
	• Obstacles included the association of the movement with the radical counterculture and the fear that environmental activism would thwart scientific and industrial progress.
	• 💬 Milestones include the **Clean Air Act of 1963,** the first federal law enacted to control air pollution, and the formation of the **Environmental Protection Agency (EPA)** in 1970, the federal agency charged with protecting the natural environment and safeguarding Americans from pollutants and other hazards.

Other Social Movements in America (1945–1980)

💬 The modern environmentalist movement is often traced back to the profound influence of a single book published by ecologist Rachel Carson in 1962. In *Silent Spring,* Carson exposed the widespread and arguably reckless use of the pesticide DDT and its harmful effects, leading to an eventual ban. She called for governmental accountability and for greater public awareness of the dangers of a hubristic and short-sighted disregard for the welfare of our planet's ecosystem.

 Ask Yourself...

Modern Americans are different from their counterparts in the 1940s: They are more likely to view negative personal circumstances, such as poverty or a lack of education, as the result of governmental failure and systemic societal injustice. Are Americans today simply a more enlightened people with a greater sense of fairness, or might the trend toward externalizing blame stifle individual capacities for critical self-appraisal? Is this a change for the better or for the worse, or, perhaps, for both?

Liberalism in the Postwar Era 🔊

So dramatic was the liberalization of America in the 1960s and 1970s that the myriad political and social changes of the period would have been downright unthinkable to most Americans just a few years before. The pervasive concern for societal reform, preoccupation with perceived injustices, demand for governmental accountability, and rejection of all forms of authority would become the hallmarks of this turbulent time. The liberalism of the sixties, however, arguably had a certain optimism to it that seemed to fade during the more somber seventies, as economic strife and unprecedented political scandal came to dominate the decade.

The Liberal Sixties 🔊

NOTABLE FIGURE: 🔊

Lyndon B. Johnson was one of the most actively liberal presidents of the modern era, as he dedicated his tenure in office (1963–1969) to the dogged pursuit of reform in many aspects of American life. He spoke of a **"Great Society"** in which there would be social, political, and economic equality for all. He vastly increased federal spending on programs for minorities and the poor and fought for legislative changes to further his agenda. Toward this end, Johnson had a formidable ally in the Supreme Court under Chief Justice Earl Warren, which is known for some of the most consistently liberal decisions of the 20th century. The **Warren Court** (1953–1969) was responsible for a substantial number of radical landmark decisions concerning civil rights, the protection of individual liberties, and the expansion of federal power.

💬 Americans immediately recognize the iconic phrase "you have the right to remain silent," a staple of every police-based movie or television show. The legal requirement that the police inform individuals who are in custody of their legal rights before interrogating them stems from the landmark case of *Miranda v. Arizona* (1966). Ernesto Miranda was arrested for kidnapping and rape and then interrogated by police, during which he admitted his crimes and signed a full confession. He later fought to have his conviction overturned because the police did not advise him of his 5th Amendment right against self-incrimination. The Warren Court ultimately sided with Miranda, holding that statements made by detainees without proper procedural safeguards (now known as "Miranda warnings") are in fact inadmissible. In doing so, the Court dramatically altered the balance of power between the state and the criminally accused.

💬

Should Miranda's conviction for such a serious crime have been overturned when his guilt was not in doubt? Some would argue that respect for Miranda's constitutional rights should not rise to the level of allowing him to rape with impunity. Others would argue that potential injustices in individual cases like *Miranda* are the price that must be paid to preserve the integrity of the system and ensure that constitutional protections remain in place for everyone. What do you think?

The Liberal Seventies ❗

While the sixties were characterized to a certain degree by idealism and the hope of a brighter future, the liberalism of the seventies was more angry and pessimistic. Plagued by political scandals, embarrassing international dilemmas, and economic downturns, Americans sharply criticized their leaders as they continually sought governmental accountability for society's various ills. The following chart describes some political crises and scandals of the seventies.

The Resignation of Spiro Agnew	The Watergate Scandal
• Involved the resignation of U.S. Vice President **Spiro Agnew** in the face of criminal charges, including bribery and tax evasion • Took place in 1973 during Nixon's second term • Resulted in an unprecedented major corruption-based scandal involving an American vice president and in increased anti-government sentiments	• Involved the alleged complicity of Richard Nixon and members of his high-ranking staff in illegal activities, such as wiretapping and burglary, and a botched attempt at a cover-up • Took place during both of Nixon's terms in office, with criminal prosecutions of major participants occurring subsequent to Nixon's presidency • Resulted in the unprecedented resignation of an American president, a substantial loss in U.S. international credibility, and a cultural devaluation of the office of the president

The Nixon Pardon	The Iran Hostage Crisis
• Involved the full presidential pardon of Richard Nixon by Gerald Ford, who had been Nixon's vice president after Agnew; Nixon had effectively made Ford president by resigning, and the pardon prevented Nixon from ever being tried for Watergate activities. • Took place in 1974, one month after Ford became president • Resulted in accusations of a **"corrupt bargain"** and in widespread cynicism among Americans concerning the shady nature of politics; it is generally believed that the scandal cost Ford a second term.	• Involved the taking of approximately 60 Americans as hostages by Iranian Islamic revolutionaries in retaliation for unpopular U.S. policies • Took place from November of 1979 through the end of the Carter presidency; the hostages were released after 444 days of captivity on the day Ronald Reagan took office in 1981. • Resulted in some loss of American international prestige and national pride, as well as some loss in confidence in the ability of government leaders to effectively protect U.S. interests; it is generally believed that the crisis cost Carter a second term.

1970s Political Crises and Scandals

NOTABLE FIGURE: 💬

The presidency of Jimmy Carter (1977–1981) was relatively free of the kinds of corruption-based scandals that troubled his predecessors in the early to mid 1970s. Nonetheless, his popularity suffered greatly as the result of pervasive economic problems. Persistent **stagflation** (a combination of high inflation, high unemployment, and slow growth) angered Americans, many of whom had little faith in the effectiveness of their leaders. The highly problematic **1979 oil crisis** left the country feeling vulnerable to the acts of foreign nations, a sentiment that was further fueled by the humiliation of the **Iran Hostage Crisis.** Voters expressed their dissatisfaction at the polls, with Ronald Reagan winning the 1980 election by a landslide.

The Rise of Conservativism

As is often the case with extreme social and political change, a conservative reaction to the stark liberalism of the sixties and seventies eventually occurred. Many Americans objected to what they viewed as the activism of the federal government and to its interference in their daily lives. Some believed that individual rights were being held sacrosanct to the detriment of society as a whole, and that the rebellious and anti-authoritarian sentiments of the time had simply gone too far. This rejection of liberal policies and ideology would further sow the seeds for the Reagan victory of 1980 and the conservative economic and social revolution that followed.

💬 Many conservative Americans of the sixties and seventies believed that their opinions and moral viewpoints were, in actuality, more prevalent than it would appear. The term **"silent majority"** was popularized by President Nixon in reference to those Americans who held traditional views but did not draw attention to themselves, as many vociferous radicals and flamboyant members of the counterculture were apt to do. Whether or not conservatives were truly the majority during this era is debatable. However, the sharp contrast between the rebellious seventies and the ultra-conservative eighties, ushered in by the Reagan presidency at the very dawn of the decade, strongly suggests that an undercurrent of traditional beliefs and values existed in ostensibly liberal 1970s America.

Ask Yourself...

Gerald Ford defended his decision to pardon Richard Nixon as an attempt to allow a wounded and beleaguered nation to heal. Some would argue that President Nixon, like every other American accused of a crime, should have been tried and held to account for his alleged misdeeds, and that the pardon was a shameful miscarriage of justice that degraded the nation. Others believe that resignation in disgrace and perpetual ignominy was punishment enough for Nixon, and that a Watergate-scarred country simply needed to move on. What do you think?

Other Cultural Changes of the Postwar Years ❗

The nation evolved in many other ways during the second half of the 20th century as well. Changes in demographics, shifts in moral values and in economic and political power, and major advances in technology converged to create the modern American cultural milieu. The following chart describes some of these cultural changes.

Demographics	• Involved an influx of non-European immigrants, especially Hispanics and Asians, and an increased percentage of younger people in the nation • Occurred as a consequence of the **Immigration and Naturalization Act of 1965,** which changed the existing policy to facilitate immigration from countries other than Europe, and as the result of the **"baby boom"** that immediately followed WWII • Resulted in increased political and social status for Hispanic and Asian Americans, and in the tremendous influence of the "baby boomer" generation, most of whom came of age in the 1960s
The Economic Boom	• Involved a substantial upgrade in the standard of living and an increase in disposable income for the average American family • Occurred in the 1950s and 1960s, in stark contrast to the frugality of the wartime years, and ended with the 1970s recession • Resulted in a dramatic rise in American consumerism that surpassed the prewar era, particularly among the middle classes, and in increased cultural materialism; the boom also widened the economic gap between the poor and the rest of the nation, leading to class-based tensions.

- Involved middle-class migration to the suburbs and to the desirable "Sun Belt" states, as affluence brought greater opportunities
- 💬 Occurred from the 1950s through the 1970s in response to poverty and overcrowding in many cities; such migration was facilitated by the **Federal-Aid Highway Act of 1956,** which created the modern interstate highway system.
- 💬 Resulted in the **"white flight"** phenomenon whereby major cities became mostly populated by minorities, as well as in a shift in economic and political power from the Northeast to the densely populated South
- Involved increasing levels of criminal activity, particularly in large urban areas, and the resultant demand for harsher penalties and more effective law enforcement
- Occurred during the latter 1970s in response to the inner city problems that increased the crime rate, and also in response to the liberal attitudes toward criminality that dominated the cultural revolution
- Resulted in harsher sentencing laws and greater demands upon police departments and prisons nationwide during the 1980s, as well as a strong cultural emphasis upon punishment and incarceration (as opposed to rehabilitative efforts)

- 💬 Involved critical accomplishments by American scientists, such as the development of the hydrogen bomb (a more powerful weapon than the atomic bomb) and the moon landing
- Occurred during the 1950s and 1960s, respectively, as the result of the arms race and the Cold War "space race" rivalry with the Soviet Union
- Resulted in increased American international prestige, as well as a dramatic increase in military might and resultant political power

Additional Cultural Changes of the Postwar Period (1945–1980)

One of the American cultural developments of the postwar era that has undoubtedly stood the test of time is the popularity of **rock and roll music**! This iconic genre, which has become a staple of our pop culture and is now celebrated throughout the world, was considered shocking and decadent by many when it debuted in the 1950s. While almost amusingly tame by modern standards, the early performances of **Elvis Presley** (known affectionately as the "King of Rock and Roll") were scandalous because the singer would gyrate his hips as he danced to the music. Many conservative and religious leaders denounced Elvis as a moral threat to America's youth, and some television stations would film him only from the waist up during his performances.

Ask Yourself...

The popular music of today that stirs controversy, mostly among the older generations, features graphic sexuality, drug references and violent imagery, and sometimes even satanic material. Might future generations rightfully laugh at how prudish and old-fashioned 21st-century Americans were to be morally offended at such music, which will seem tame by then, just like we might find it amusing that the 1950s generation was offended by Elvis's hips? Alternatively, is there in fact an objective moral difference between the two, and a line between acceptable and unacceptable influences on young people that can at some point be crossed? If so, have we crossed it yet?

Cultural Conflict !

The postwar period is perhaps best known for the deep and painful cultural divisions between Americans who valued tradition and orthodoxy and those who favored radically different lifestyles. The conflict tended to fall along generational lines, with older individuals dismayed at the seemingly self-centered and irreverent behavior of the young people of the "**counterculture**" movement. The following chart outlines the differences between the counterculture and the conservative traditionalists.

	The Counterculture	The Conservative Traditionalists
Prominent or Notable Members	**Beatniks:** The 1950s forerunners of the hippies who expressed their creativity and nonconformity through poetry, unconventional art, and bohemian lifestyles **Hippies:** The most prominent members of the counterculture movement, who dominated the 1960s and early 1970s **Yippies:** Hippies who were known for extreme left-wing political activism	The **Religious Right,** an informal coalition of Americans with traditional Christian values; the term is often associated with fundamentalist and evangelical Protestants. Other Religious Leaders Various Americans, often middle-aged or older, who rejected liberal principles and radical social change
Stance Toward Authority	Vehemently challenged and rejected most forms of authority, particularly those associated with the established order	Promoted respect for established authority, so long as that authority acted within accepted moral boundaries
Sexual Morality	Eagerly supported the **sexual revolution,** which involved greatly relaxed standards of sexual conduct; the counterculture is often associated with the "free love" philosophy, in which sex is encouraged without fidelity or ongoing commitment to a partner.	💬 Denounced sexual relations outside of marriage as immoral and detrimental to the well-being of the nation

Drug Use	Adopted the use of certain drugs (especially marijuana and hallucinogens such as LSD) as an integral part of their culture	Condemned illegal drug use and fought for the criminalization of LSD
Religious Views	Frequently explored Eastern religions or rejected formal religious teachings altogether, while sometimes seeking "purer" and more authentic adherence to established Christian doctrine (e.g., communal living)	Valued spirituality in accordance with traditional (usually Christian) teachings
Political Opinions	Typically advocated strongly for civil rights, equality for the disenfranchised, and environmental concerns; expressed opposition to military action and were highly critical of the U.S. government; were much more likely to support abortion rights than were conservatives	Were more likely to want to maintain the domestic status quo and to support U.S. government action; opposed abortion
Gender Attitudes	Advocated somewhat inconsistently for women's rights and gender equality, with women in the counterculture much more likely to adopt the cause; the feminist movement gained greater support among men in the 1970s.	Tended to reject nontraditional gender roles

Fashion and Appearance	Favored controversial fashion statements such as long hair and sideburns for men, revealing clothing for women, and flamboyant styles for both	Preferred traditionally conservative clothing and grooming for both men and women

The Counterculture vs. the Culture of Conservative America

The Supreme Court and the Sexual Revolution ❶

Counterculture values, along with the women's movement, got a major boost with two critical Supreme Court decisions concerning contraception and abortion. With some of the fear of unwanted pregnancy and forced parenthood abated, Americans were considerably more willing to reject the conventional sexual morality of the previous generations.

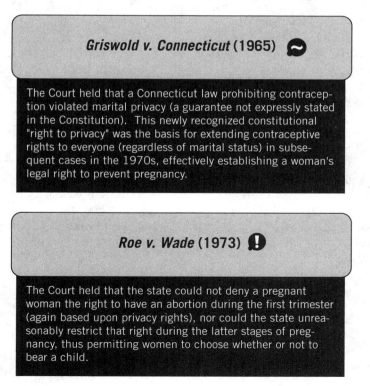

Griswold v. Connecticut (1965) 〜

The Court held that a Connecticut law prohibiting contraception violated marital privacy (a guarantee not expressly stated in the Constitution). This newly recognized constitutional "right to privacy" was the basis for extending contraceptive rights to everyone (regardless of marital status) in subsequent cases in the 1970s, effectively establishing a woman's legal right to prevent pregnancy.

Roe v. Wade (1973) ❶

The Court held that the state could not deny a pregnant woman the right to have an abortion during the first trimester (again based upon privacy rights), nor could the state unreasonably restrict that right during the latter stages of pregnancy, thus permitting women to choose whether or not to bear a child.

The Culture Clash and the Era of Assassination ⓘ

The anger and intolerance that arose during the 1960s as the result of cultural discord is exemplified by a shocking string of assassinations of prominent political figures. While the perpetrators of these various crimes had very different motivations and agendas (some of which were actually nonpolitical), the murders of so many liberal leaders served to fuel the existing "us versus them" mentality. The following chart describes four of these assassinations.

John F. Kennedy	Malcolm X
• The 35th president of the United States • Shot on November 22, 1963, by Lee Harvey Oswald, an attention-seeking and emotionally troubled young man (although various conspiracy theories question Oswald's guilt and whether or not he acted alone) • The assassination caused cultural conflict because of Kennedy's popularity and liberalism, and because of the accusations of conspiracy and governmental cover-up that surrounded his murder.	• A civil rights activist and highly controversial leader of the **Nation of Islam** African American political movement, who advocated violence and was frequently accused of racism • Shot on February 21, 1965, by Nation of Islam members with whom he had quarreled (having recently left the organization), although some have questioned the guilt of the purported murderers • The assassination caused cultural conflict because Malcolm X was such an extremely divisive figure, and also because conspiracy theories of white involvement were proposed.

Martin Luther King, Jr.	Robert F. Kennedy
• The most prominent civil rights leader of the postwar period, known for nonviolent methods of protest • Shot on April 4, 1968, by James Earl Ray, a white fugitive and petty criminal; some have suggested that Ray did not act alone. • The assassination caused cultural conflict because the murder was interracial, resulting in widespread rioting, arson, and looting by blacks, and many deaths occurred; theories about government conspiracies and a contract killing were rife.	• The younger brother of John F. Kennedy, a former U.S. Attorney General, and senator from New York; a presidential candidate at the time of his assassination who was known for his liberal political stance • Shot on June 5, 1968, by Sirhan Sirhan, a Palestinian immigrant angered by Kennedy's support for Israel in the Middle East conflict • The assassination caused cultural conflict because Kennedy had been an iconic figure to many Americans, some of whom, after so many assassinations, doubted that change could occur through peaceful means.

Prominent Political Assassinations in 1960s America 💀

Ask Yourself...

While the heyday of the counterculture ended decades ago, in many ways the movement still exerts an influence. From fashion and music preferences, environmental awareness, and egalitarian politics, to an ever-present willingness to question authority, one could argue that Americans today still have a little bit of "hippie" in them. In what way do you think the counterculture youth of the 20th century made their most indelible mark on 21st century America?

PERIOD 9 (1980–Present):
Entering into the 21st Century

The post–Cold War period of American history is still being created. Some of the ongoing story is a reaction to recent history, such as conservative and liberal backlashes to past events. Other factors shaping our current history have to do with technology and globalization—both of which have brought people in closer contact with one another in recent years than any period in human history.

Conservatism and the "New Right"

By the late 1970s, many Americans had grown tired of the conflicts of the previous decade. Many were uncomfortable with the growing cynicism toward political leaders. Jimmy Carter hit a raw nerve—and disturbed many Americans—when he complained in a speech that the people were letting themselves be overtaken by a "crisis of confidence." This came to be known as "the malaise speech," though Carter never used the word *malaise* in it. The next couple decades would usher in a new wave of conservatism.

Ronald Reagan

Republican **Ronald Reagan** saw that the nation was ready for a major change and won the 1980 election by a landslide.

NOTABLE FIGURE:

Appeal of Ronald Reagan
- Reagan stressed the positive aspects of America (seemingly in contrast to Carter).
- His likeable, "can-do" attitude appealed even to those who disagreed with his politics.
- He presented himself as an "outsider" (ironically so, too, did Jimmy Carter four years previous).

Trickle-Down Theory

Central to President Reagan's domestic policy was the idea of **trickle-down economics**, later known as "**Reaganomics**." Economists called the theory "**supply-side economics**" because its purpose was to stimulate the economy by increasing supply (creating an environment for businesses to develop more goods and services) rather than demand (giving consumers more opportunity to purchase goods and services).

The Theory	
Removing obstacles to the creators of supply (industries) would increase the wealth of American businesses.	The wealth at the top of the economy (both corporate and individual) will "trickle down" to the middle class and working class.

The Policies			
Corporate tax cuts	Deregulation in banking, industry, and the environment (all of these, Reagan argued, stood in the way of businesses maximizing profits)	Cutting the income tax across the board	To pay for the tax cuts, Reagan advocated cutting spending on federal programs such as welfare, food stamps, and Medicaid.

The Results			
The tax cuts increased Reagan's popularity initially, but many complained that the tax cuts hurt the poor, who pay little in income tax, but depend on federal enfranchisement programs to survive.	The country continued in a recession for almost two years before the economy revived. Even then, results were mixed.	Rather than reinvesting in the economy, as supply-side economics suggested, the rich used the money saved on taxes to buy luxury items, which did not see the money trickle down.	Although inflation subsided, there was continued criticism that, under Reagan, the rich were getting richer while the poor were getting poorer.

"Read My Lips"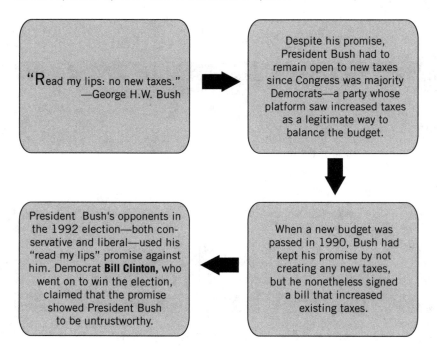

Riding the wave of tax cuts, President Reagan's vice president, **George H.W. Bush** won the 1988 presidential election over Democrat Michael Dukakis. In the 1988 Republican National Convention, Bush delivered his acceptance speech with a memorable quote:

"Read my lips: no new taxes."
—George H.W. Bush

Despite his promise, President Bush had to remain open to new taxes since Congress was majority Democrats—a party whose platform saw increased taxes as a legitimate way to balance the budget.

When a new budget was passed in 1990, Bush had kept his promise by not creating any new taxes, but he nonetheless signed a bill that increased existing taxes.

President Bush's opponents in the 1992 election—both conservative and liberal—used his "read my lips" promise against him. Democrat **Bill Clinton,** who went on to win the election, claimed that the promise showed President Bush to be untrustworthy.

Contract with America

Two years into the Clinton presidency, the Democrats lost their long-standing majority in Congress. Following a rough start in which the Clinton Administration experienced some stumbles in getting legislation passed, notably Health Care Reform and Campaign Finance Reform, the GOP enjoyed an enormous victory in the 1994 midterm elections. Led by Newt Gingrich, who would become Speaker of the House, Republicans rallied behind a common set of promises known as the Contract with America.

Contract with America

- Reduce taxes
- Consolidate government programs
- Reform welfare entitlement programs

Welfare Reform Act 🛈

While the Republicans won back control of the Congress in 1994, their power was limited by Clinton's executive power. Clinton cooperated with the Republicans in Congress on some matters, especially reforming welfare and giving the states more control over administering welfare benefits. This led to him winning the 1996 presidential election over Bob Dole.

💬 In 1993, Bill Clinton made a speech to Congress to announce his intentions to create universal healthcare. He appointed his wife, Hillary Clinton, to lead the campaign. Heavy conservative opposition (and funding form the health insurance industry) led to widespread opposition to the plan with critics dubbing it "Hillarycare." Sixteen years after the bill died, President Barack Obama signed the Affordable Care Act, which achieved many of the same goals of universal coverage outlined by the Clinton plan. In contrast to the 1994 bill, Democrats wore the derisive label, in this case "Obamacare," as a badge of pride.

Block Grants 💬

Many conservatives who felt that the federal government played too large a role in their lives advocated for **block grants**, which limited the influence of the federal government on local issues. Advocates for categorical grants, the more traditional form of grant distribution, claimed that block grants could not always ensure that those who most need the federal aid would receive it.

- Traditional Federal Grants (categorical grants): Money is given to a local entity (state or municipality) for a specifically defined purpose.
- Block Grants: Money is given to a local entity, allowing that entity freedom to decide how it is to be spent.

Ronald Reagan frequently claimed that he sought to decrease the size of the federal government. He called his plan the **New Federalism**, but it was quite the opposite of federalism—its goal was to shift power from the national government to the states. Reagan suggested that the states take complete responsibility for welfare, food stamps, and other social welfare programs currently funded at the national level; in return, the national government would assume the entire cost of Medicaid. Reagan's goal was never accomplished, however. The states feared that the shift would greatly increase the cost of state government, which would require unpopular tax increases at the state level.

Growth of the National Debt 🔔

Government spending increased while government revenues shrank, forcing the government to borrow money. Congress blamed the deficit on Reagan's tax cuts and called for a tax increase. Reagan, on the other hand, argued that the fault was with Congress, which refused to decrease funding for social welfare programs at the rate the president requested. Neither side budged, and as a result, the federal deficit reached record heights during the Reagan administration.

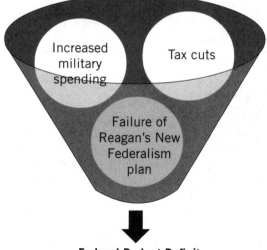

Federal Budget Deficit

It was not until the Clinton presidency that the budget was finally balanced (and then returned to deficit status in the George W. Bush administration).

Debate over Social Security Reform 💬

One of the primary drivers of the federal deficit is Social Security. Created as a safety net for the elderly and disabled during the New Deal, Social Security encountered a major test in the 1990s and 2000s as Baby Boomers began to reach retirement age. For the first time, there was more money being paid out by the Social Security Administration than was being paid into the system.

On the one hand...
- Social Security is the government's largest spending program.
- Reforming Social Security could mean increasing payments from workers, means-testing (not paying to those who are well off), or decreasing payments to recipients.

But on the other hand...
- People have spent a lifetime paying into the system. It would not be fair to suddenly cut them off from receiving what has been promised.
- Many elderly and disabled people have little to no income outside of Social Security benefits. Major alterations to this program would involve creating an alternate social safety net.

Liberal Backlash ❗

Frustrations with Republican president **George W. Bush**'s War in Iraq and his handling of Hurricane Katrina, as well as stories of corruption in the Republican ranks, led to Democrats retaking the House of Representatives in 2006. One reason this election was historic was that it led to the election of Nancy Pelosi to Speaker of the House—the first woman to hold this position.

The election of **Barack Obama** in 2008 and his reelection in 2012 led many political observers to conclude that the conservative resurgence has ebbed and that American history has entered a new phase. However, the 2016 election of Donald Trump may have called that speculation into question.

Citizens United vs. FEC 🔊

During the 2008 Democratic primary election, a group called Citizens United tried to air an ad critical of candidate Hillary Clinton. However, their film violated a Federal Election Commission rule. In the 2010 case *Citizens United vs. FEC*, the Supreme Court ruled 5-4 that such rules were a violation of 1st Amendment rights, declaring that money donated for political speech was indeed free speech. This ruling changed the dynamic of the 2010 midterm election, as well as future elections, since it eliminated restrictions on how much money individuals could donate to **Super PACs** (groups that raise money for political purposes).

Rise of the Tea Party 💬

Buoyed by resentment over the passage of the **Affordable Care Act,** (colloquially known as "Obamacare"), a law that removed barriers that had previously prevented Americans from receiving health insurance, conservatives around the country organized under a banner known as the **Tea Party**, a reference to the 1773 Boston Tea party that rebelled against British taxation. The group even adopted the Gadsden Flag of the American Revolution as its symbol. Conservative organization paid off in the 2010 midterm elections:

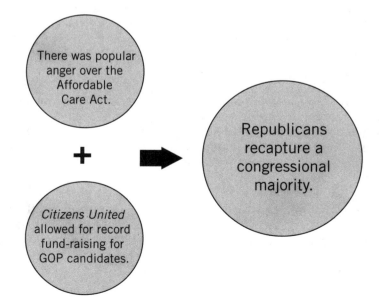

Ask Yourself...

Which elements from the social, political, and legal changes of the 1960s and 1970s contributed to the conservative resurgence of the 1980s and 1990s?

Science, Technology, Business, Banking 🔊

The close of the 20th century brought with it radical changes in the way Americans do business. Local economies could no longer be viewed in isolation, as the affect of the larger global community needed now to be considered. Further, the economy was jump-started by a revolution in digital technology that brought about new business opportunities, as well as fast-paced breakthroughs that quickly made relatively new technology obsolete.

Globalism 🔊

One significant change from the 1990s was the acceleration of **globalism**. As opposed to nationalism, in which a nation's affairs are focused inward, globalism promotes an interconnectivity of nations by way of economic agreements (typically promoting free trade reducing tariffs), immigration, and military intervention.

Trade Agreements 🔊

The first significant event of the Clinton presidency was the establishment of the **North American Free Trade Agreement (NAFTA)**. Although the treaty had been negotiated by the administration of George H.W. Bush, Clinton signed it into law in 1993. In a way, it was similar to the global treaty from 1947, the **General Agreement on Tariffs and Trade (GATT)**, which sought to reduce trade barriers such as tariffs and preferential treatment. In the case of NAFTA, the agreement focused on eliminating trade barriers among Canada, Mexico, and the United States. The agreement was largely supported by American corporate interests and derided by unions.

| American companies could increase their business in neighboring countries without the fear of high tariffs. | Companies could easily move factories out of the U.S.in order to reduce costs with lower wages and operation costs. |

Digital Revolution ❗

The worldwide interconnectivity caused by globalism is both a cause and an effect of the **digital revolution**. As digital technology such as personal computers and cellular phones became easier to produce, they became cheaper to purchase. Americans moved both personal and professional business to these technologies due to the exponential increases in data storage offered by new devices. As you can probably guess from the data below, the twenty years between 1990 and 2010 saw significant changes in the ways Americans lived.

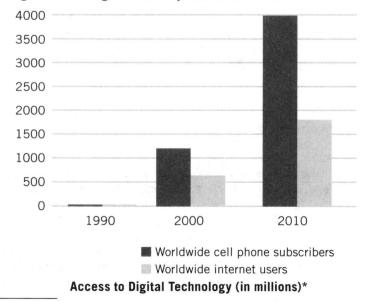

■ Worldwide cell phone subscribers
▧ Worldwide internet users
Access to Digital Technology (in millions)*

*Source: www.worldmapper.org

Manufacturing Jobs Go Away ❗

From 1990 until 2010, manufacturing jobs in the United States decreased by a third. Around the turn of the century, those jobs became retail jobs. However, those retail jobs were impacted by the 2008–2009 recession and many Americans found new jobs in the booming healthcare industry.

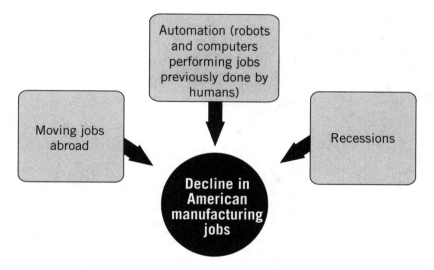

Decline of Unions ❗

Throughout the second half of the 20th century, and in particular, its final three decades, union power and membership declined. Besides increased spending on the part of industry to advocate for anti-labor legislation, there are some key factors at play:

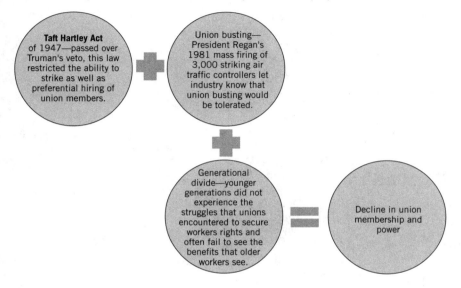

Wage Stagnation ❗

Economists have noted that one of the most notable effects of a decline in union membership is the growth in income inequality starting in the latter part of the 20th century. The inability to collectively bargain on the scale that unions could from World War II through the 1970s has led to a stagnation in wages. As union membership, which was 34 percent in 1979, fell to 10 percent in 2010, there has also been a notable consolidation of wealth in the upper echelon of American earners:

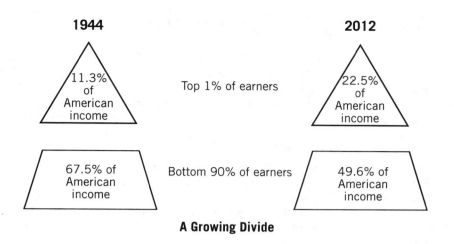

1944		2012
11.3% of American income	Top 1% of earners	22.5% of American income
67.5% of American income	Bottom 90% of earners	49.6% of American income

A Growing Divide

Repeal of Glass-Steagall ❗

In 1933, President Roosevelt signed the **Glass-Steagall Act** (also known as the **Banking Act of 1933**). The act stemmed from the volatility of American banks leading up to the Great Depression. Banks were able to use their commercial deposits (from individuals and businesses) to speculate in the investment market. Since the investment market was not always predictable, banks that used commercial deposits for this purpose were often unstable. The Glass-Steagall Act forced banks to avoid a conflict of interest by deciding whether they would be commercial banks or investment banks and prohibited them from participating in more than one of these operations.

The **Gramm-Leach-Bliley Act** of 1999 effectively did away with this provision. Many economists, such as Joseph Stiglitz, argue that it is no surprise that within a decade of the repeal of Glass-Steagall, the American economy was brought to its knees by a recession stemming from banks offering home loans based on speculation of the value of those homes.

 Ask Yourself...

1. How did the digital revolution impact American culture?
2. How did the American economy at the dawn of the 21st century differ from the economy of the mid-20th century? What factors account for this difference?

Demographic Shifts 🔴

The latter decades of the 20th century ushered in some dramatic changes in demographics and the opportunities offered to those who were previously kept at a distance from mainstream acceptance. As was the case a century ago, when predominantly Eastern European immigrants arrived by the millions onto America's shores, immigration in recent decades has significantly affected the shape and tenor of American society. In 1890, approximately 86 percent of immigrants to the United States were from Europe. From the 1970s through today, however, the fastest-growing ethnic minorities in the United States have been **Hispanics** and **Asians**, and according to the 2000 census, Hispanics now outnumber African Americans as the largest minority in the United States. Much of this growth among Asians and Hispanics has been fueled by immigration.

Migration to South and Southwest 🔴

As jobs in the "rust belt" (Northeast and Midwestern manufacturing towns) began to fade due to automation and outsourcing, many Americans moved south and west to find employment in the growing service and technology industries.

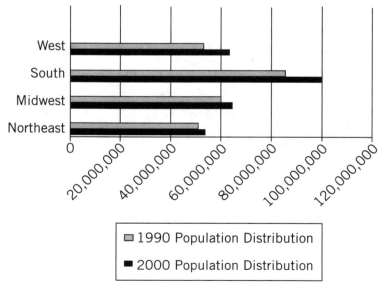

Population Distribution in the United States

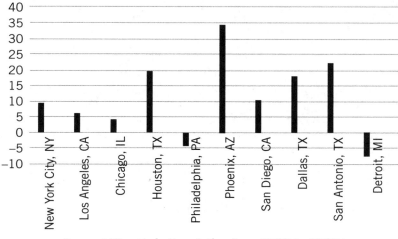

**Percent Change in Population from 1990 to 2000
in the Ten Largest U.S. Cities**

Increased Immigration ❗

With each new wave of immigration, ethnic enclaves sprout in big cities and neighborhoods, contributing to America's unique mixture of
peoples. A century ago, there were communities such as Little Italy in
New York City or Chinatown in San Francisco. Today, reflecting more
recent population trends, there are places like Little Havana in Miami
and Little Saigon in Orange County, California.

Who?	Hispanic	Asian
How many?	Population increased from 6 million in 1960 to 50 million today.	Population increased by 70% in the 1980s (about 3 million in the decade). Today there are about 12.8 million Asian immigrants.
From where?	Mexico, Puerto Rico, Cuba, El Salvador, Guatemala, Honduras, and Nicaragua	Mostly Philippines, China, South Korea, India
To where?	California, Texas, Florida, Southwest	Largely settled in California

Anti-immigration Sentiment ❶

As with other immigration waves, such as during the mid- and late 19th century, opposition to immigration generally stems from a fear of an oversaturated labor market, a strain on public resources, and/or xenophobia and racism. The increasing racial and ethnic diversity of our population has sparked heated debate not only on immigration policy but also on issues such as bilingual education and affirmative action. The discussion of immigration policy can take on various forms:

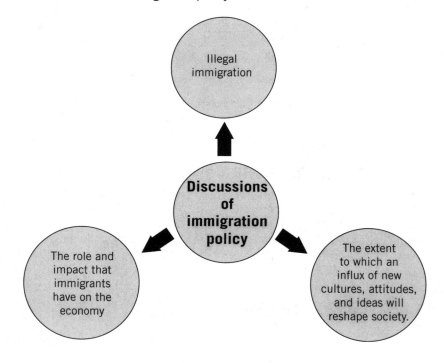

Solutions to Illegal Immigration 💬

Tensions created by this new wave of immigration have resulted in various measures to curb **illegal immigration**.

Left-wing solutions include amnesty, or offering a permanent home in the United States to undocumented immigrants.	Moderate solutions do not offer amnesty, but may allow both low-skilled and high-skilled workers into the United States on a temporary basis to provide needed labor and services.	Right-wing solutions make it difficult for undocumented workers to continue living in the United States, including deportation and abolishing bilingual education.

In 1986, Congress passed the **Simpson-Mazzoli Act** (also known as the **Immigration Reform and Control Act of 1986**), which outlawed the deliberate employment of undocumented immigrants and granted legal status to some of those who entered the United States before 1982.

Diversity: Asset or Liability? ❶

It is clear that the United States is in the midst of major demographic changes that are visible today. Even political parties openly attempt to attract Hispanics in recognition of their potential political influence.

Arguments for diversity as an asset
- Immigrants enrich the development of our economy and society.
- American identity has always evolved with new waves of immigration, and the economy and American culture are well served by the market forces that encourage access to groups who were previously excluded.

Arguments for diversity as a liability
- Immigration places a burden on social services.
- There exists an American identity that is threatened by the presence of cultures that are not presumed to fit into that identity. This can be observed by frustrations with an increase in multilingual services and media outlets offering access to Hispanics and Asians.

Gender Roles ❗

Women have taken on larger roles in professional settings in the 21st century; however, many claim the glass ceiling (unfulfilled promises for advancement) still remains. The fact that the average age for first marriage has increased points to the fact that women are prioritizing their careers before settling down to have families. Further, the 2008 recession affected jobs traditionally held by men more than it affected jobs traditionally held by women. Therefore, women were increasingly a family's primary breadwinner at the start of the second decade of the 2000s.

Dramatic Increase in Women Elected to Political Offices 💬

Along with changing gender roles, the United States has seen an increase in women elected to political office since the dawn of the 21st century. Besides Hillary Clinton's presidential campaign in 2016, both Geraldine Ferraro and Sarah Palin were nominated as running mates in the presidential campaigns of 1984 and 2008 respectively. Further, the number of women elected to Congress has increased sharply.

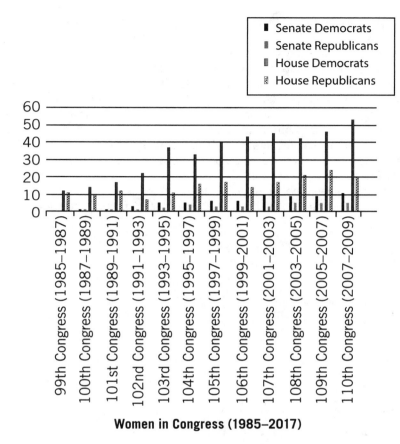

Women in Congress (1985–2017)

Rise of Nontraditional Families ❗

In addition to changing demographics, analysts have also noticed new patterns in family structures over the latter half of the 20th century. While 87 percent of children lived in a two-parent household in 1960, only 73 percent did in 2000, and 69 percent do today. Consistent with this is the rise in one-parent households: 9 percent of children lived in a one-parent household in 1960 compared with 26 percent today.*

---

*Source: Pew Research Center. http://www.pewsocialtrends.org/2015/12/17/1-the-american-family-today

LGBT Rights 〜

The 21st century also saw rapid developments in LGBT rights (although not all groups, in particular the transgender community, received full legal protections). As recently as 1993, the federal government created a **"Don't Ask, Don't Tell"** policy, which was intended to keep gay, lesbian, and bisexual soldiers from being unjustly dismissed from the military. The LGBT community harshly criticized the policy as it forced sexual minority servicepersons to keep part of their lives secret. The policy was repealed in 2011, among a decade long wave of states recognizing same-sex unions and marriage. In 2015, the Supreme Court declared in *Obergefell v. Hodges* that, under the 14th Amendment, neither states nor the federal government can prohibit full marriage rights to same-sex couples.

 Ask Yourself...

1. In what ways have changing demographics presented political challenges in the United States?
2. To what extent do America's changing demographics reflect continuities in American history?

1980s and 1990s Foreign Policy ❗

In foreign policy, Reagan sought to end the Cold War by winning it on every front he could in any way he could. He went as far as to support repressive regimes and right-wing insurgents in El Salvador, Panama, the Philippines, and Mozambique, all because they opposed communism. However, following the Cold War, the U.S. foreign policy of George H.W. Bush and Bill Clinton shifted its focus toward the Middle East and human rights.

Fall of the Soviet Bloc 🔔

Reagan's greatest successes in foreign policy came in U.S.-Soviet relations.

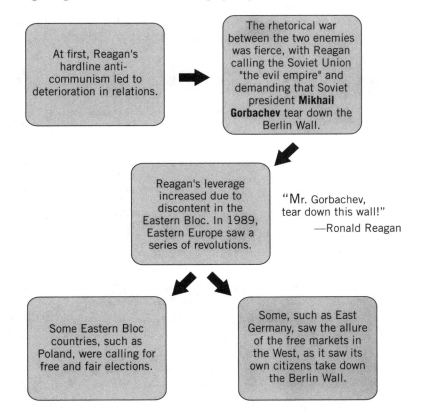

At first, Reagan's hardline anti-communism led to deterioration in relations.

➡️

The rhetorical war between the two enemies was fierce, with Reagan calling the Soviet Union "the evil empire" and demanding that Soviet president **Mikhail Gorbachev** tear down the Berlin Wall.

Reagan's leverage increased due to discontent in the Eastern Bloc. In 1989, Eastern Europe saw a series of revolutions.

"Mr. Gorbachev, tear down this wall!"
—Ronald Reagan

Some Eastern Bloc countries, such as Poland, were calling for free and fair elections.

Some, such as East Germany, saw the allure of the free markets in the West, as it saw its own citizens take down the Berlin Wall.

Diplomacy between the United States and U.S.S.R. 🔔

American-Soviet relations were actually helped by Mikhail Gorbachev's rise to power. Gorbachev is best known for his economic policy of **perestroika**, or restructuring, and his social reforms collectively referred to as **glasnost**, or openness. Gorbachev loosened Soviet control of Eastern Europe, increased personal liberties in the Soviet Union, and eventually allowed some forms of free-market commerce in the Communist country. Reagan and Gorbachev met frequently and ultimately negotiated a withdrawal of nuclear warheads from Europe.

Nuclear Weapons ❗

As they turned more toward diplomacy, rather than rapidly escalating larger nuclear weapon stockpiles, the two superpowers were left wondering what to do with the thousands of warheads they had compiled. Negotiations to limit stockpiles began as early as the 1960s.

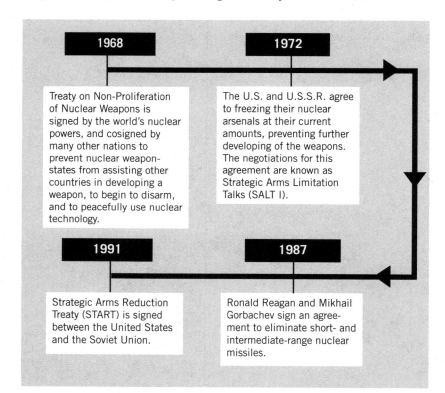

1968

Treaty on Non-Proliferation of Nuclear Weapons is signed by the world's nuclear powers, and cosigned by many other nations to prevent nuclear weapon-states from assisting other countries in developing a weapon, to begin to disarm, and to peacefully use nuclear technology.

1972

The U.S. and U.S.S.R. agree to freezing their nuclear arsenals at their current amounts, preventing further developing of the weapons. The negotiations for this agreement are known as Strategic Arms Limitation Talks (SALT I).

1991

Strategic Arms Reduction Treaty (START) is signed between the United States and the Soviet Union.

1987

Ronald Reagan and Mikhail Gorbachev sign an agreement to eliminate short- and intermediate-range nuclear missiles.

Increased Military Spending ❗

Faced with mounting concerns about the capabilities of the "evil empire" (even though Gorbachev had declared his intention to stop the arms race), Reagan convinced Congress to greatly increase military spending. However, he would face blowback due to the impact that this plan had on the deficit (a condition that occurs when government spending outpaces revenues).

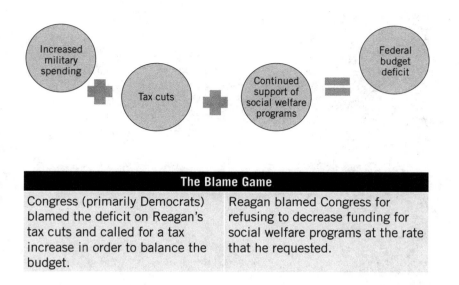

The Blame Game	
Congress (primarily Democrats) blamed the deficit on Reagan's tax cuts and called for a tax increase in order to balance the budget.	Reagan blamed Congress for refusing to decrease funding for social welfare programs at the rate that he requested.

Neither side budged, and as a result, the federal deficit reached record heights during the Reagan administration.

End of the Cold War 🛈

Following the revolutions in Eastern Bloc countries and slow economic development in the wake of *perestroika*, the Soviet Union seemed to be on the verge of collapse. In 1991, Soviet republics met to withdraw from the Soviet Union, turning the once-great superpower into Russia and a series of newly independent countries. Gorbachev resigned immediately following the dissolution of the U.S.S.R.

Post–Cold War Military Interventions 🛈

U.S. foreign policy in the post–Cold War era has largely focused on political stability in the Middle East and defending human rights.

Persian Gulf War	• Years: 1990–1991 • President: George H.W. Bush • Conflict: **Saddam Hussein,** the leader of Iraq, invaded Iraq's tiny but oil-rich neighbor Kuwait. When Saddam seized Kuwait's oil fields and threatened the world's access to Middle East oil, Washington reacted immediately. The war ended quickly with a U.S. victory and few American casualties. • Outcome: Although Iraq was required to submit to UN inspectors to ensure that there were no **weapons of mass destruction,** Saddam Hussein remained in power
Somalia	• Year: 1993 • President: George H.W. Bush and Bill Clinton • Conflict: Food and supplies sent to aid starving Somalians were being seized by warlords. The United States sent forces to protect the supplies. • Outcome: After U.S. troops were killed in the Battle of Mogadishu, the intervention lost support at home. The president heeded popular opinion and withdrew troops the following year. Somalia went on to suffer from a fractious power vacuum.
The Balkans	• Year: 1999 • President: Bill Clinton • Conflict: Slobodan Milošević, president of Serbia, was conducting a brutal policy of "ethnic cleansing" against Balkan Muslims. Clinton supported a bombing campaign in the former Yugoslavia under the auspices of NATO. • Outcome: Milošević was eventually tried and convicted for committing "crimes against humanity."

 Ask Yourself...

1. To what extent did U.S. foreign policy accelerate the collapse of the Soviet Union? To what extent was the collapse internal?
2. How did American foreign policy after the Cold War differ from its foreign policy during the Cold War?

Post 9/11 Foreign Policy ❗

The 21st century has seen the United States proceed in many ways as the world's "leading superpower." With the absence of a Soviet Union, the United States moved into the new millennium with unquestionably the strongest military and economy. Many American leaders see the United States as having a responsibility to provide international leadership.

9/11 ❗

America entered a new phase of foreign policy when **Osama bin Laden**'s **Al Qaeda** organization attacked the World Trade Center and the Pentagon on September 11, 2001. Two planes flew into the World Trade Center's Twin Towers, and one flew into the Pentagon. A fourth plane was allegedly planned to hit the White House, but passengers overcame the hijackers long enough to crash the plane into a field in Pennsylvania. In total, almost 3,000 civilians were killed on 9/11.

Bin Laden offered three reasons for the attacks:

- The United States supports Israel, which his organization would like to see removed from the planet.
- The United States has troops stationed in Saudi Arabia, which is considered sacred land in Islam.
- The United States is the primary agent of globalization, which Al Qaeda believes is infecting Islamic culture.

There were two main policy consequences of the 9/11 attacks, one domestic and one foreign:

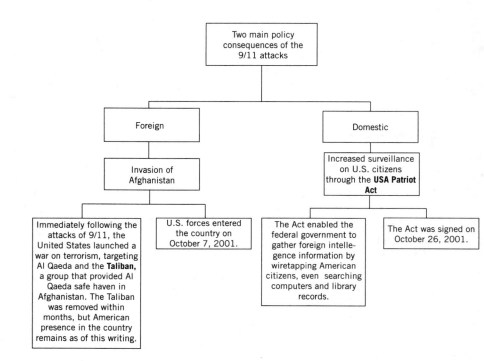

Iraq War !

Allegations, not supported by any evidence, that Saddam Hussein helped to orchestrate 9/11, as well as his ongoing human rights violations against his own people and rumors of weapons of mass destruction (which were later found to be false), led the Bush administration to invade Iraq in March of 2003. United States armed forces remained in Iraq until 2011. Both the War in Iraq and the War in Afghanistan fell under the United States' larger foreign policy known as the **War on Terror**.

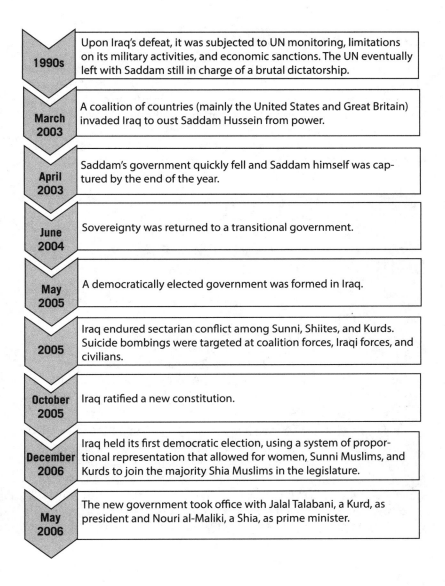

1990s
Upon Iraq's defeat, it was subjected to UN monitoring, limitations on its military activities, and economic sanctions. The UN eventually left with Saddam still in charge of a brutal dictatorship.

March 2003
A coalition of countries (mainly the United States and Great Britain) invaded Iraq to oust Saddam Hussein from power.

April 2003
Saddam's government quickly fell and Saddam himself was captured by the end of the year.

June 2004
Sovereignty was returned to a transitional government.

May 2005
A democratically elected government was formed in Iraq.

2005
Iraq endured sectarian conflict among Sunni, Shiites, and Kurds. Suicide bombings were targeted at coalition forces, Iraqi forces, and civilians.

October 2005
Iraq ratified a new constitution.

December 2006
Iraq held its first democratic election, using a system of proportional representation that allowed for women, Sunni Muslims, and Kurds to join the majority Shia Muslims in the legislature.

May 2006
The new government took office with Jalal Talabani, a Kurd, as president and Nouri al-Maliki, a Shia, as prime minister.

Climate Change 🔰

In the age of globalization, it has become impossible to keep environmental policy local. The United States, along with the rest of the world, has seen increasing global temperatures in the final decades of the 20th century and the first decades of the 21st century. While the scientific community largely has come to a consensus that human activity, such as carbon emissions, has accelerated an overall increase in global temperatures, policy makers in the United States are split on the issue.

Consequences of Climate Change	• Increased temperatures raise the sea level, threatening coastal towns and cities. • Unpredictable weather events • Damage to animal habitats, particularly in arctic regions
Solutions to Climate Change	• Some government programs have incentivized alternative energy sources, such as wind and solar energy. • The global community has investigated ways to cooperate to reduce carbon emissions, such as the 1997 **Kyoto Protocol,** which the United States agreed to under President Clinton, but subsequently refused to ratify under President Bush.
Challenges	• While Democrats have largely supported legislation to limit carbon emissions, Republicans and large businesses have provided a stumbling block, questioning the science behind climate changes. • Dependence on fossil fuels remains, with ongoing calls to find new sources of petroleum, including in the **Arctic National Wildlife Refuge (ANWR)** in Alaska.

 Ask Yourself...

In what ways are the challenges of the 21st century rooted in 20th-century events?

NOTES

The Princeton Review®
International Offices Listing

China (Beijing)
1501 Building A,
Disanji Creative Zone,
No.66 West Section of North 4th Ring Road Beijing
Tel: +86-10-62684481/2/3
Email: tprkor01@chol.com
Website: www.tprbeijing.com

China (Shanghai)
1010 Kaixuan Road
Building B, 5/F
Changning District, Shanghai, China 200052
Sara Beattie, Owner: Email: sbeattie@sarabeattie.com
Tel: +86-21-5108-2798
Fax: +86-21-6386-1039
Website: www.princetonreviewshanghai.com

Hong Kong
5th Floor, Yardley Commercial Building
1-6 Connaught Road West, Sheung Wan, Hong Kong
(MTR Exit C)
Sara Beattie, Owner: Email: sbeattie@sarabeattie.com
Tel: +852-2507-9380
Fax: +852-2827-4630
Website: www.princetonreviewhk.com

India (Mumbai)
Score Plus Academy
Office No.15, Fifth Floor
Manek Mahal 90
Veer Nariman Road
Next to Hotel Ambassador
Churchgate, Mumbai 400020
Maharashtra, India
Ritu Kalwani: Email: director@score-plus.com
Tel: + 91 22 22846801 / 39 / 41
Website: www.score-plus.com

India (New Delhi)
South Extension
K-16, Upper Ground Floor
South Extension Part-1,
New Delhi-110049
Aradhana Mahna: aradhana@manyagroup.com
Monisha Banerjee: monisha@manyagroup.com
Ruchi Tomar: ruchi.tomar@manyagroup.com
Rishi Josan: Rishi.josan@manyagroup.com
Vishal Goswamy: vishal.goswamy@manyagroup.com
Tel: +91-11-64501603/ 4, +91-11-65028379
Website: www.manyagroup.com

Lebanon
463 Bliss Street
AlFarra Building - 2nd floor
Ras Beirut
Beirut, Lebanon
Hassan Coudsi: Email: hassan.coudsi@review.com
Tel: +961-1-367-688
Website: www.princetonreviewlebanon.com

Korea
945-25 Young Shin Building
25 Daechi-Dong, Kangnam-gu
Seoul, Korea 135-280
Yong-Hoon Lee: Email: TPRKor01@chollian.net
In-Woo Kim: Email: iwkim@tpr.co.kr
Tel: + 82-2-554-7762
Fax: +82-2-453-9466
Website: www.tpr.co.kr

Kuwait
ScorePlus Learning Center
Salmiyah Block 3, Street 2 Building 14
Post Box: 559, Zip 1306, Safat, Kuwait
Email: infokuwait@score-plus.com
Tel: +965-25-75-48-02 / 8
Fax: +965-25-75-46-02
Website: www.scorepluseducation.com

Malaysia
Sara Beattie MDC Sdn Bhd
Suites 18E & 18F
18th Floor
Gurney Tower, Persiaran Gurney
Penang, Malaysia
Email: tprkl.my@sarabeattie.com
Sara Beattie, Owner: Email: sbeattie@sarabeattie.com
Tel: +604-2104 333
Fax: +604-2104 330
Website: www.princetonreviewKL.com

Mexico
TPR México
Guanajuato No. 242 Piso 1 Interior 1
Col. Roma Norte
México D.F., C.P.06700
registro@princetonreviewmexico.com
Tel: +52-55-5255-4495
+52-55-5255-4440
+52-55-5255-4442
Website: www.princetonreviewmexico.com

Qatar
Score Plus
Office No: 1A, Al Kuwari (Damas)
Building near Merweb Hotel, Al Saad
Post Box: 2408, Doha, Qatar
Email: infoqatar@score-plus.com
Tel: +974 44 36 8580, +974 526 5032
Fax: +974 44 13 1995
Website: www.scorepluseducation.com

Taiwan
The Princeton Review Taiwan
2F, 169 Zhong Xiao East Road, Section 4
Taipei, Taiwan 10690
Lisa Bartle (Owner): lbartle@princetonreview.com.tw
Tel: +886-2-2751-1293
Fax: +886-2-2776-3201
Website: www.PrincetonReview.com.tw

Thailand
The Princeton Review Thailand
Sathorn Nakorn Tower, 28th floor
100 North Sathorn Road
Bangkok, Thailand 10500
Thavida Bijayendrayodhin (Chairman)
Email: thavida@princetonreviewthailand.com
Mitsara Bijayendrayodhin (Managing Director)
Email: mitsara@princetonreviewthailand.com
Tel: +662-636-6770
Fax: +662-636-6776
Website: www.princetonreviewthailand.com

Turkey
Yeni Sülün Sokak No. 28
Levent, Istanbul, 34330, Turkey
Nuri Ozgur: nuri@tprturkey.com
Rona Ozgur: rona@tprturkey.com
Iren Ozgur: iren@tprturkey.com
Tel: +90-212-324-4747
Fax: +90-212-324-3347
Website: www.tprturkey.com

UAE
Emirates Score Plus
Office No: 506, Fifth Floor
Sultan Business Center
Near Lamcy Plaza, 21 Oud Metha Road
Post Box: 44098, Dubai
United Arab Emirates
Hukumat Kalwani: skoreplus@gmail.com
Ritu Kalwani: director@score-plus.com
Email: info@score-plus.com
Tel: +971-4-334-0004
Fax: +971-4-334-0222
Website: www.princetonreviewuae.com

Our International Partners

The Princeton Review also runs courses with a variety of
partners in Africa, Asia, Europe, and South America.

Georgia
LEAF American-Georgian Education Center
www.leaf.ge

Mongolia
English Academy of Mongolia
www.nyescm.org

Nigeria
The Know Place
www.knowplace.com.ng

Panama
Academia Interamericana de Panama
http://aip.edu.pa/

Switzerland
Institut Le Rosey
http://www.rosey.ch/

All other inquiries, please email us at
internationalsupport@review.com